DIARY OF A LADY'S MAID

Diary of a Lady's Maid

Government House in Colonial Australia

Edited by

Helen Vellacott

MELBOURNE UNIVERSITY PRESS
1995

Melbourne University Press
PO Box 278, Carlton South, Victoria 3053, Australia

First published 1995

Text © Helen Vellacott 1995
Design and typography © Melbourne University Press 1995

Designed by Lauren Statham
Typeset by John Sandefur, Usitech Pty Ltd, Melbourne
in 11½/14 pt Adobe Caslon
Printed in Singapore by KHL Printing Co Pte Ltd

National Library of Australia Cataloguing-in-Publication data

Southgate, Emma.
    Diary of a lady's maid: Government House in colonial
    Australia.
    ISBN 0 522 84698 X.

    1. Southgate, Emma—Diaries. 2. Domestics—
    Australia—Biography. 3. Australia—History—
    1851–1901—Biography. I. Vellacott, Helen, 1911– .
    II. Title.
640.46092

Contents

ILLUSTRATIONS

Preface

WHEN MY earlier book *A Girl at Government House* first appeared, I began to receive letters from all over Australia asking for more information about its heroine, Agnes. Which one of her suitors did she choose? This was the usual question. Some said they had sat up all night to come to the end of the story and were still left wondering. As the book was not on sale in England, it came as a surprise to get letters from there, from people who had presumably been sent the book by friends in Australia. The first of these was addressed to the publishers; it was on the notepaper of Lieutenant Colonel Charles Earle of Queen Camel, Yeovil, and commenced, 'Gentlemen—As the grandson of Sir Henry and Lady Loch and the only son of Edith their elder daughter, "A Girl at Government House" gave me the greatest pleasure. It is so true to all the family lore I heard from my mother and grandmother. I have stayed at Government House with the Delacombes, so I was able to savour the very full diary of Lady Loch's maid which I possess'. Thinking that the diary might be of interest to Australian Archives he had offered it to them, but the only person interested was the Tasmanian Archivist. Lieutenant Colonel Earle confessed that he did not know the diary writer's name, but he could remember her giving the diary to his mother in the 1920s, and he offered his help if it were to be published.

Just as it took many years to discover the surname of the kitchen maid Agnes, and to trace her history, the details of Emma's life are proving even more elusive. Old census returns and ships' passenger lists revealed only that her maiden name was Emma Southgate and that she had been born in England. From the diary itself we learn that she had her forty-ninth birthday during the voyage to Australia, but little else emerges.

Charles Earle and his wife asked me to spend a few days with them when I was in England, and when I reached Yeovil they drove me to their 'new' house. I put 'new' in inverted commas, for the Earles had recently moved from a large old manor house into a huge medieval tithe barn, its exterior revealing the huge timbers with which it was constructed, but its interior now converted into two spacious sets of apartments, complete with air conditioning and with every kind of electronic security device that can be imagined. It was prudent to have these devices for the Earles' rooms were full of family treasures and other precious possessions. On the wall of the dining room, for instance, were two letters in frames, one from the Duke of Wellington and one from Lord Nelson, in the course of which he apologises for the uneven writing saying, 'It is but two weeks since the surgeon removed my right arm'. When I admired these, Charles Earle said, 'Do you mind coming into the downstairs loo?' And in here were two more frames of letters, apparently hung there because this room possessed the only blank walls left in the house. One large frame contained letters signed by every British sovereign from George I to the present day. The letters of the first two Georges, who usually spoke German, were written by an amanuensis and merely signed by them, but George III's was in his own clear flowing hand. Queen Victoria's letter was written, of course, on notepaper with a wide black border, and the first to be typed was Edward VIII's, thanking Colonel Earle for the splendid way in which the men of his regiment had kept watch round his father's bier as he lay in State in Westminster Hall.

The Earles and I had several long talks about Emma and her diary, which they hoped to see published. Charles Earle said the name Southgate sounded familiar, though Lady Loch and her children always called her 'Titty'. She had been with the family when the children were born, they all loved her, and presumably 'Titty' was their first lisping attempt to say 'Pretty' when she delighted them with colourful toys.

Lord Loch was another of Sir Henry's grandsons who helped with the diary. He had written to me about *A Girl at Government House* and when I was in England asked me to go across to their house, close to Stonehenge, for lunch. When the train pulled in, he was easily recognized—very like pictures of his grandfather but more heavily built, and accompanied by a large, smooth-haired, black labrador, very similar, no doubt, to Benson, the family's labrador, who is mentioned frequently in Emma's diary. I evidently passed the luncheon test, for the Lochs very kindly asked me if I would be able to stay with them at their castle in Scotland, where many family treasures were in the library. It fitted in well with my journey to Edinburgh for the Festival, and before leaving Edinburgh I telephoned to confirm my travel arrangements. After I had spoken to Lord Loch he said, 'My wife is here and she would like to have a word with you'. Lady Loch confided, 'We are looking forward to seeing you tonight, but be sure to have a bath before you come, we haven't any water here, you know'. Was I really going to the notoriously damp west coast of Scotland? But I need not have worried, for next day the spring that supplies water to the castle began to trickle again, and we were allowed to have baths as long as they were not deeper than two inches.

I spent happy hours in the library with the Lochs. It was full of interesting books and pictures, and I particularly enjoyed the huge old photograph albums with their excellent pictures of life in Victoria. Benson was often included in family photographs, but alas, there were no pictures of Titty. However, I did gain more insight into her time spent with the Lochs in Melbourne.

ACKNOWLEDGEMENTS

My sincere thanks go to the many people who have helped me to amplify Emma Southgate's diary and to find pictures of the many colourful characters whom we encounter in its pages.

It was Sir Henry Loch's grandson, the late Lieutenant Colonel Charles Earle, who first showed me the diary and expressed the hope that I would publish it, and I would like to thank his son, Richard Earle, for his continued help and encouragement, and Lady Loch for her interest and her help with illustrations.

My thanks also go to the staff of the British Library, the Cambridge City Library, the National Library in Canberra, the State Archives in Hobart, the La Trobe Library and the Parliamentary Library in Melbourne, the Mitchell Library in Sydney and the State Library in Adelaide, and to the librarians of Bendigo, Ballarat and Castlemaine, of the South African Library in Cape Town, the Archives of the Isle of Man, and the editor of *Manx Life*. It was the historical societies of Macedon, Gisborne, Warrnambool and Bairnsdale who were able to provide many of the details for this book. My thanks are due, too, to the many friends who have assisted me in gathering information, especially Judith Brown, Julia Vellacott, Mary Lloyd, Winifred Faulkner, Barbara Johnston, Mary and Miles Lewis, Jessie Serle, Jennifer Bleakley, Meg McArthur, Bet Stonehouse, the Reverend Neville Connell, Frank Cumbrae-Stewart, Geoffrey Stillwell, Kim Brownbill, Ian Smith and Wal Larsen.

I must thank especially Elizabeth Sherriden for coping so patiently with my untidy handwriting and for turning my pages of scrawl into a pile of immaculate typescript.

Helen Vellacott
Castlemaine

CONVERSIONS

1 inch	2.54 centimetres
1 foot	30.5 centimetres
1 yard	0.91 metres
1 mile	1.61 kilometres
1 acre	0.405 hectares
1 pound	0.45 kilograms
1 hundredweight (cwt, 112 pounds)	50.4 kilograms
1 ton (2240 pounds)	1.02 tonnes

Currency

On 14 February 1966 Australian currency changed from pounds, shillings and pence (£, s, d) to dollars and cents at the rate of £1=$2. Twelve pence made up one shilling; twenty shillings made up one pound. One guinea was equal to twenty-one shillings.

PUBLISHER'S NOTE

Emma's handwritten diary is sometimes illegible, and her spelling and grammar are frequently incorrect. To facilitate reading of this published edition of the diary, spelling, punctuation and capitalisation have been slightly modified, although some inconsistencies and irregularities have been retained to convey the original style of the author's work.

Lady Loch with Evelyn, Douglas and Edith. (La Trobe Collection, State Library of Victoria)

INTRODUCTION

THERE IS A widespread belief among Australians that, in the past, those great houses of Britain that are admired so much today, were only maintained by the employment of an army of servants who lived in fear of the senior staff, and never dared to question their commands. These domestic servants are presumed to have been illiterate, and this impression is reinforced when prosperous Australians start to compile family histories, and discover with a shock that their grandfathers or great grandfathers, who came out and founded the family fortunes, were themselves only able to 'make their mark' on their marriage certificates. Of course many remote or mountain villages in Britain were without schools last century, and as country girls were preferred as domestic servants and believed to be harder workers than their city counterparts, no doubt there were many uneducated girls in the great houses. On the other hand though, some maids had received a good, though perhaps narrow, education, and their copperplate writing, in the book of 'Servants Wages', where they signed each week for their pitifully small wages, would put many present day scholars to shame.

The staff in those days had to work extremely long hours for the few shillings that they earned each week. They had to remain on call until supper had been served and cleared away, until lamps and candles had been prepared for people going up to bed, and until hot-water cans had been carried to bedrooms, before their duties finally ended. And occasionally they used some of these hours of waiting to record the day's happenings.

We are lucky that the vivid impressions of a young kitchen maid named Agnes Stokes, who came to Victoria last century, have survived until our own day. When these were published as *A Girl at Government House*, descendants of the governors for whom she worked declared that her narrative exactly corresponded with everything that their grandparents had told them of their life in Marvellous Melbourne, and indeed it gives us an insight into the life of the times that no history book could give us.

Agnes joined the staff of Government House in Melbourne in 1888. She probably scribbled away on a corner of the kitchen table. In view of the persistent belief that the domestics of old were quite uneducated, it comes as an added surprise to discover that, some years earlier, another of the governor's maids was recording her experiences as she sat in a quiet corner awaiting the return of her mistress from the ball. The maid was Emma Southgate, older than Agnes, who had been Lady Loch's trusted lady's maid for a number of years.

While Agnes's rambling narrative was scribbled on any scraps of paper she could lay her hands on, Emma's record was written in a large black note book, given her, no doubt, when she was about to set out on that voyage to the other side of the world. Both journals were written in pencil, and although Emma had obviously received a much better education than the young kitchen maid, both journals are somewhat lacking in punctuation! While Agnes views life from 'downstairs', Emma gives us what Dr Davis McCaughey, in *Victoria's Colonial Governors*, calls a 'between stairs view'. Emma lived and worked with the other servants, but when she accompanied Lady Loch to Sydney, for instance, she shared Lady Loch's luxurious railway carriage and marvelled at all its fittings—'lavatories, brushes, combs, towels, sponges and dressing room'.

Emma's journal, with its revealing 'between stairs view' of life at Government House, sadly ends when Sir Henry and his wife were at the peak of their popularity. It ends, naturally enough, when the writer comes to the last page of the book. If she continued it in another book, this second volume has not come down to us, and the one that is printed here has only survived because Emma, when over ninety, gave it to one of Lady Loch's daughters, saying that it might amuse the children.

The journal begins on 26 May 1884, when a group of people assembled on London's West India Dock to board the *Coptic*, the ship that was to carry them to Australia for Sir Henry Loch to take up his appointment as Governor of the colony of Victoria. As well as Sir Henry and his wife and their children, the party included his two aides-de-camp, Lord Castlerosse and Mr Hughes, and his private secretary, Captain Traill. The Lochs' two daughters, 'Miss Edith', aged eight, and 'little Miss Evelyn', six, were accompanied by their special attendants, Lucy, the nursemaid, and Mlle Heyman, their French governess. To speak French with the correct accent was an essential accomplishment for every young lady at that time, and most children of prosperous families began to acquire this skill while still in the nursery. And the Lochs' 11-year-old son, 'Master Douglas', was accompanied by his tutor, Mr Sturgess, under whose supervision he was to continue his lessons during the weeks they were at sea. Bringing the number up to seventeen were the members of the domestic staff, headed by the capable Mr Hawkins, the butler. The others were Mrs Calla, the middle-aged cook, Emma, the author of the journal, and three other servants, Mary, Henry and William. With them, though not appearing on the passenger list, was another important member of the family, Benson, the Lochs' large black retriever.

Sir Henry stood out conspicuously in any group of people. At fifty-seven he was a man of upright bearing, over six feet tall, with a magnificent flowing beard, which was soon to become known as 'the best beard in Melbourne'. The number seven is universally considered to be lucky and Sir Henry, who was the seventh son of a Scottish MP, certainly seemed to bear a charmed life. He had come unscathed through forty years of service in the Navy, the Army and the public service in some of the world's greatest trouble spots, and has left us an account of his adventures in his book, *A Narrative of Events in China*. He had been in that vast country with Lord Elgin, and had been despatched under a flag of truce, which guaranteed his safety, to carry a peace treaty to Peking, when he was seized, bound with chains, and dragged through the streets to be reviled and spat on by the excited crowds. He and his companion, still bound with chains, were thrown into China's worst prison, 'The Board of Punishment', where wrong-doers were tortured. Loch had lapsed into unconsciousness after his beatings, when one of his captors noticed that he wore a gold ring and, in trying to drag it off, caused so much pain that Loch struggled to sit up again. Twice the two Englishmen were taken into the courtyard to be beheaded, but each time something inter-vened and they were then placed in dark cells, far apart, and during this period each tried to discover if his colleague were still alive by singing 'God Save the Queen' and listening anxiously in the hope of hearing an answering verse. When finally released they were able to rejoin Elgin's main force, and Loch was ulti-mately to return to England with the completed treaty.

After his marriage in 1862, Henry Loch was appointed Governor of the Isle of Man, a small island about thirty miles long and ten miles wide, lying between England and Ireland, a deci-dedly peaceful spot. But he found plenty to do there, planning a new pier where ships could berth even at low tide, reforming the education system and the postal service, encouraging the develop-ment of the island's first railway, modernising the mental health provisions and, as early as 1881, introducing votes for women. After ten years of marriage, the Lochs' son was born on the Isle of Man, and was christened Douglas after the principal port, Douglas, which Henry Loch had chosen as his residence in pre-ference to the smaller ancient town of Castletown. It came as a great blow to the islanders when Sir Henry—for he had been knighted—resigned from his post after eighteen years of close involvement with the day to day life of the people. As their local historian recorded, it brought a shock of dismay. Then, after a year of valuable work with the department of lands in Britain, Sir Henry had received news of his appointment to Victoria and at once began preparations for his departure, as his predecessor there, the Marquis of Normanby, had already left the colony, which was temporarily administered by the Chief Justice, Sir William Stawell.

As they set out for that distant land, which was to be their home for the next five years, what did the travellers know of it? Sir Henry was the only one of the party who had actually set foot there, though Mr Hawkins, the butler, had an aunt in Victoria and was no doubt able to impress the rest of the staff with things he had learnt from her letters.

Sir Henry's visit to Melbourne had taken place thirty years before and although he may have been able to assure the others that they would find themselves in a delightful spot where the sun was always shining, he may not have been able to answer all the other questions that troubled them. When he had stepped ashore from the *Fottel-Oheb* all those years before, he had gone straight to Passmore's Hotel, at the corner of Lonsdale and Elizabeth streets, and he still had notes in his diary of the charges—'bedroom 2/6, sitting room 7/6, breakfast 2/6, luncheon 2/-, dinner 3/6'—but these prices could scarcely have remained unchanged. During that visit he had met some of the district's leading men, Mr a'Beckett, Mr Sturt and Sir William Stawell, and had dined with Mr La Trobe and his wife at their official residence at Jolimont, now replaced, he knew, by a large and impressive Government House. At the La Trobes' table he had also met some of the great landowners, down from the country: Mr Ferrars, who had extensive kennels and hunted with his own pack of hounds, and Mitchell from the Campaspe, who described how all his Barfold shepherds had run off to the goldfields—for the year was 1852—and left his flocks untended. These tales of the goldfields made Henry Loch anxious to see them himself, so he had made his own way to Ballarat, a vast city of tents, and ridden on to

Cambell's Creek and Castlemaine, the headquarters of the mounted police, whom he found 'a splendid body of men'. And he had survived the dangerous ride back to Melbourne through the Black Forest.

But if the travellers had sought more up-to-date information about Marvellous Melbourne than this, what would they have found? In one of the handsome volumes that had been published about the growth of the colonies they might have read:

> At this moment there is nothing to differentiate the city from one of the capitals of Europe. Its streets are as well paved, as well channelled, as well lighted and as well watered as those of London, Paris, or Vienna.

Another volume declared,

> There is nothing in Melbourne but the broad streets, the warmer atmosphere, the brighter sun and the newness of the public and private buildings, to efface the impression that you are in an English city. Carriages, with their liveried coachmen and footmen, are drawn up outside the principal linen drapers, jewellers and booksellers, and showy posters announce such and such operatic performance for the evening at the four theatres, with a concert perhaps at the Town Hall.

And if the staff wondered if their favourite sports would be played in the colony, they had only to read a little further:

> There are in Melbourne seven rowing clubs, fifteen cricket clubs, a boat club, a coursing club, two or three amateur dramatic clubs, two yacht clubs, several football clubs, besides bowling, lacrosse, baseball, tennis, and rifle clubs. [Add to these the] associations of anglers, of canary and pigeon fanciers, of bicyclists, of old blues, of temperance societies and missionary societies [and what else could one need?]

Sir Henry was looking forward not only to taking up residence in Marvellous Melbourne, but to the weeks at sea which would precede it. He loved the sea, having entered the Navy as a lad of fourteen, and in later years having made voyages to India, to Australia, and twice to China.

Lady Loch, too, was a seasoned traveller; in fact, she had spent her whole life travelling, for her father, Edward Villiers, had died in the south of France while she and her twin sister, Edith, were still babies, and his distraught young widow, feeling that she was too impecunious to maintain an establishment of her own, had spent the rest of her life moving, with her children and her servants, into whichever of their houses her relations could lend her. When her relations moved to town for 'the Season', for instance, she moved into the country house that they had just vacated, and when no family residence was available, she took her three daughters over to France, where living was so much cheaper than in England. The girls had never been to school, and except for an occasional visiting tutor, they had received no education apart from travel. They were in England when Sir Henry, returning as a hero from his exploits in China, had met and fallen in love with the lovely young Elizabeth, many years his junior.

But while Sir Henry and his wife looked forward with delight to the weeks at sea, the members of their staff viewed the voyage in a very different light. Admittedly, in the course of their years in service with the Lochs, they had many times crossed and recrossed the straits that separate the Isle of Man from the mainland. On that noisy little ferry, however, they were always in sight of land, but here they were sailing to unknown seas and an unknown country. And they would be so far away from their friends and their relatives. They were only persuaded to accompany the family by the Lochs' promises of a beautiful country with an ideal climate, and of work that would be far less arduous than that required to maintain the houses of the old country.

THE VOYAGE

26 May–8 July 1884

THE *Coptic*, which was to carry the Lochs' entourage to Australia, was one of the Shaw Saville Line's fleet, a vessel of 4367 tons, used on the Hong Kong run as well as to Cape Town, Hobart and the New Zealand ports. She had been constructed in Belfast in 1881, and was considered the last word in comfort, her cabins being lit by electric light. This ship was to survive, under the name *Persia*, and after being sold to a Japanese company, as *Persia Maru*, until she was finally broken up for scrap in Osaka in 1926.

The Lochs' party must have had an extraordinary amount of baggage, for the family carried with them not only clothes for both formal and informal occasions, but many household belongings, including their huge stocks of monogrammed household linen and all the crested family silver, and the children's books and toys. The silver was carried in locked boxes, many of them individually constructed to fit large pieces of unusual shape. Much of the clothing, too, travelled in specially shaped boxes—hat boxes, bonnet boxes, helmet cases, and very long narrow boxes to carry guns and ceremonial swords. One wonders where the passage money for this large party came from, for though Sir Henry belonged to a well-known Scottish family, it was not a particularly wealthy one, and during the eighteen years that he had spent on

The Lochs and their children travelled First Class and enjoyed the comforts of the dining saloon on the upper deck.

the Isle of Man, his salary was an extremely modest one. Lady Loch, however, possessed a considerable fortune. Her mother, the charming young widow, had numerous male friends who found her company fascinating, and one of these left his enormous fortune to her daughters.

The Lochs, their ADCs, and their children, of course, travelled in the ship's best cabins, and so did Mlle Heyman, sharing the little girls' cabin, while Mr Sturgess, the tutor, shared with Master Douglas. The rest of the staff travelled in the Second Class section of the ship, though Emma was privileged in sleeping in a tiny First Class cabin, near Lady Loch's, so that she would be at hand to dress or undress her mistress at any hour of the day or night. This does not imply that Lady Loch was incapable, of course, but merely that fashionable ladies found it useful to have someone at hand to help with the elaborate clothing that they habitually wore. First there were their lace-trimmed underclothes of linen or fine muslin, with their freshly ironed frills and tucks, and before the days of press-studs these were all fastened by small white linen buttons or narrow silk ribbons. The boned corsets, too, had to be correctly laced up and tied very firmly, and the 'improvers' placed correctly. These improvers were of two kinds—bust improvers, made of soft padding that filled out the bodice of the dress so that its embroidery could be displayed to the best advantage, and bustle improvers, which were tied on at the waist to help support the frilled bustle and the train. Ladies who had to dress themselves had round, long-handled mirrors set at an angle so that when the glass was held at shoulder height, it reassured the wearer that her improver was in its right position and was supporting her bustle and train correctly. The elaborate hair styles that were fashionable in the 1880s also called for skilled attention. Travel guide books of the times advised ladies who were going on a sea voyage always to take with them three 'transformations', the name given to the fashionable wigs of that time. One transformation should be suitable for morning wear, and an elaborate or curled one for evening wear, and the third was to be kept in reserve, to use when one of the others was being washed or recurled.

A huge variety of clothes, too, was needed for the voyage. The large shipping companies all issued guides for their passengers, sometimes of three or four hundred pages, giving information about the clothes they should take, and about the things they might expect to see on the voyage. One guide warned ladies to take plenty of warm clothing as 'recent investigation confirms all experience in giving woollen fabrics first place as regards health', and went on to insist that in the tropics, nothing but flannel should be worn next to the skin. It explained that sleeping on deck was advisable for healthy passengers during the few days at certain seasons when the temperature below was not easily borne, but again warned the passengers that flannel must be worn and a resting place under cover selected.

The shipping companies' guides listed the birds likely to be seen on the voyage, and the fish, and gave charts to help identify the unfamiliar stars that would appear in the heavens when the ship reached southern latitudes: thus we find Emma commenting on the first sighting of the Southern Cross. The guides also gave detailed descriptions of all the ports of call, but as the *Coptic's* passengers were only to come in sight of land twice during the whole voyage these were hardly relevant.

Many passenger ships printed a weekly news sheet while they were at sea, with articles, serious or frivolous, contributed by those on board, but the *Coptic's* passengers, who certainly did not lack talent, must have been feeling lethargic when a weekly paper was suggested, and the attempt to start one came to nothing, so that the only record of the day-to-day happenings on the ship is that given in Emma's journal. It starts in late May 1884.

May 26th 1884

Left the Euston Hotel at 9 for S.W. Indian Docks and went aboard about 10.30. The Coptic *did not sail till 2, reaching Gravesend about 4 p.m. We stayed there all night and as it was smooth might have slept well. Some way one could not manage to rest; all the noises were so great taking on cargo. We left Gravesend about 10.40. Sent off postcards and letters. Most beautiful quiet night.*

Wednesday May 28th

Arrived at Plymouth at 12 noon. Several passengers came on board. A stiff breeze blowing from east. Captain found 18 stowaways on board and sent them off. Pilot left at 2 p.m. We nearly all succumbed to seasickness. Young ladies sick, Mrs Calla, Mary and self.

FOR SOMEONE who considered herself a seasoned traveller and sea lover, as Emma did, this was a new and devastating experience. The English Channel bore no terrors for her as she had been unaffected by it on the many occasions she had crossed it with her employers, sometimes, indeed, ministering to them when they were prostrated. Even more frequently she had made the journey

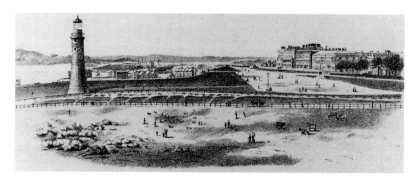

The Hoe, Plymouth.

from the Isle of Man to the various English and Scottish ports that ran regular services during the summer months. Everyone looked forward to these journeys on the paddle steamers and even the shortest crossing meant being at sea for about four hours. The steamers had an arrangement to synchronise their departure times, two vessels leaving at the same time and trying to race each other to the landing stage, a race which created tremendous interest and excitement among the passengers. There was usually a large crowd of people on the wharf, cheering on the ship they had tipped to win. In the 1880s the return fare for first class passengers was only four shillings, for second class three shillings—with a bottle of beer thrown in—so the ships, some of which could carry 2000 passengers, were usually crowded.

Thursday May 29th

Lovely weather. Got into Bay of Biscay at 2 this morning. Heavy ground swell. We have sighted lots of vessels. They don't come very near. We have altered our watches half an hour.

Friday May 30th

Lovely bright day again. Out of the Bay into the Atlantic Ocean. Heavy ground swell. Each day we find the heat greater. Got a glimpse of Portugal. All keeping well. Reading, knitting and

*resting. The time glides away imperceptibly. Great delight to think
one week has already passed away.*

Saturday May 31st

*Heavy swell and very much warmer. Awnings are up in all parts of
the vessel to shade the decks as there are so many children. Have
suffered all day with windy spasms. Nothing seems to touch them.
Cannot enjoy anything.*

Sunday June 1st

*Had a wretched night. Wind reached my heart and at 1 this morn-
ing I thought I should die on the floor of my cabin. I grew cold and
faint with pain. At last summoned up courage to go to Lady Loch's
cabin opposite but she did not hear or see me, so crept back and lay
across my box and after an hour or two began to feel better. The
glands of the stomach are still so sore from pain I am afraid to cough
and almost to speak. Nice service in the Saloon at 10.30. Lady Loch
played that beautiful hymn 'For Those in Peril on the Sea' and two
others well known that all might join in. The Purser read the
service. The Captain has a sweet tenor voice. The heat has been
steadily increasing. All passengers dressed in the white and Sunday
best, look smart and just as they should do on Whit Sunday.*

Monday June 2nd

*Tenerife. When we got up this morning we looked for the beautiful
rugged rocks of Tenerife and about 10 reached the Bay. It is very
beautiful, each rock a different shape and the water blue as a
sapphire. Sir Henry, Lady Loch, the two young ladies, Master
Douglas, Lord Castlerosse, Captain Grant and Mr Sturgess went
ashore early. Mr Hawkins, Mary, Henry and William also went
later on, but had great difficulty to get into a small boat. The swell
was great and Lucy hung to a rope ladder ever so long, making us
all so nervous for fear she should fall. Mrs Calla gave up all thought*

Tenerife.

of landing after seeing Lucy hang over the deep for nearly a quarter of an hour. Luckily she had someone below her very brave, which helped to give her nerve. Such lots of Spaniards came aboard with straw hats, lemons, bananas, oranges, singing birds, parrots, etc. They look a very dirty race—and no great beauty to my mind. We take on coal here and then some weeks before another chance to land. Mr Hawkins came back with Mary, loaded with biscuits, chocolate, apricots, tangerines, oranges, green figs, etc., which we have paid our respects to and enjoyed. We were to leave at 6 tonight. The coaling is not finished so hope we may get a quiet night. An accident happened this morning which made us feel sick, involving a young woman who was watching a party that was leaving for the shore. She had her hand on a pipe and a rope from the coal barge broke the pipe and her poor hand was wedged in a vice. The seamen were prompt and knocked a wedge in and the poor fingers were released. One is much bruised but she was very brave and neither screamed nor uttered one word—though she fainted later on. The doctor had gone ashore but the Captain was very kind and did his utmost to soothe her. The ladies and gentlemen all came back looking hot and weary—tho' they seem to have enjoyed the little change.

THE RUGGED ROCKS OF TENERIFE that greeted the travellers' eyes were the twin summits of its tallest mountain, the Peak, over 12 000 feet high—some 'rock' indeed. The island of Tenerife is one of the Canary Islands and contains the capital, Santa Cruz, a busy port, shipping the island's fruit crops to many parts of the world. Mr Hawkins, the butler, a veritable Admiral Crighton, returned from his visit to the shore bearing a selection of its choicest subtropical fruit, a very welcome addition to the *Coptic*'s menu.

The Peak, which is visible on a clear day from nearly a hundred miles away, is composed of lava and white pumice stone, and gives its name to the island, 'Tenerife' meaning 'white mountain'.

In contrast to the Peak's great height, Table Mountain, looming behind Cape Town, the only other land that the passengers saw, rises to only 3600 feet.

Wednesday June 4th

Fine bright morning, very fresh on deck. Close below. I felt good for nothing first thing for want of air. Soon recovered upstairs. Mr Hawkins says they had a great desire to get up a weekly paper and have applied to 1st Class Cabin passengers, but they don't seem equal to anything of the kind and I fear it will drop thro' for want of support. A French steamer passed us about 3 p.m. Plenty of music. The piano is always going, then the Purser plays the accordion very well as accompanist. Several play concertinas. There is a great demand for a piano in the Second Saloon. As there are many passengers and none too much room there is a fear the request may not be granted.

June 4th

African Coast near Ashanti. Quite a nice gathering in the Steerage. Our head steward in the 2nd Class Cabin sang a sweet song. Henry also obliged with a song and the men cooks are quite like Christy's minstrels. Such a merry party always singing. It was quite warm. The Captain said we cross the Sun today.

Thursday June 5th

Very hot. The hottest day we have had. I could not sleep for the heat of the cabins last night and fear the heat will be terrific tonight. Mrs Calla made us some nice lemonade for dinner and we had some ice to cool it. We need cooling. Everyone looks half-baked except the Captain, officers and Chief Stewards, who have donned their white costumes and look so clean and fresh. Thermometer is 83 degrees [Fahrenheit] in cabin. Same last night. 'Tis rather trying.

Friday June 6th

Fine bright hot day. We all feel the heat very much. Poor Benson more than anyone. He pants and seems so restless. I hope he won't go mad poor dear. We should be sorry and everyone has got a pat or kind word for him. The sooner we cross the Line the better. There will be some hope of cooler weather.

Such a storm of rain. It came all in a minute without any warning and lasted about half an hour. It caused quite a panic in our cabin as the water came down in large drops from the ventilator. We rushed to remove all wearing apparel. We hope the rain will cool the vessel and the air too. A poor woman has been fainting away again and again from the heat and want of nourishment. Unfortunately she cannot relish the food cooked on board and has scarcely eaten anything since she came aboard. The doctor ordered her some eggs at once, and we hope she will obtain great benefit from them.

Saturday June 7th

Wet, damp, muggy morning. We have not had much sleep and feel very limp. Poor Lucy so sick and faint for want of air. I can't imagine how people live in such a climate. It is simply killing. Rain eased about 12 noon and the air is lighter and more bearable. Still squally. The days are drawing in so fast. Quite dark at 6 p.m. We seem to have jumped from the height of summer to the depth of winter in a fortnight—it is really wonderful. An entertainment was given in Second Saloon for Sir Henry, Lady Loch and party. Mr Cox first showed off with some sleight of hand tricks, which greatly amused the company. Then some ladies sang a duet; they were both so nervous I much dreaded a breakdown and there was a sad want of music to accompany the singers. Mary sang the 'The Skipper and his boy'. She sang bravely tho' I believe it was more pain than pleasure to her. The German recited a piece in the German language so clearly that everyone seemed to have a good idea of what he was saying tho' few know German. The party broke up at 10 p.m.

Sunday June 8th

Trinity. Lovely morning, fresher than yesterday. Attended Divine Service on upper deck at 10.30. Very solemn and well conducted. Good singing. Lucy better today I am glad to say and able to attend.

We collected together after tea in Saloon and sang hymns— 'Abide with me' and several favourite and well-known hymns. The heat was great and our sacred concert was soon over. We had a good walk and went to cabin at 9 p.m. We enjoy these moonlight walks more than anything. Several places vacant today at meal time— two from our table. Many are suffering from faintness. The doctor must find plenty to do.

Monday June 9th

Very hot again. We all feel very weak and languid. Poor Lucy has scarcely eaten anything these last two days. At 1 this morning the heat was almost unbearable. Got up several times and tried to make a little air with my fan—if this heat was to last I feel sure we should collapse. Sat on deck all morning. Benson has been moved forward and seems to feel the heat less. Quantities of flying fish to be seen. Two flew on board and were caught. They are beautifully marked. We crossed the Line about 12.15. No ceremony. There has been such rough work carried on at this place and many complaints about it. The Captain will not sanction or allow anything to be done to those who cross for the first time. The joke was carried too far. There is to be a little fun this evening I have just heard.

About 7 p.m. Father Neptune arrived over the bow of the steamer with his retainers, who carried a gong and dinner bell, which they did not fail to use. One would have thought the demons of the deep had been loosened, such a noise and uproar they made. They seemed to have a pretty good idea who had and who had not crossed the Line before. Each victim was led to a place screened off with sails or canvas. Here he had to take a pill or some harmless medicine—then if he happened to open his mouth when spoken to, a brush with soft soap, or something very like it, is popped in and he is pushed backwards into a bath and the hose well used. All the gentlemen of Sir Henry's suite were handed down one after the other, but got off by paying ten shillings each. They came for Master Loch but Miss Edith and Miss Evelyn cried so bitterly, he too was let off with a fine. We were all very excited when they hunted out of his hiding place Mr Hawkins, who paid his footing and got off. William also paid but Henry suffered going thro' the ceremony and bore it very bravely.

Tuesday June 10th

Another hot day. Slept fairly well and felt a little more strength coming. Sat on deck all morning, reading and chatting. Lucy very seedy again, can eat nothing—seems to lose all pluck and won't even try. It makes her look so weak and thin. Champagne has been recommended by the doctor as it did her good last week.

Had a nice evening on deck and saw the Southern Cross very distinctly. The stars are very brilliant tonight. The Evening Star is so wonderfully bright. The reflection in the water beautiful. Sat on deck till 8 p.m., chatting and buzzing, and then put little girls to bed and after reading for a short time turned in and slept better on the whole than I have done for a week.

Wednesday June 11th

Dull morning, not actually raining but I much fear close at hand. Fine all day and not so warm as yesterday. Thermometer is 79 degrees in the cabin. Had several trots on upper deck and felt all the better for extra exertion.

A concert in Steerage lasting till 9.30. Some capital songs were sung. One gentleman played a solo on a whistle very nicely. Another played the concertina and sang 'Down by the river side where the sweet lilies grow' extremely well. Another gave a reading of 'The Wreck of the Hesperus'. It was altogether a very pleasant time. The Southern Cross very distinct tonight. An hour or so ago it was pitch dark—not a star to be seen—and now the heavens are all glitter.

Thursday 12th June

Dull grey morning. Came out clear and fine about 11. Sat on deck till 12 noon, then went to my sanctuary and commenced a letter to Jenny.

Such a nice cool night. All slept better. Lucy a little better. Unequal to any exertion. I wish she could throw off this attack, it makes me so depressed and she looks as if she is fading away. There is a dear little white-headed boy in our Saloon. Youngest child of Mr and Mrs Cox. He is a perfect picture. So round, fat and good tempered. Goes trotting about in such a careful but independent way. There is another child called Daisy, a girl, equally attractive, so good tempered, plump and easy-going—everyone has something to say to her. There is a large family of them—father, mother and six children.

Friday June 13th

Nice cool morning. Thermometer is 74 degrees. Busy morning getting out linen for the week from the box room. It takes up a lot of time and helps to pass the long morning pleasantly. Lucy better today I am glad to say.

Had a rubber in the evening. Mary and Mr Hawkins against Mrs Calla and me. We beat them—it was rather an exciting game. We both got 9 holes and we only just saved ourselves. Went to bed at 9.30. Heavy swell. Had some difficulty to fix myself in bed. Everything in the cabin seems on the move and I am afraid of getting a nasty blow when I am asleep and not on the alert for No. 1.

Saturday June 14th

Fine bright, sunny morn. The freshness seems quite delightful after the great heat. Washed some stockings then worked in cabin till dinner time.

PROGRAMME OF CONCERT GIVEN IN SALOON.

Pianoforte and accordion: Captain Traill
Cotten song 'When the Tide comes in': Mlle Heyman
Song 'Drink Puppy drink': Mr Seymour Hughes
Duet 'I would that my love': Mlle Heyman and Mr Thomas
Comic song 'He always comes home to Tea': Mr Rhe
Song 'Sailing': Captain Kidley

Interval of twenty minutes. Claret cup handed round. Cakes and dried fruits. Very amusing. Each and all did their part well. Concert ended at 10 p.m.

Sunday June 15th

My birthday. Many good wishes and nice presents. A Tenerife silk handkerchief from Lady Loch. A book marker from Miss Evelyn. A book and card from Ted, handed over to Lucy to give on 15th. A pretty card from Lucy and Mrs Carote. It was kind of them to be prepared so long beforehand and I feel very grateful for their kind thought—a line from those at home is indeed valuable now I am so far from them all. We had some singing at 7 in the Saloon, quite a nice party. Mrs Cox started the hymn then all joined together. My birthday has been a very happy day. Went to bed at 9.30. A very rough night. We had very little sleep for fear we should topple over such a heavy roll.

Mrs Calla tried her hand at gymnastics down the cabin stairs, and stood on her head on the mat below to the great astonishment of those who sat in the Saloon below.

THE NUMBER OF presents Emma received on her forty-ninth birthday shows how highly she was regarded both by the Lochs and by her fellow employees. Book markers, one of which Miss Evelyn gave her, were at the height of their popularity in the 1880s, and ranged from those depicting clowns or acrobats, to ones embellished with religious texts or verses of hymns, while Stevens, a firm in Coventry, made exquisite silk ones, costing at least half a guinea. One wonders whether Miss Evelyn's gift had been made on board, either painted or embroidered under Mlle Heymann's guidance, or whether it had been bought as a birthday gift before they came on board.

Monday June 16th

Fine morning, heavy swell. 'Tis difficult to get any exercise today. The Coptic is showing us how nicely she can dance today. Each day 'tis getting colder. I am glad of my new under-flannels—quite a boon. Have seen some Cape pigeons flying about this morning. They are small and milk white. They look like foam a little distance off. Looks rather cloudy, I trust we shall get no rain. It will be dull work shut down in one's cabin all day without air or exercise. We have now had three weeks without a single wet day.

Everything upon the tramp, 'tis laughable. Takes all one's time to hold on and keep the perpendicular. Cups, saucers, plates, and bottles are all running about the table. Mrs Calla feels rather stiff today from gymnastics last night. Lucy sick again. Can't throw off these attacks.

Tuesday June 17th

Roughish night. Went to bed at 8.30, very tired. Slept till 12. Heavy rolling sea. A little steadier from 1 till 4, then very rolly again. Don't feel quite so well as normal. Mrs Calla says she aches all over. Lucy very poorly again. Looks thin and haggard. I don't believe her food does her any good.

Sir Henry has taken a chill and seems in great pain. The pain is so bad it makes him sick. Evening: glad to say Sir Henry is a little better. The sea has gone down, wonderfully calm night. Sir Henry has had a fairly good night. Lucy not well. Fed the fishes again this morning. I am afraid the sickness will continue so long as she remains on sea. The days have been gradually shortening. We had tea by electric light tonight. We could not see what we had on our plates at 5.15 p.m. Very cold after 4—just like a cold evening in October.

AT THIS POINT in the diary Emma herself seems rather under the weather, and days and nights merge so that more than one day's events appear under the one date.

Wednesday June 18th

All slept well. Very quiet night. Bright sunny morning. Sir Henry much better, had a cup of tea and biscuit at 5 a.m. There are some large birds following us this morning—albatrosses. They don't come very close. I am told they are very large when you see them close.

Lucy no better. Could not induce her to go on deck. At 7.30 p.m. went with Mr Craig, Chief Engineer, to see the machinery and the stoke holes. We first inspected the electric machinery for supplying the steamer with the electric light, then the indicators and then the stoke holes. They remind me of Dante's Inferno. *I was glad to get out. The huge boilers and fires were enough to alarm a stronger nerve than mine. It is altogether a miracle how they escape taking fire. At 8.30 there was dancing on deck. I had a turn or two with Henry—a polka. Finished with Mr Hawkins. Had an evening party in my cabin after. Sir Henry not quite so well.*

Cape Town.

Thursday June 19th

Got up in good time and before I could dress Mrs Walsh came with a cup of tea and said we were close to Table Mountain, then we were all excitement. I threw on my clothes and went to Lady Loch who was all anxious to get on deck to send off letters. Alas, alas. The fishing boats refused to take them, so our efforts are all in vain. We are passing Cape Town now. The rocks look lovely, all shapes, and the silver sand on them looks like snow. It is a sight I never expected to see and we have such a beautiful bright morning, warm and sunny. It is a real treat to see the land again, tho' there is a sad want of vegetation, not a speck of grass to be seen anywhere. We passed False Bay, and after dinner we could only see sand very indistinctly. Rough all afternoon and cold. Difficult to walk about.

Did not get on deck after dressing. Such a heavy sea washing over both sides. Read a little and retired early.

Friday June 20th

Such a night I never spent at sea. I don't know what they call a rough sea if this is nothing. Hardly slept at all. Everything in my room on the tramp: leather box, 3 bags of books, umbrellas, photographs and books, boots and shoes, combs, water bottle, glasses, ink, pin cushion and camp stool. It is amusing and I laugh heartily when I see all huddled together in a mass, sliding from one side of the cabin to the other. I often wish Ted could be here to enjoy the confusion—he is the only one that would. And I aren't quite sure he won't be prone against these heavy seas. Showery this morning. Could not risk getting wet. Had a long talk with the Captain this morning. He spoke so kindly of his old nurse.

The sea washes right thro' the deck every now and again. Several are injured from slipping on the wet deck. Mrs Griffiths has sprained her ankle badly thro' a fall and Mr Harry Smith tripped up and had got a nasty cut on his shin. He fears the bone is injured. We played cards. Mrs Calla, Mr Williams, Mary and me, and then we had a game of whist and rummy. Had a nice sharp walk on deck with Mr Hawkins, Mrs Calla and Mary. Got nice and warm and returned to my cabin at 10 p.m. Very weary of everything. This lazy life would not suit me. I like to be at work and wish I could settle down either to work or reading or writing.

Saturday June 21st

Longest day in old England. It was not light till 7.30 here. Wet morning. Rather anxious night. From some cause or other the engines stopped early this morning, at 5. I heard a strange noise last night and heard that one of the valves were broken. We are under sail and going very slowly. They are repairing the damage. I am told it is anxious work, and one cannot take in that the damage is insignificant hundreds of miles from land. God grant it may be. Engines started again about 11 a.m. and as it is calm we are going at a fine pace. We shall soon make up for lost time. As we sat at tea an invitation came to meet in the Saloon at 8 p.m. Very nice concert by the Captain, Lord Castlerosse, Mr Hughes and the Purser, Mam'selle

Concerts were held in the music saloon.

and Mr Sturgess, who read a lovely piece of poetry about 'Billy'. Mr Thompson gave another reading about that 'Vulgar Boy at Margate', beautifully given. We all enjoyed ourselves immensely.

Poor Lucy very unwell still. Sent the children to bed and tucked Lucy up with a mustard plaster on her stomach. I wish she was well soon. [Note inserted at the foot of the page 'Sail torn to shreds at 4 a.m.']

Sunday June 22nd

Very cold morning. I was glad to put on my fur cloak. Had a nervous night. Got a panic about the engines. Such a squall at 1 this morning. Another sail blown to pieces. Thermometer 42 degrees on deck— 'tis cold enough for snow. Had a nice service in Saloon at 10.30 and after kept Mr Hawkins birthday. Then Mrs Calla, Mary, me and Mr Hawkins had an hour's exercise on deck, then a heavy shower of *hail stones fell. We all made a good dinner (except poor Lucy, who is not much better and can only take light milk food) and had a cup of cocoa to keep us warm. There was a slight fall of snow about 1.30 p.m. Had a nice nap in afternoon from 3 till 4.30. Sea rather rough after tea. Could not attend the singing class held at 7 p.m. Water was washing over lower deck. Sat with Lucy some time. She is certainly better tonight, more spirit.*

Service of Song at 9. Could not attend. Weather squally. Seas washing lower deck. Afraid I might slip. Mr Furst played the flute. Went to rest at 10.30. No sound rest for me—not sick, but dreadfully nervous.

Monday June 23rd

Very rough. Wet morning. Sleet and rain. For once found I was too soon for breakfast. Cause: a heavy sea caught the pantry steward, who was standing at the galley door waiting for the dishes. Galley cooks and boy up to their waist in water. Pantry boy washed in head first. He has hurt his hand and broke no end of plates. I think Lucy is certainly better this morning and only trust the improvement will last. Poor girl, she has suffered. Mr Jones, 2nd Steward, so very kind—anything she fancies she's to have. Took her on deck at 12 noon for a little exercise. We trotted up and down till dinner time. Lovely sea behind us today. Waves as blue as a sapphire and the size of mountains.

Read East Lynne *after dinner. At 3.30 went on deck for more exercise. Very difficult and so bitterly cold. It seems very wonderful only a month since we left London, the height of the Season and summer close at hand. Now plunged into winter weather. Hail and snow storms. Glad to wear furs and can't keep warm.*

Tuesday June 24th

Such a good night. Really rested all night. More snow during the night. Very cold still. Heavy seas. Had a narrow escape last night. A heavy sea broke just as I peeped out of the Saloon. To avoid a wetting I rushed to the stairs and bruised my arm against the iron rail and caught my left shin against the last step. It was painful, but thankful the shin was not broken. We saved ourselves, and that was all. The water rushed over and out the other side. People are caught nearly every time. But I don't seem to care for a wetting. There is no place to dry wet clothes aboard ship.

Very stormy. Did not go to see Mrs Calla or Mary after tea. Went to Ladies Room on upper deck for a little change. Read in my cabin and went to bed at 11 p.m. Slept till 12. Heard the Captain call Sir Henry and felt very anxious and nervous. Peeped out of my cabin door, but saw no one (tho' the Captain says he saw me). Such heavy seas kept falling on deck and washing to and fro. The screw [engine] is fighting hard with the large waves. Had little or no rest. Feel worn out.

Wednesday June 25th

Such a stormy night. Squally and such heavy seas. Very anxious night. Heard the Captain's voice calling Sir Henry about 12 a.m. Could not think why? We shipped some heavy seas and I thought of the poor sailors who have to be out in such cold tempestuous weather. Had little rest after 12. Feel worn and weary for want of rest. Could not go and get my breakfast with the others. Mr Hawkins said I had better not attempt. Seas as high as the funnel sweep the deck. Went to Ladies Room in upper deck for a while. A heavy sea came in at the door and washed right down the cabin stairs. All hands at work to clear up the water. Sponges, flannels, towels. Stewards without shoes or stockings, trousers rolled up to their knees clearing up the mess. The seas are running as high as the funnels. It is a mercy the wind is in our favour or we should be buried in water.

Thursday June 26th

Passed a better night, tho' it was a very heavy, rough sea. Rolling and tossing all night. Thank God we have a better time of it this morning. Tho' rough we can get out. I went to breakfast soon after

8 and had about half an hour on deck when a hail shower came pelting down. I was obliged to take shelter. Fine foam washing thro' second deck. Had a capital walk after dinner till 3.40. Bitterly cold. Snow showers falling every few minutes. Mrs Calla had another tumble on deck. At 7.30 p.m. they had a quiet sort of entertainment —songs, recitations and choruses. Wound up at 9.30 by singing the National Anthem.

Mr Hawkins saw me home as the seas were washing between decks. Saw the new moon. A welcome sight, the nights have been so dark the last week or so.

Friday June 27th

Fine night. Slept beautifully. In capital health and spirits. Have got a little colour in my face now. Most people tell me I look much better than when I came aboard ship. This pinching cold seems to brace everyone up. Went for the usual constitutional on deck at 10. Sun shining, blue sky and lovely sea. Had a capital trot till 12, then the cold wind was more than I could fight against. Heavy snow storm directly after. We are bowling along splendidly. Wind favourable. Sails are set. It will soon be time to pack up. The time seems long since we had news from the dear folks at home. I must try and write. Alas, I have grown so lazy with having little to do. I do nothing.

Evening intensely cold. I long for the sight of a bright fire. Retired at 10.30. Bitterly cold. Consequently could not rest at all.

Saturday June 28th

Slept very badly. Feel as if I had no head. Quite dazed. Fancy I shall be unequal to labour of any kind if this stupid feeling continues. Just when I ought to get up I could sleep beautifully. Had a nice turn on deck after tidying up my cabins. It rained so Lucy and myself came below at 11 a.m.

Busy afternoon for the performers who have commenced an entertainment in the Saloon for tonight. It is sure to go off well. Had to get some rest after dinner. So worn out for want of sleep. Rough sea and such a noise with the screw [engine] right over my head. I am getting very nervous about my clothes now I see how impossible to keep anything dry. It will be sad if they are all spoilt after the expense of buying such a stock. The glass [barometer] has fell very much again, nearly 9-10ths, which may account for these miserable nights. Mrs Calla is not much better. She also suffers from sleeplessness.

Sunday June 29th

Very little sleep I am sorry to say. The entertainment was most successful last night. The first piece was well acted by Mr Hughes, Mr Sturgess and Mr Ray—the Purser—most laughable farce (No. 1 round the corner), then the gentlemen with their faces blackened sat in a circle as they do at Christys, St James Hall, and sang many laughable nigger songs, and asked each other conundrums. The doctor made a stump [soap box?] speech, which was quite killing— his get up also. Altogether most enjoyable evening. The entertainment was not concluded till 10.30, and it was 12 before the black faces were made white and all quiet.

THE CHRISTY MINSTRELS, who caused so much amusement at the ship's concert, were perhaps the first band of popular musicians to gain worldwide recognition. The original Edwin Christy began his career in the United States in 1842, singing with two assistants in the bar of a Buffalo hotel. The Christy Minstrels were soon in demand in New York and London, and as many of the best singers in the group were American Negroes, the others blackened their faces to match them. They wore top hats, and huge bow ties in unexpected colours, and their popularity was instantaneous. During the American Civil War Christy became so distressed by the strife between blacks and whites that he killed himself by jumping from an upstairs window. However, right into the present century concert parties repeated his songs and his jokes with great success, and when it was difficult to procure elaborate costumes, the easily achieved black faces and bow ties brought instant applause.

June 29th [cont.]

Had some bromide and went to bed at 10.30 p.m. Strong wind and high sea. Dull rainy weather.

I forgot to describe Master Douglas' get up. His face was blackened. He wore a red turban and a white dress of Mam'selle's, and a bright table cover for an apron, pinned cornerwise. He was enough to make one burst over the improver—which he declared should not go on his body, if he could help it. It was managed tho' and he made a very graceful lady and distributed the programmes amongst the company.

It was a very stormy night and I did not get to sleep till it was time to get up, and felt too seedy when Mrs Walsh came in, but managed to dress Lady Loch and felt a little better after breakfast. Attended the service at 10.30 in Saloon, then went to bed, but got no rest. After dinner went to bed and slept for one hour and a half, then went on deck to see what the weather was like. Such a grand sea. Had a chat with Mr Patterson, Captain and one of the sailors, who said they had a hard time of it since we left the Cape. One sailor nearly lost his life this morning by a heavy sea. Washed overboard but managed to catch a rail. A mercy he did poor fellow. With such a heavy sea he would never be seen again. Another was hurt with the windlass. They have had a hard time of it and not much pay (£3 to £5 a month). At 7 p.m. Mary and Mrs Calla came over to see how we were going on and Mr Hawkins. We returned with them and had a Service of Song for an hour. We were thrown to and fro by the rolling of the ship and when time to leave there was such a heavy sea washing between decks we did not know how we should get back to the cabin. Mr Chapman kindly volunteered to carry Lucy and me to the steps. So we managed to get back without a wetting. We clung to each other on the upper deck, for the wind blew very hard and

The promenade deck.

when going full steam, it's as much as one can do to keep the perpendicular, hold one's hat on and keep from falling.

Monday June 30th

Very stormy night. I thought we should capsize, such heavy lurches. A heavy sea struck the porthole in the ladies retiring room. Broke the glass and flooded the ante-room. The Chamber Steward went and put up all the dark ports along the weather side for protection. Lady Loch does not feel very well. An attack of indigestion she thinks. Lucy is much better, but looks very thin. Had a good trot on deck from 10 till 12, then sat in my Cabin and worked till dinner time. Had a long talk with the German and Mr Williams. The latter so pleased to talk about his native place, Wales. He seems a most respectable young man, a total abstainer and evidently a good-living man. Jeered at because he does not enter into bad ways on board.

Wet afternoon and rough night tho' thank God I slept well. There was a great noise from some cause. I cannot find out what it was. Sounded like a pump at work. 'Tis no use to ask, one never gets the right version—they are so afraid of alarming those who are the least nervous.

Tuesday July 1st

Rough, wet, dark morning. Too late for breakfast with the others. Lucy and I collected things that will not be required any more and packed them away. Had to remain this side. Mr Frost said I might be injured with such a heavy sea if I was caught and said 'twas better not to risk it. Had dinner with Lucy on the floor of her cabin. The wind is high today. The thermometer fell very much last night. I went up to watch the sea and thought I would have a peep at Mary and Mrs Calla, had asked if it was safe. The door was shut and I could see a heavy sea coming, so rushed back and had just reached the galley. They told me to jump in, which I did and just saved myself a wetting, then crept into the Saloon when another lurch seemed to carry everything with it, Mr Frost told me to hold onto the stair rail and not move—it was a roll. This boat is very unsteady. I hope, please God, we shall all arrive in safety to our journey's end. Poor Captain Traill had a nasty fall on deck again today. He has hurt his leg, but not much he says. Lucy complains of sickness again today. Her digestion seems very much out of order. Lady Loch, Mam'selle Heyman and Miss Evelyn were all rolled off their sofas on to the floor this afternoon when the steamer lurched.

This has seemed a very long dreary day and no chance of clearing. The thermometer has gone down to 28 degrees and we have lost our top gallant sail. The wind is very high and the sea very confused. Went to my cabin early. Did not undress. I felt something must happen before morning. We all felt anxious. It was difficult to walk, and the heavy lurches and seas that came over our side was something not easily forgotten. Lady Loch gave me some bromide and I lay down in my clothes, only taking off my dress. The wind kept howling, doors slammed and the night seemed a long one. I dozed but woke up with every bang. I thought we were settling down over and over again. Never, never can I forget this night. May I never experience such another.

Wednesday July 2nd

Still rough, very rough. It is a mercy we are spared to see another day dawn. Everyone has had little or no sleep. A new sail torn to shreds during the night. Lady Loch and Mam'selle tried to get a little rest. I took charge of the young Ladies. Heard from Mr Hawkins that Mary was nearly washed overboard. They went on deck as usual, keeping between the engine house and the funnels, when a sea rose up and came down upon their heads and swept Mary against a boat. A large lump has appeared on her forehead, which must be painful. Her hat was washed away, a tam-o'-shanter made on board. The doctor has been to see her and seems to think she will soon be alright again. Her knees are both very much grazed and swollen.

Thursday July 3rd

Fine bright sunny morning. We have all had a good night's rest. The sea was rather rough when we went to bed but calmed down and the vessel sailed along fairly smooth. Awoke at 7 and got off to breakfast in good time. Then had a walk on deck. It was dipping a good deal and we had to be very careful. Mary came up for a turn. She has got one eye black and her nose swelled up and grazed. The lump is just at the top of her nose and had the rail struck her on her temple I don't know but the consequences might have been very serious. Lucy don't seem well yet. She complains of feeling sick after eating.

Had a bad night's rest. Awoke with a nasty fit of coughing and in a great heat. Everything was moving in my cabin. Such a heavy roll. Such a clatter with the crockery-ware smashing up and the boxes sliding about in the box room. You might see one any minute coming thro' the partition.

Friday July 4th

Beautiful dry sunny morning. A goodly number on deck. All the invalids visible. It is a grand sight to see the decks dry after so much rain and storm.

In afternoon had boxes out and pack up all that can be spared. I had the pleasure of seeing my box that had been hidden in the hold ever since we came on board, tho' a good deal knocked about, the water had only got in just in two or three places. Not sufficient to do any harm. There was a good entertainment in the steerage by the crew. All dressed in Nigger fashion with faces blackened and white shirts with various collars and decorations. There was a chorus first, then some good songs, a dance, stump speech 'Poor ole Joe' in character, a march past, Mr Samson (Men's chief cook) leading with a drum made with a tub and covered with canvas. He hammered away. The men all carried something, one a pan and brush with which he managed to make a fine din. Mix up with the noise of two violins, one concertina, triangle, castanets, trombone, etc. etc. etc. The Captain, Sir Henry, Lady Loch and Master Douglas, Miss Edith and Miss Evelyn, seemed to enjoy the fun immensely. The doctor, Purser, Mr Jones, Mr Thompson and all the staff were there. They broke up at 10 p.m. and we all sang the National Anthem and scrambled out on deck where the moon was shining so clear and the sea so calm. After wishing all good night, we marched off to our quarters in First Saloon. Lucy and me had biscuits and went to bed. Such a quiet night's rest. Forgot for the first time we were on the sea and slept like a log till the Stewardess brought me a cup of tea and said it was 7.30. A good night's rest has made my head feel much clearer. I have felt so thick and stupid all day—cannot think why. Many are complaining of the same thing, perhaps we don't get sufficient exercise. Now the days are so short and the air so keen we are obliged to stay in our cabins more. It seems very strange that we are again having short days and winter weather instead of fine hot long summer days.

Saturday July 5th

When I went on deck at 8 a.m. the sun was shining brightly tho' the air was thick and hazy. Soon after breakfast the fog increased and rain came on so we only had a turn or two on the deck as it was very wet and slippery. Hardly safe, even for those who have found their sea legs.

A wet afternoon. Did not venture out after dinner. Sat in my snuggery and wrote to Jenny Clark as a friend has promised to post my letter when they reach Wellington. Dear little Miss Evelyn has got cold. I hope it will not be much. So many people seem to have taken colds. Either the cold wind or fog has been too much. Henry is very poorly with a sore throat. The doctor has sent him to the hospital. I hope he will soon get round to his own quarters again. It will be so lonely in the hospital all alone. We think something must have happened to the engine. We are going so very slowly and as there is no wind all sails are down. I fear there is now no chance of getting to Hobart Town Monday next.

Sunday July 6th

Fine dry bright morning. Going very slowly all night. We all slept well but think we are losing much time. We hear the engine has broken down. Saw Mr Chapman, who we just recognised as he was covered with black and iron dirt. Looks fatigued. Says he has been at work since 4 yesterday morning. Thirty-six hours! Mr Craig I didn't know—he was in a fine pickle. They were very chirpy and asked me to go and help them. Gave me 15 minutes to dress. We had service in the Saloon this morning. Not a great many people. I cannot think why they neglect the opportunity of meeting to give thanks for mercies received during this long and perilous journey. Miss Evelyn stayed in bed for breakfast and her cold seems much better.

'We had a time of it during dinner.'

Had a nice walk on deck after service. Almost an hour. Went to enquire after Mr Lawson, who is seriously ill from pleurisy. They said he was asleep then but not much improvement. He is such a nice little man. How anxious his wife would be if she only knew. 'Tis a mercy we do not hear what occurs till the worst is over. A fine breeze sprung up after dinner and the deck's nice and dry. We, Mrs Calla and me, stayed out till 4 p.m., then read a little and wrote a few more lines to Jenny. At 7 we had some singing in Saloon. Mr Williams led. Mrs Cox was not very well. When I returned it was blowing hard and difficult walking, the lower deck so slippery. Had a peep at Henry. The hospital is very small: two shelves and he lays on one of these, a small porthole to light the little place and a ventilator. He must feel like a rat in a trap. He seems very depressed.

Monday July 7th

Very rough again this morning. Engines going I am thankful to say. There is a strong breeze which will help us to make up for lost time, tho' 'tis very difficult to put our clothes in the boxes. Had breakfast with Miss Evelyn and Lucy in their cabin as the sea is washing over the main deck again.

Went up but only stayed a short time—the sea was so high and the Coptic *just did pitch. Magee helped me down to dinner. I just reached the cabin door. They hauled me in, Mr and Mrs Thomas, or I should have been half drowned by the heavy sea that came over-board. Poor Magee was wet up to his waist. We had a time of it during dinner. First one thing slipped then all went together like a regiment of soldiers—glasses, bottles, meat and vegetables, rolls, knives, forks, plates, salt and pepper. Everything that can move does move, and with a vengeance. It makes me rather vexed when one feels hungry. I got such a drenching after dinner. Went up the steps that lead to the upper deck. Just as I reached the top a heavy sea broke right over the upper deck. I held on for life. I felt the wind would hurl me over the rail if I didn't. Mr Hawkins held me too, and laughed ready to kill himself. He wanted me to get one, as I had luckily escaped the whole six weeks. Very rough. Did what packing we could but 'tis difficult when the things go rolling all over the cabin. Lucy and me had some arrowroot and went to bed in good time. The seas fell on board two or three times like a clap of thunder. One in particular very heavy (as Mr Frost said, things one reads of but seldom saw).*

Tuesday July 8th

A fine morning. Sun shining brightly. Did some of the packing and went on deck just in time to see a lovely rainbow. Beautiful colour. It looked small, or I thought so. So shallow. All in high spirits at the thought of seeing land tomorrow.

We had such a feast in Saloon today, our last dinner on board. All the invalids appeared, for a wonder. Perhaps the bill of fare was an inducement to some of them. One of the lads caught a fine alba-tross with a piece of pork fat on a hook attached to some string. We expect to be at Hobart Town tomorrow morning. Sir Henry has just proposed the Captain's health as 'tis their last dinner on board. There are loud cheers for him, and for the Purser, Mr Ray, doctor, stewards, cooks and all who have helped to make things go smoothly. Sir Henry told me the lights could be seen, and land, distinctly at 11 p.m. Steamer going very slow. The engines have kept us back. Coal getting very low. 'Tis calm at any rate and we shall get a good night.

The steamer that left two days after the Coptic *passed us. They must have gone further south and had better weather, or it may be a faster boat. We have been going half speed the last 12 hours. I am told that one of the boilers leak. We ought to feel very thankful that it is nothing serious and that we are so near our journey's end. We are all tired of this easy, lazy life.*

AUSTRALIA AT LAST

10 July–15 July 1884

WHY, one might well ask, did the Lochs book their passages on a ship that was going to Hobart when their real destination was Melbourne? The *Coptic* was probably the first passenger ship that was available. Sir Henry was anxious to reach Victoria as soon as possible for it had been without a resident governor since the Marquis of Normanby had sailed for home in early April, and the colony had merely had an administrator since that date. Various causes had contributed to this long delay in appointing a successor to Normanby. Several distinguished people had been suggested for the post, including Queen Victoria's youngest son, Prince Leopold, Duke of Albany, but not one of these was found to be entirely suitable. It was probably fortunate that Prince Leopold was not formally offered the post, for he had inherited the family's tendency to haemophilia, and died while still very young. In 1867, Australia's first royal visitor, the Queen's son Alfred, Duke of Edinburgh, had been shot and seriously wounded at a function in Sydney, and if Prince Leopold had become the second royal visitor only to die soon after reaching our shores, Australia would indeed have had a black record.

When the *Coptic* reached Hobart, a group of officials boarded her and escorted the Lochs to the wharf, where a crowd of citizens was waiting, anxious to be the first to catch a glimpse of the distinguished Sir Henry and his family. Among the welcoming officials was the manager of the railway, offering a special train to take the Governor to Launceston, on his way to Melbourne, whenever it suited him, and making arrangements for some of his staff to proceed there immediately to prepare Government House for the family's arrival. Despite the chronicle of woes in Emma's journal of the voyage, the Tasmanian papers were able to report that:

> The Vice Regal party are in the enjoyment of perfect health, and fine weather was experienced to the Cape of Good Hope, but from thence the passage was rather rough. The health, not only of His Excellency and family, but all on board the "Coptic" was excellent, no disease of any kind having broken out during the voyage. Sir Henry made himself popular amongst the passengers in sports and pastimes.

The Lochs' party were fortunate that their first glimpse of the country that was to be their future home was Tasmania for, as the shipping guide informed them,

> . . . the general aspect of the country, both physical and social, is more English than that of any other part of Australia. The homesteads with their stone built houses, trim lawns, well kept gardens and luxurious hawthorn hedges, recall the scenery of the English counties, while the orchards delight the eye with all the fruit of the northern country produced here in even a greater abundance and perfection. Nowhere are such apples and pears, strawberries and gooseberries, as in Tasmania.

When they reached Hobart's Government House, where they were to be the guests of Sir George Strahan, the visitors could not fail to be impressed. Second in size only to Melbourne's palatial Government House, it was admittedly too large for Strahan, who was a childless widower, but its huge reception rooms with their carved ceilings and sets of folding doors, made it ideal for entertaining. It followed the plan of many houses built in England last century, in having high ceilinged rooms upstairs and a set of smaller basement rooms below ground level, where the servants lived and worked. To increase its similarity to English houses, all the furniture, most of which had been purchased in London, was of dark mahogany. Its extensive grounds, which in those days contained a miniature 'home farm' with chickens and cows, were adjacent to the Botanical Gardens, and possessed one of the very few 'fruit walls' ever to be built in Australia: these structures, very popular in Britain, consisted of double brick walls with a cavity between the two walls. In the late afternoon a small fire was lit in this cavity and left to smoulder all night. Its purpose was to warm the bricks and keep the adjacent fruit trees safe from frost, ensuring large and perfect fruit for the household.

Government House Tasmania Thursday July 10th

Lovely morning. Oh, the views from the windows are splendid, the bush in the distance makes one wish to penetrate and see something of the life they lead there. Lady Loch was up early. Lucy and me then had a walk to Hobart Town. It is all so different to anything I have ever see before. This is their winter and the trees look so funny. They peel from top to bottom, they don't lose their foliage as in England. The leaves are green all the year round. We saw some magpies and other large birds but no sparrows or small birds of any kind. We returned to Government House at 1.30 well pleased with our outing. I have a wretched cold and went to bed after dinner for a time, I feel so used up. After Lady Loch was dressed wrote a little, then as soon as I could do so after supper went to bed. They made me a poultice and was so good to me. Had something hot and a good fire, hope to be well quickly.

THIS WAS A day of relaxation, not only for Emma, but for the whole party as Sir George had been careful to leave the Lochs' first day ashore free from engagements of any kind. He felt that they would appreciate a rest before they faced Friday's round of engagements—the morning visit to the Charitable Institute, the afternoon reception and Bishop Sandford and his wife to dine in

Government House, Hobart.

the evening. He knew that Sandford would have much in common with Sir Henry, for he was a fellow Scot who had worked for years with the Bishop of Edinburgh.

Mrs Sandford, too, must surely have looked forward to the evening although she made no secret of the fact that she detested life in the colony, and shortly after this, returned by herself to the Old Country. This must have added to the Bishop's sorrows: he had already suffered the loss of six of his children, only two sons and a daughter surviving to adulthood.

Sandford had thrown himself into the work of his huge diocese, and as well as church work did much to foster the growth of hospitals and other caring institutions. He was highly regarded not only by the church people, but by the whole population, and he was clear sighted enough to realise that for the church to form an integral part of the community, its clergy should be Australian born. Because of his wife's inability to reconcile herself to life in Tasmania, Sandford resigned from the See after a few short years, to be succeeded by Bishop Montgomery, whose young son, 'Monty', the World War II leader, has become a household word.

Government House Friday July 11th

A fine morning, all well and down to breakfast. Afterwards, we went to see the grounds as it was a bright sunny morning. Mrs Paisy went thro' the houses with us, her husband was up in the house arranging the decorations for the reception. The garden is very large, all kinds of flowers out tho' 'tis winter here. Geraniums, heliotrope, mignonette, lettuce, figs. The soil must be very rich, it looks so black, and everything seems to thrive. At 2 p.m. the band arrived and at 3 the company began to assemble, such troops of ladies, very, very smart in every sort of colour. They walked up and down the lawn and then a regular rush for tea, all seemed to go at once and the same time. They soon dispersed after tea. The Bishop and his wife dined here.

THIS RECEPTION would have been an event of great importance for the ladies of Hobart, for Government House had been without a hostess for the years that Sir George, a widower, had been there. Now was their opportunity to see, and be seen, in the most stylish costumes in their wardrobes: no wonder Emma found them 'very, very smart'. She, of course, would have dressed Lady Loch in a different costume for each of these engagements, and would certainly have taken special care with every detail of her dress for this first public appearance in the new country.

The *Hobart Mercury* reporter, clearly a man with a mind above the triviality of dress, informed his readers only that:

 Sir Henry and Lady Loch. Yesterday afternoon a reception took place at Government House, at which about 200 ladies and gentlemen were present, in order to welcome and be introduced to Sir Henry Brougham and Lady Loch, who are at present the guests of Sir George Cumine Strahan . . . The reception continued from 3 to 5 o'clock. Previous to the reception His Excellency Sir G.C. Strahan, Sir Henry Loch, Lady Loch and family, drove out on the New Town-road, and visited the New Town Charitable Institution. The distinguished party appeared to take a very great interest in the inmates, both of their Excellencies entering freely into conversation with those who take advantage of the hospitalities of the institution. Sir Henry Loch expressed himself as highly pleased with his visit, and also referred to the complete and admirable way in which the institution was managed.

Government House Tasmania Saturday July 12th

Wet early this morning. Got such a bad cold, feel so thick and stupid. Went for a turn with Lucy soon after 11 but felt the cold terribly, went to see Benson but found William had taken him for a walk. He is so miserable tied up. I had such a fright this morning. Mrs Smith's rosella does not care for strangers, it flew from her shoulder on to my hand and pecked me rather hard. I felt such a coward but perhaps it's from feeling so poorly. We had a turn in the garden, such beautiful shrubs and plants in flower. Geraniums like trees, prickly pear, mulberry, figs, and such a store of fine fruit in store for winter use, apples, pears, pumpkins, figs, etc., etc. This is their coldest month of the year, they have walnut trees, a nice clump of tall trees. Some snow fell today and the hills are covered which may account for the bitter cold air. Had to lie down for an hour or two felt so wretched from heavy cold, the wind so very high, sounds as if the windows would come in during the night.

While Emma stayed indoors again and nursed her cold, the Lochs braved the icy winds to return the Premier's call:

 On Saturday morning, Sir Henry Loch and family returned the call made by the Premier (Hon. W.R. Giblin), and had an interview with the members of the Ministry in the Chief Secretary's room . . . A short but interesting conversation ensued; and, in passing, it was incidentally mentioned that this is not

Hobart, Tasmania.

 the first visit that the new Governor of Victoria has made to Tasmania. In 1852, just before the commencement of the war in China, in which Sir Henry was so cruelly treated by the Chinese, when acting as an envoy under a flag of truce, in company with Lord Stuart Wortley and Mr. Colvin, now Sir Auckland Colvin, who was afterwards well known in India, the new Governor of Victoria included Tasmania in a travelling tour, and it seemed to afford him great pleasure to renew his acquaintance with Hobart after so many years. At the close of the interview the party returned to Government House.

Government House Tasmania Sunday July 13th

Fine morning but very cold. I am thankful to say my head feels clearer today. Packed up a great many things after breakfast, Lucy helped me. Lady Loch and Sir Henry, young ladies and Master Douglas and the gentlemen of the suite have been to church. (One felt a distinct shock of earthquake at 2 p.m., Lucy and me were

45

sitting in my room waiting for the dinner bell when everything seemed to heave. The wind was quite still at the time and we could not think what had caused the commotion at first. It must be terrible when a severe shock comes.) We went to dinner and told Mr and Mrs Smith. They treated the matter very lightly and said if we lived in that part of the country we should soon get accustomed to such little things as they were very common. After dinner 3 p.m. Lucy found Mam'selle in the passage leading to her room in a very uneasy state of mind. She said everything in the room have been moving. The jug rattled in the basin, fire irons and the sofa on which she was lying heaved up and down, so we concluded there had been another shock, just one hour after the first. Rather alarming to have two shocks in one day. We leave early tomorrow, thank God.

THE PRESS did not mention the earthquake, but observed that:

On Sunday forenoon the party attended Divine service in St. David's Cathedral. There was a large congregation, and the service was conducted by Rev. Canon Bailey, assisted by Revs. John Gray and J.C. Whall. As the Vice-Regal party proceeded to their carriage, they were respectfully recognised by a number of the congregation, the recognition being graciously acknowledged by both Sir Henry and Lady Loch. Sir Henry, Lady Loch, and Sir George drove in the afternoon to the Fern Tree Bower, and the distinguished strangers were greatly struck by the beautiful surroundings of this charming spot.

Monday July 14th–15th

All up at 6 a.m. Packing done and downstairs before 8. We had a good breakfast and left Government House at 8.30 for the station where a special saloon carriage was in waiting to take Sir Henry Loch and family to Launceston. Lucy and me were the first to arrive in a carriage and pair with all small things, then Sir Henry and the gentlemen in waiting and Mam'selle Heyman and the young ladies. William went off at 8 with the luggage, and Benson (who will be glad enough when his travelling days are done) was popped into the guard's van and off we went. A reporter jumped in the last minute to give his version to the press. We waved handkerchiefs as we passed Government House. Mrs Smith was at the window. The way in which the train jumped and thumped us all about was laughable. The corners were so sharp, but we held on and got no unlucky blows.

Such lovely country we passed thro' where the timber had been cut down and now large sheep farms. Timber seemed abundant, land very rich and a mass of berries and flowers tho' 'tis winter time, must be lovely in the summer. We had a good hot cup o'tea at Oatlands. It is a good arrangement to have both tea and coffee ready when the train arrives. Bread and butter and sandwiches are also to be had.

We arrived at Launceston soon after 1.40 and went on board a tender for the Flinders *s.s., where Sir Henry was received with loud cheers. The flags were up and it all looked very gay, but small after the* Coptic. *We have one small cabin between Miss Evelyn, Lucy and me. Mam'selle and Miss Edith, Sir Henry and Master Douglas. Lady Loch has one to herself, Mr Sturgess, Capt. Traill and Lord Castlerosse occupy one—they won't have very much room. There was a good lunch, or I may say dinner, flowers on the table and everything nicely done. One long table the whole length of the saloon quite full of ladies and gentlemen. Sir Henry and Lady Loch and party at one end, we managed to get seats at the other end and Lucy, me and William had a good meal as we had 8 o'clock breakfast and nothing but a sandwich till 4 p.m.*

We did unpacking then lay down. Lucy was not feeling well. We did not undress. Slept fairly well and rose early to dress Lady Loch for early breakfast. After we passed the Heads the guns began to fire, the steamer was dressed with flags and at 11 some gentlemen came on board to welcome Sir Henry. Soon after we saw the Aus-tralian Squadron in view. The Nelson *stopped and when opposite loud cheers were given, a steam launch came alongside and took all the ladies and gentlemen on board the* Nelson *where a luncheon was given to Sir Henry, Lady Loch and family, after which several speeches. One gentleman presented Lady Loch with a beautiful*

The naval reception for Sir Henry Loch. (National Library of Australia, Canberra)

bouquet. After luncheon all were landed at Melbourne and went off to the Treasury midst much cheering, where Sir Henry was sworn in, then left for Government House escorted by a guard of mounted police. All very tired out with the long day's excitement, they reached Government House soon after 5.

We arrived at 3 p.m. straight from the steam ship Flinders. *Found Mrs Calla and Mary well, but we all think this House too large for the staff and fear some will regret coming all this way only to find at the end of the term they are worse off than when they landed. It is a grand looking place but, oh, so inconvenient, nothing of use. We are all in despair, it will be quite impossible to have any sort of order or comfort unless more hands are added. Mr Hawkins looks tired and depressed. There is so much ground to walk over before you can reach the rooms occupied I am afraid we will all be used up instead of getting a new lease as we were promised.*

ON THE MORNING of the 14th, they were all up early, and were greeted by blue skies. But despite the carefully made plans for the special train 'with Mr C. H. Grant in charge', which was to convey the Lochs and their entourage to Launceston to connect with the Bass Strait ferry, the *Flinders*, there was a slight hitch. As the papers reported next day 'the *Flinders* was detained at the bar for some little time owing to the quantity of luggage to be put on board'. But it was all eventually stowed away and the passengers were assured that despite this slight delay, there was every possibility of the steamer reaching Port Phillip Heads on time.

 Sir Henry and Lady Loch. Sir Henry, Lady Loch, family, and suite, who, after their voyage from England, have spent a pleasant week as the guests of Sir George Strahan at Government House, before proceeding to Victoria, leave for Launceston this morning at 8.45, by special train, which is timed to catch the express at Evandale junction, which will arrive in Launceston at 1.45, in time for the *s.s. Flinders*, posted to sail for Melbourne at 2 o'clock in the afternoon. The distinguished party will be accompanied as far as Launceston by His Excellency the Governor. The train will be in charge of Mr. Grant.

As THE DATE of the Lochs' arrival in Melbourne drew closer, elaborate plans were made for every aspect of their reception. The Premier, Mr Service, announced that Tuesday 15 July would be a public holiday, and that Excursion Tickets would be issued on all railway lines on the previous day, and these would be available up until Wednesday evening so that country people would have an opportunity to witness the ceremony. Large crowds were expected along the route, and fortune seemed to smile on the occasion, for as one newspaper announced, 'If Sir Henry Brougham Loch had picked his weather, he could not have been blessed with a more perfect day than that which greeted him on 15th July. After a capital passage from Tasmania, the *Flinders* reached the heads about half past nine'.

The Melbourne papers seemed to vie with each other in the length and enthusiasm of their reports of the occasion, and to quote from them would take up many pages. They described in detail the flotilla that would sail down the bay to meet the Governor, and to list all the distinguished persons who would be on board. The provincial newspapers gave equally enthusiastic, though slightly shorter accounts, and the 'Melbourne correspondent' of one of these, after describing how Sir William Stawell, who had administered the colony till the new governor's arrival, being accompanied by the Premier, boarded the *Flinders* to welcome the Lochs and to escort them onto the *Nelson*. This was the pride of the Victorian Navy, a grand British warship built of oak but by this time fitted with auxiliary engines to increase her speed and manoeuvrability. For this special occasion she was decked with flags, and for Sir Henry's reception, her yards were manned and a salute fired from her guns.

 As soon as he boarded her another salute rang out, accompanied by deafening cheers from the spectators who crowded the poop, and His Excellency, who seemed astounded by the warmth of his reception then proceeded to the bridge, where Sir William Stawell also conducted Lady Loch. Lady Loch's appearance produced quite a remarkable impression, and to use a sporting phrase she won from the jump. Simply but elegantly attired in a brown costume, with a brown bonnet and pheasant feather, there was a grace accompanied by a pleasant kindliness in her manner, which made her at once the theme of approving conversation, and it was easy to see that we had at last received a Governor's lady who would revive the lost popularity of Government House and easily queen society . . .

About one o'clock the Luncheon was served on the gun-deck, the caterer, Clements, rising to the occasion, and surpassing his best previous efforts. The collation was a cold one, but wine flowed freely, and the chablis with which everyone was enraptured increased the genial flow of conversation. The *Nelson* was kept under easy steam the whole time, the gunboats closing upon her, so that they could be clearly seen through the open ports, and after the edibles had been disposed of, the usual loyal toasts were drunk.

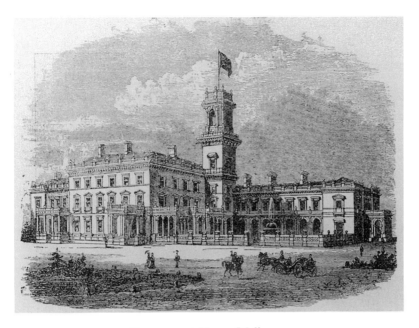

Government House, Melbourne

TOAST FOLLOWED TOAST, and one speech followed another. At about three o'clock the official party stepped on to the town pier at Port Melbourne, and after acknowledging the cheers of the dense crowds there, they proceeded in carriages, drawn by four horses, to the Old Treasury where the Governor was sworn in. This time there were not only long speeches of welcome and con-gratulations, but no less than four illuminated addresses were presented to Sir Henry, the last one, which seemed to give him particular pleasure, being from the Manx Association of Victoria. Eventually, a little before 5 o'clock, when the last of the welcoming speeches had been acknowledged and responded to, the Lochs were able to sink into their carriage and depart for Government House. It was no wonder that the Lochs had been astounded by the size of the crowds along the route, and overwhelmed by the length and number of the speeches, for although Sir Henry had been extremely popular as Governor of the Isle of Man, he had never before been greeted by such numbers of people. In fact, the total population of the Isle was just over 50 000, and Douglas, its capital, had a mere 14 000 people, in contrast to Melbourne's 200 000.

As the Lochs' cavalcade wound up the driveway of Government House in the early evening, after a long and tiring day, they had their first glimpse of the imposing building that was to be their home for the next five years. Inside the large mansion, their staff, also very tired after a long day of moving and unpacking, were feeling dismayed at the size and inconvenience of the place. How could they reconcile this with the promise of an easier life that had influenced them to travel to Australia?

THE SOCIAL SEASON BEGINS

16 July–8 August 1884

AFTER THE DAY of brilliant sunshine that greeted the
Lochs' arrival, Melbourne's cold winter weather returned,
but the staff were probably glad to have some comparatively quiet
days so that they could get on with the unpacking and sorting, and
could familiarize themselves with their new quarters. Apparently
some extra staff were engaged to help with the work of the enormous house, for three new names appear in Emma's diary, and
these extra staff members were able to assist with the round of
entertaining that was soon to begin.

Wednesday July 16th

*Began to unpack and kept on the whole day without making much
show. Feel so heavy with cold, but must work and get the clothes in
their places.*

Sunday July 20th

*Went to St Paul's Church in the morning. Got our first walk to Mel-
bourne. It is rather farther from Government House than I expected.
Mrs Westlake went with us. The church reminds me more of a lecture
room than God's house. A want of reverence in every way. A clever*

Sir Henry, Lady Loch and their daughters welcome guests to a reception at Government House, Melbourne. (National Library of Australia, Canberra)

sermon by the Dean about the life of Saul. I felt as if I wanted a special service to offer up thanks for our safety from the peril of the deep.

Wednesday July 30th

Lady Loch's first reception from 3 till 5 p.m. The people streamed in. Me, Lucy, Jane, Christine, served tea and coffee in Refreshment Room adjoining Ballroom. Some of the ladies were elegantly attired, others looked dowdy. It was a rare mixture of society, all sorts of respectable citizens came to offer their congratulations, in all 1200 callers. It was very amusing. We all felt rather stiff next day. There was a good string band playing in the Ballroom so it all passed off merrily.

THE *Age* was able to report that:

The first reception held by Lady Loch since her arrival in the Colony took place at Government House yesterday and proved a brilliant success. About 1,200 ladies and gentlemen attended to pay their respects to her Ladyship, the numbers being greater than at any reception held by the wife of any previous Governor. From 3 to 5 o'clock, the hours during which it was announced that Lady Loch would receive visitors, there was a continuous stream of vehicles up the drive to Government House, their occupants alighting at the main entrance. In the ante-room the callers inscribed their names in a visitors' book and left their cards. They then passed into the drawing room where they were announced and presented to Lady Loch, after which they passed through into the ballroom which was used as a promenade for the time being. At the lower end of the ballroom Herr Plock's band played a number of pleasing selections of music. Light refreshments were also provided.

It need hardly be said that nearly all the visitors were ladies, and a large number of handsome winter costumes were worn. The rooms were beautifully arranged with cut flowers and plants, supplied from the Botanical Gardens, by the curator, Mr Guilfoyle.

Friday August 1st

Lady Loch's second At Home. About the same number, tho' there seemed many more. They were as a rule quietly dressed and seemed very amiable. We had quite done by 5.15. The string band was here again and the tea and coffee was in great demand. We had no leisure from beginning to end.

THIS SECOND RECEPTION was even more largely attended, it being estimated that over 1500 ladies and gentlemen were present, and within a few days even larger functions took place in Melbourne. The first of these was a gathering at the Exhibition Building, where some hundreds of gentlemen had assembled. Punctually at 1 o'clock the Governor, accompanied by Captain Traill, drove up to the entrance, where he was met by the Premier and other officials, and conducted to the main hall for a wine tasting, to enable everyone to sample the wines that had been sent to the Calcutta International Exhibition by Victoria's forty-two wine growers. After 'God Save the Queen' on the grand organ, loyal toasts were drunk, and the company invited to partake of light refreshments, and to congratulate the growers on the thirty-six medals that they had been awarded at Calcutta.

August 5th

Mayor's Ball at Town Hall Melbourne. Sir Henry and Lady Loch went to the Ball at 9 p.m. and the four gentlemen in waiting, Captain Traill, Lord Castlerosse, Mr Hughes, Mr Sturgess, returned home about 12.30. There was a great many ladies in high dresses. How strange, as they are wealthy and might dress in good taste at any rate.

In the evening of 5 August, after the wine tasting at the Exhibition Building, the Lochs attended the Mayor's Ball in the Town Hall, and this glittering event was fully described in the columns of the *Argus*. Sir Henry was so amazed at the wealth that was in evidence at the ball, that he felt he must make a comparison of the Melbourne of the day with the Melbourne he had visited as a young man.

The ball given by Mr C. Smith, M.L.A., Mayor of Melbourne, last night, was one of the most brilliant gatherings which has been seen in the Town-hall for a long time. The guests numbered about 1,600 ladies and gentlemen, and as a considerable portion of the latter were officers wearing military or naval uniform, the aspect of the throng was very striking. Special preparations were made for beautifying the interior of the hall, which, by the time the guests began to arrive was very tastefully decorated. On either side, above the balconies, were trophies consisting of the Imperial shield, the Prince of Wales's coat of arms, the four quarters of the Royal standard, two shields bearing the civic arms of Melbourne, and other devices. Large mirrors were hung on the walls underneath the balconies, where there were other flags and coats of arms. The orchestra and choir in front of the organ were filled with beautiful ferns, which entirely concealed the seats, and small electric lamps were placed in positions where their brilliant light was softened in its passage through the thick foliage. Coloured electric lamps were hung at intervals round the front of the balconies. In the south gallery, where Warnecke's band of 25 performers was stationed, there were ferns and shrubs, and the bleak aspect of this portion of the hall was thereby modified. The general appearance of these decorations was highly creditable to Mr. W. Morgan of Swanston-street, and Mr. Joseph, the latter of whom had charge of the electric light apparatus. Up to 9 o'clock—the hour announced for commencing—long lines of vehicles rolled along Swanston-street to the Town-hall steps, where the guests alighted and passed into the building. His Excellency Sir Henry Loch and Lady Loch, accompanied by Captain Traill, private secretary, arrived at 10 minutes past 9, and entered the hall at the Collins-street door, where they were received by the aldermen of the city, who also conducted them into the ball room. As the Governor and Lady Loch proceeded to the dais, in front of the platform, the band played the National Anthem. The Mayor and Miss Smith having received their distinguished guests, and the necessary introductions having been made, his Worship retired to take off his huge robe of office, in order to facilitate his movements in the dance. It was then observed that he, as well as other members of the civic body, was in full civic costume, though this would hardly have been suspected when he was disguised in his imposing robe . . .

The Mayor having returned from his transformation, and the proper positions having been taken, nothing was wanted but for the music to begin. An awkward pause was broken by Mr. Fitzgibbon, who, airily waving his hand to the band, like an enchanter working a wonder, gave the company to understand that the leader of the instruments was keeping a very close eye on him indeed. The floor was crowded to inconvenience during the first half-hour, and the efforts of the dancers seemed to come short of realising the full enjoyment of their pastime. In the square dances the difficulty was not so great, but those who took part in the walzes—and nearly everybody did take part in them—found the poetry of motion in many cases converted into a series of collisions, for which no-one in particular was to blame. If any could be held deserving of censure more than others, it was those couples who when walzing reached out their arms stiffly like sema-phores of danger, plunging them into the sides of all who came within reach, and sweeping them round in eccentric and puzzling circles. As soon as it was realised that comfortable dancing was an impossible thing for every one at the same time, large numbers of guests made their way to the balconies and platform, from which elevated positions they were enabled to watch the interesting movements going on below. At 11 o'clock a general move was made in the direction of the supper-room in the basement. His worship the mayor presided, and the repast was admirably prepared by Mr. T. Clements.

After replying to the loyal toasts, Sir Henry went on to assure the gathering that:

Lady Loch and I will enter as one of yourselves into your interests. (Cheers.) Whether they be interests of a social character, or interests connected with the happiness and welfare of the community, it will always be our endeavour to respond to that confidence by identifying ourselves with all movements that may tend to the improvement and advantage of this great colony. (Cheers.) When I see the great hall in which we assemble this evening, and witness this large assembly, I am almost inclined to think that my ever having been here in Melbourne in former years is a dream of my imagination. (Hear, hear.) For in that dream I saw no great public buildings, no grand Town-hall, no well-equipped carriages driving through wide streets, with shops on either side which might be said to rival in appearance those of Paris and London. But in that dream I saw low one-storied buildings, mostly of wood, and in the streets instead of carriages, heavily laden drays, with occasionally a few open waggonettes full of excited shouting men, down on a spree from the diggings. (Laughter and cheers.) But if it is not all a dream, I wonder how these great changes have taken place—how many great institutions like the hospitals, the museums, and many benevolent societies have been organised, and brought to their present state of completion, equalling in their government and management similar institutions in the old country which have taken centuries to mature.

August 7th

First large dinner, Parliamentary, eighty gentlemen who sat down at 7.30 to a first class dinner cooked by Mrs Calla, and much credit is due to her and Mary who have worked very hard that all might be satisfactory. At 9 p.m. Lady Loch received the wives and daughters of the gentlemen who dined—we had to serve tea in the corner of the front Hall. All looked very well dressed and seemed very easy. All over at 11.30. We then had to clear the way, consequently nearly 1 a.m. before we retired all tired out. Very stiff day for one and all.

TWO DAYS AFTER the Mayor's Ball Sir Henry held this parliamentary dinner, which was a huge success from every point of view. In Parliament an understanding was reached that the

Assembly should rise at the refreshment hour to allow the honourable members to attend the dinner, and when they arrived they found a dazzling spectacle in the State dining room. The long table had been set with the Lochs' crested silver, probably the first time it had been used in Victoria. The *Argus* was able to inform its readers that:

> His Excellency the Governor last evening entertained at dinner at Government-house, about 70 gentlemen—members of the Legislative Assembly, the Executive Council, the judicial bench, and officers of Parliament. The invitations to members of Parliament, &c, extended only half-way down the alphabetical list, and the remainder are invited for Monday evening. His Honour the Chief Justice was prevented by illness from availing himself of the Governor's invitation for last evening. After the dinner Lady Loch was "at home", and about 200 ladies were received by her. A very pleasant evening was spent, the visitors coming away agreeably impressed with Sir Henry and Lady Loch's efforts to minister to their pleasure.

August 8th

Up at 7, Lady Loch dressed, early breakfast 8.15, started at 9 for Sandhurst. Out all day. Returned to Melbourne 11.30 p.m.

THE *Argus* gives us a more detailed description of the day's events:

> The time of His Excellency the Governor will be very closely occupied to-day during his first visit to Sandhurst [Bendigo]. His Excellency will be accompanied by the Premier, the Chief Secretary, the minister of Mines, and will start by special train from Spencer-street station at 9.40 a.m. The train is to arrive at Castlemaine at 11.55 a.m., and a stay of 20 minutes will be made at the station there to enable the local borough council to present an address of welcome to Sir Henry Loch. Sandhurst will be reached at five minutes to one o'clock, and

The city of Bendigo in the 1880s.

an address will be immediately presented to His Excellency by the mayor and councillors of the city. A luncheon will be ready at the Shamrock Hotel by 1 o'clock, and when it has been partaken of His Excellency and party will be conveyed to the public gardens, and from there will drive past the mechanics's institute, the hospital, the asylum, and other public buildings. They are also to visit the lake, inspect the Garden Gully mine, and make a flying journey to Eaglehawk, and arrive back in Sandhurst in time for His Excellency to lay the memorial-stone of the new public offices at half-past 4 o'clock. The banquet to His Excellency will commence at 6 o'clock, and the special train will start on the return journey to Melbourne at 8.10 p.m.

SANDHURST is today's Bendigo: it had begun as the Bendigo gold-field, named, it was believed, after a particularly lucky boxer of the day, but when it achieved city status in 1861, it decided to adopt a

Castlemaine.

more dignified name, and chose 'Sandhurst'. And Sandhurst it was to remain until 1891 when the original name was restored.

It was a triumph for Sandhurst that it had the honour of a visit from the new Governor before its rival Ballarat had one. The two cities had long been competing with each other. Ballarat could boast a larger population of 40 000, while Sandhurst, lagging behind by only a few thousand, prided itself on the diversity of its industries. The day of Sir Henry's visit was declared a public holiday throughout the district to enable everyone to take part in the celebrations.

Despite a somewhat longer than anticipated halt at Castlemaine as it sped north, the train managed to reach Sandhurst on time, and what was an even greater feat, the Governor managed to get through every one of the engagements that had been crammed into the programme.

Castlemaine people felt annoyed when the Station Master declared that no more than fifty people could be safely accommodated on the platform to witness the presentation of an illuminated address to the Governor—why, they asked, was the presentation not moved to the outside of the station, where the people could have stood round in a semicircle and caught a glimpse of the function?

There was some consternation felt in Sandhurst, too, for it was after 11 o'clock that a telegram arrived to say that the Governor would be accompanied by Lady Loch. No present or addresses had been prepared for her but a large bouquet was hastily contrived and by the time of their departure that evening, the Mayor was able to present to Lady Loch a large satin and plush card on which were the words 'Souvenir to Lady Brougham Loch: memento of her ladyship's first visit to Sandhurst, August 8th 1884'.

Sandhurst's satisfaction with all the events of the day and its prophecies for the colony's rosy future under Sir Henry's administration are expressed in the editorial of its Saturday newspaper.

Other Governors have been met by the Bendigonians in the most loyal manner, and with every assurance of their attachment to the throne. The same spirit was strongly exhibited yesterday in the welcome given to Sir Henry and Lady Loch. So much had been heard in their praise that the citizens were anxious to do them honour independently of the desire to afford proof of fidelity to the beloved "little lady" who occupies the British throne. It is to be hoped that His Excellency will carry away with him pleasant reminiscences of his visit to Sandhurst. He, together with his amiable wife, won the hearts of all who had the honour and pleasure of being introduced to them, and here as elsewhere their great affability placed all persons with whom they were brought in contact at their ease, and as Mr. Berry remarked at the banquet at the Shamrock "They are no sooner known than they become one of ourselves." The general opinion is that Sir Henry Loch will become the most popular Governor the colony has yet known.

Government House, from Melbourne's Botanic Gardens.

ANOTHER ROUND OF VISITS

11 August–16 October 1884

S IR HENRY was indefatigable in visiting the distant parts of
the colony and getting to know their inhabitants, and on his
official visits he was always accompanied, of course, by some of his
suite. If Lady Loch went with him, Emma was usually in the
background; she was responsible for the packing and the
unpacking, and for helping Lady Loch into those elegant gowns
and bonnets that gave country people perhaps their first glimpse
of Paris fashions. All nineteenth-century clothes were volu-
minous, formal evening gowns still had trains, and to be prepared
for the hot, cold or even pouring wet days that Victoria's notoriously fickle climate could produce, a vast wardrobe had to be
packed for every country visit.

August 11th

*Second large dinner, for eighty. All went off successfully and the
ladies arrived at 9. Many very well dressed and good looking, but to
my mind rather fast going some of them—there was a large
gathering altogether. We served tea, coffee and sandwiches, claret
cup, champagne too in the corner close to the State Saloon. All left
before 12, we did not finish till after that hour. Nearly sixty dishes of
cakes and dessert to stow away. We feel nearly used up. So much
standing is very trying to old folks.*

August 17th

Went to Christ Church this morning. A nice service. Such a good choir sang above while the offertory was collected—'Be of good Courage' and 'I will Comfort thine heart'—oh, so beautifully. It was a very wet morning and we had to take shelter on our way home under a doorway, such a heavy downpour. After dinner Lucy, me and Mr Hawkins mounted the tower for the first time. It's a good pull but nothing like the Arc de Triomphe in Paris, we had a splendid view of Melbourne as it was a very clear day. Worth the effort.

August 18th

Very wet again. Went with Sir Henry, Lady Loch, Capt. Traill at 11 a.m. in the carriage to Melbourne. Lady Loch went to a photographer in Bourke Street. In the afternoon Miss Cross came to see me, Mrs Hounsell's niece. She seems a dear lady-like little woman, and so pleased to get some token from her aunt, whom she has never seen. I am going to 99 Cremorne Street to see her first opportunity.

August 24th

Lovely morning. Lucy, me, Mr Strickland and Mr Hawkins went to Christ Church. Such a full church and nice service. We were rather late home. Weather too warm to hurry. Mr Drury came about 3 (a friend of Mr Hawkins). He is Engineer on board the s.s. Ballarat, *P. & O. Co. We all went to the Botanical Gardens and stayed till nearly five. The gardens are beginning to look splendid.*

Tuesday August 26th

Our second visitor left by 11 a.m. Mr Fitzclarence and his valet, Mr Strickland, for England. They sail at 1 p.m. by s.s. Ballarat *from Williamstown. Mr S. has kindly taken some little parcels for us.*

August 27th

Dinner party for twenty. Sir Wm. & Lady Clarke came to sleep for the night and a sister of Lady Clarke, Miss Snodgrass. The maid is a Miss Shannon, rather amusing, not like the usual type. Sir Wm. is enormously rich, the richest man (I am told) in Melbourne.

August 31st

Fine morning, high wind. A fire took place near Melbourne in the cricket ground. The grandstand took fire from some cause—carelessness 'tis supposed—it looked alarming even from Lady Loch's boudoir. No houses near so there will be no loss of life we hope. Lucy and I had two letters each by the English mail today. It is nice to think they don't forget one in old England. Dear old Ted has just seen our arrival in the Times. *Went to church with Mr Lovegrove and Lucy, Christ Church, South Yarra. Not such a good sermon as last Sunday but very full congregation and nice hymns, 'Holy, Holy, Holy' for once beautifully sung.*

THE PAPERS gave all the details of the fire.

BURNING OF THE M.C.C. GRANDSTAND

In the morning a fire broke out in the grand stand of the Melbourne Cricket-ground, and although there was a very large proportion of brick and iron work in the building, it burned so fiercely that within an hour it was in ruins. Owing to the light pressure of the water supply, the 10 or 11 brigades on the spot could do little to check the violence of the flames. The timbers supporting the roof were bound together with iron rods, and when the woodwork had burned through these fell in a mass, dragging down the iron roof. The wooden framework in front fell bodily inward, and the destruction was complete. At noon the flames had burned out, and an inspection of the building showed that the masonry work was cracked in so many places that it was entirely useless for re-

The fire-devastated ruins of the grandstand at the Melbourne Cricket Ground.

building, and must all come down. Even the blue-stone foundation was partly destroyed at the eastern end. The origin of the fire is not known. The grand stand was built in 1877, on debentures, taken up principally by members of the club. It occupied an area of 240ft, by 80ft., and was intended to seat 2,000 persons, but as many as 3,000 have been accommodated when intercolonial and international cricket matches were played in the M.C.C. ground. From a purely architectural point of view it was not a very elegant structure, but its plainness was more than counterbalanced by its usefulness. The novelty about it was that it could be reversed, so that in the football season, when matches were played on the ground adjoining, the same accommodation was given to spectators as at the most important cricket match. It was, in reality, a two-story building, the ground floor being occupied by ladies' rooms, a skittle alley, a large luncheon room, and two refreshment bars. The sitting accommodation was above this, and was reached from the lawn in front of three broad stairways.

This spectacular fire at the neighbouring Melbourne Cricket Club grounds was the main excitement for the staff in the next few weeks. As the flames and sparks shot high into the air they were terrified that Government House itself might be ignited.

The staff were glad of these few quiet weeks, free from the enormous parties that had meant so much hard work for them. Early in September a visit to Ballarat took place, and as the Lochs were to stay overnight there, Emma of course went, too, to assist Lady Loch in changing into the elaborate costumes that were called for at each separate reception. This visit to Ballarat proved to be one of the few occasions when Sir Henry's proverbial good luck with the weather deserted him, and to add to their misfortune he woke up on the second morning feeling violently ill. However, despite these disasters, the Lochs carried out the entire programme of events that had been arranged for them and, as usual, won the admiration and affection of everyone they met.

The opening paragraphs of the *Ballarat Courier*'s report, and Emma's diary, enable us to visualise the wintry conditions with which they had to contend.

 The invitation to his Excellency had been delayed somewhat in order that the weather, always wintry and boisterous in August and September, might become settled; but the delay did not altogether achieve the end aimed at, for a disagreeably cold and, at times wet, day had to be encountered by the visitors. The programme for the day was published in our columns yesterday, and it may at the outset be observed that, notwithstanding the unpleasantness of rain and cold, it was faithfully adhered to. The early risers yesterday morning were greeted with a fall of snow and a barometer which remained studiously low and solid, forecasting a raw September day. Showers of hail in the morning also promised discomforts for the day, but ever and anon the returning sun got in atween the clouds and brightened everything. On the whole the sunshine was happily timed, for the worst showers fell before the visitors came, or fell when they were under cover.

September 11th

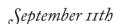

Left Government House at 8.20 a.m. for Spencer Street Station where a special train was in waiting to take Sir H. and Lady Loch,

Lake Wendouree, Ballarat.

Capt. Traill, Mr Hughes and Lord Castlerosse to Ballarat. Mr Lovegrove, Charles and myself were in attendance and had a nice saloon carriage all to ourselves. Unfortunately it was such a very cold morning and rained heavily now and again. We stopped at Geelong for 10 minutes and were told it was snowing at Ballarat, which is what one might expect considering how dreadfully cold it is. We reached Ballarat about 12 noon and the Volunteers were there, and their band, to receive the Governor and Lady Loch. The Major also read an address, then they were taken to the hotel and afterwards to open the Art Academy. Triumphal arches were made of evergreen and hundreds of people lined the streets and especially round the hotel door to get a sight of them. Lady Clarke and Sir Wm. are staying at the same hotel, Craigs, it is nice to see someone one knows. Miss Shannon is with Lady Clarke. After came luncheon, then we went to see the lake. Had not been there many minutes when Sir Henry, Lady Loch, Lady Clarke, Sir Wm., Lord Castlerosse, Mr Hughes, Capt. Traill and all the party came and crossed the lake. We went in a steam launch behind. It was very pretty, but oh the cold! I cannot say what it was like. Then after a heavy shower it was warmer but too wet to enjoy the gardens where hundreds of lovely drooping willows were to be seen and fountains. It must be a charming retreat in the summer. We returned home [to the hotel] and at 5.30 commenced dressing Lady Loch for the banquet at 6.30. After that was over, speeches etc., they dressed for a ball given to Sir Wm. and Lady Clarke, a Masonic Ball, to which they went at 9 p.m. precisely. Miss Shannon, Charles and a young lady friend went to the hall and had a peep at the dresses. I was tired and went to bed.

The ladies and gentlemen returned about 1 a.m. Friday morning. Sir Henry was very unwell before breakfast with a bad sick headache. It was very bad for him as he has to hold a service at 10, which he got thro' very well, then came back to the hotel and prepared for the races, and we had some dinner and took a cab and went round the town. Saw the Chinese quarter, looks dreadfully dilapidated, windows broken and very dirty. The cabman pointed out the first gold mine that was worked, and another place in the road where an immense nugget was found. Miss Shannon and myself were much pleased with our drive. We saw all the principal buildings, Jewish Synagogue, chapels, churches, Post Office, Town Hall, etc., etc., and, in time to come, Ballarat will be a fine place. The streets have trees down each side and will form a fine effect. Mr Lovegrove and myself left, after a cup of tea, for the station. A crowd had collected to see our people. The special train left the station at 5 and we reached Melbourne soon after 8, Government House 8.30. We have enjoyed our first visit very much.

THE LOCHS' next expedition, about a month later, was a private visit to the Clarkes at Rupertswood, only about twenty miles to travel, and, for once, no speeches to respond to when they stepped out of the train. For the Lochs this was to be a quiet weekend with congenial friends, and Emma, too, looked forward to the company of Miss Shannon, Lady Clarke's personal maid, who had become a firm friend of Emma's when she had stayed at Government House with her mistress. On the Clarkes' first visit to Government House Emma had described Sir William as 'the richest man in Melbourne' but the Clarkes were famous for far more than the size of their bank balance. Believing that the possession of wealth brought with it the responsibility of helping others, the Clarkes were the most generous benefactors Melbourne has ever known. Sir William had been born in Tasmania where his father had vast estates, and his wife, Janet, was the daughter of a Victorian MLA, but their benefices went far beyond this continent, for they included a generous scholarship for music students as far away as London. Lady Clarke's name is familiar to today's generation from Janet Clarke Hall, originally a hostel for the early women students of Melbourne University, which she endowed, but so widely distributed and so lavish were her gifts that her name might equally have been given to the hospitals, the nursing organizations and the cultural bodies that she also encouraged.

The 'nurses' in Emma's diary would have been the young women who cared for the Clarkes' children: Lady Clarke had first come to Rupertswood as the governess of Sir William's children, and had married him two years after his wife's death. She was to prove an inspiring mother to her stepchildren and to the six children of this second marriage.

October 11th

Left Government House at a few minutes before 3 p.m. for Spencer Street Station and left by train at 3.30 for Sunbury. We found a buggy waiting to take Mr Lovegrove and myself to Rupertswood. It was only about a mile thro' the grounds. Got a fine view of the house as we drove down. The lake is very nice and a model of Sir Wm. Clarke's yacht, The Janet, *with colours flying, was on the lake, and swans, pleasure boats. Miss Shannon, Lady Clarke's maid, and Mr Smith received us at the door. We have got beautiful rooms and all are most anxious to make us comfortable. Mrs Maclean, the nurse, and her niece are both most kind. This is quite open house—anyone and everyone passing thro' the country seems to walk in and get what they want to eat and drink. Such a pity the weather is so unfavourable, heavy showers constantly falling.*

Thursday [?]

Bright morning but every place so wet we cannot venture out till some of the wet dries up. Dined rather late in the nursery with the nurses, then about 4 took a turn by the lake and rosewalk with Miss Shannon. Had a turn about the house, which is beautifully furnished by Gillow of Oxford Street, London. The ballroom is splendid and drawing room very nice, dining room rather small. Had tea in the nursery, dressed Lady Loch for dinner. It was a large party, then afterwards sat on the stairs and listened to the singing. It sounded well, some good singers.

Monday October 13th

Lovely morning. Went out for a trot to the lodge. Quite warm and oh, so sweet after the rain. The trees are all full of bloom, lilac, salt trees and another white blossom, so sweet, like orange blossom. Jenny came out and met me. We went thro' the kitchen garden and stayed out till dinner time. I am not up to much walking so did not go out again.

The weather was apparently too wet to tempt Emma into the Clarkes' beautiful garden. There were sixty acres of it, beautifully planted and maintained, but she does not seem to have ventured beyond the rosewalk and the kitchen garden. An article in the *Australasian*, however, gives a detailed account of the garden at this time, and if today's train traveller looks out of the carriage window, a little to the north of Sunbury, many of the features described in this article can still be seen. None of the Clarke family live at Rupertswood now, but the house fulfils a useful role as a secondary college.

❀ You enter the grounds through a set of ponderous and elegant iron gates, hung on massive iron piers, supported by expansive wing walls, and a commodious gate-house, embowered among a mass of evergreens. A wide carriage drive, over a mile in length, winds through clumps of plantation and flowering shrubs, varied by extensive glades of grass, studded with various specimen trees. About midway after passing through a dense clump of timber you emerge into an open valley, where the road runs along the embankment of the lake, which covers an area of some four acres. This fine sheet of clear water, with its bays and inlets, its wooded isles, gondola, and miniature yachts, its white swans and other wildfowl, forms altogether one of the most pleasing and interesting features in the grounds. After passing the lake, the drive winds round the hillside up to the front, and a considerable amount of excavation had to be done to make the gradient fit for vehicle traffic; opposite the entrance-front the drive encircles a handsome marble fountain.

The house is an elegant modern mansion with balcony round three sides of the main building . . . The building stands on an elevated plateau, with a rapid declivity on three sides; the position such as might have been selected by a baron of the 'middle ages' as a suitable site for a residence and stronghold . . . The grounds are intersected by numerous walks leading to various points of interest . . . Near the house, on the southern slope, a natural depression was selected as an eligible site for a fern gully. The ground was set out with a view to add as much as possible to its apparent extent; a deep and wide passage was excavated, with high banks, to afford the necessary shelter. Large recesses, with grottoes, pools of water, and jets were formed at various points; rustic stone steps introduced in the steeper parts, and the banks supported and rusticated with rockeries, the intersections serving as receptacles for small ferns. The slopes were covered with rich friable loam and planted with hundreds of tree ferns . . .

Along the top of banks umbrageous trees are planted, with a dense undergrowth of evergreens, affording in the hottest summer day a cool and impenetrable shade, the whole presenting such a wild and natural appearance that it requires little flight of fancy to imagine yourself in the middle of some distant mountain ravine. Perforated pipes are laid all along the banks, so that it requires a minimum amount of manual labour to keep the soil always moist; a rill of water runs down along the path, and flows into a pool at the lower end, which is margined with lofty weeping willows. Beyond the fernery is a perfect gem of a tennis lawn, not a parallelogram patch such as we usually find devoted to lawn tennis, but a wide expanse of close-shaven velvety sward of irregular outline, where any number of sets can be played, the whole surrounded on three sides by a dense belt of shrubbery, with roses and other flowering plants in the foreground . . .

The grass is mown every second day. At the west end of the lawn, under the shade of a weatherbeaten sheoak, is a rustic summer and tennis house. A little to the east of the lawn is a rosery, where the strong dark chocolate soil produces blooms of amazing size and substance of petal. On the opposite side of the walk that winds along the valley north of the tennis lawn and under the shelter of the hill is a large irregular bed for dahlias, tuberoses, perennial phlox, and other autumn flowers. A shady walk leading around the base of the hill brings the visitor to a large camellia bed on the eastern slope . . . From the camellia-ground the path leads up to the door of a handsome and lofty conservatory on the east side of the mansion . . .

The orchard and kitchen garden are situated behind and away from the house on a bend of the river; and, as vegetables have to be raised for an average household of 50, it is no light tax on the resources of this important department to keep up a constant supply; there are immense breaks devoted to peas, French beans, marrows, and other seasonable vegetables, and a large area devoted to salad raising, asparagus beds, etc. Fruit trees do not grow large in the heavy soil, but are unusually productive, and there is an avenue of fine orange and lemon trees in full bearing. A large square is devoted to cherries, which are planted 8ft. apart . . . On the bank of the river is a large water-wheel, which supplies motive power to a set of force-pumps that raise a fine stream of water to a height of 100ft. into cisterns on the roof of the house, and also feed a large reservoir on the highest point of the ground; the wheel is placed in a brick chamber cut out of the solid rock, and the floods sweep over the top without doing the slightest injury; besides this supply there is a large dam at a high level in a branch creek out on the estate, which supplies abundance of water for irrigation . . .

The aspect of the house from the main entrance is very pleasing, the light iron traceries of verandahs and balconies and the marble pavements laid in squares softening the effect. The front portion is of two storeys of considerable loftiness, but the servants' quarters on the south rear are of three storeys. Off the main entrance to the right is a magnificent suite of three rooms, fitted with revolving shutters, and capable of being converted into one large salôn of 65ft. long by about twenty-five in width. At the end of these are a conservatory, with seven large fern trees growing in the centre . . . Upstairs, a magnificent view is to be had from the balcony, of all the surrounding country. The landing is very spacious, and orna-mented with handsome iron columns, painted to resemble marble. Both upstairs and down, the windows, which look into the paved courtyard, are painted, chiefly with sporting scenes, in the highest style of glass-staining. The boudoir, drawing rooms, and bedrooms are all elegantly furnished, the carvings upon some of the marble mantel-pieces being espe-cially fine . . . It is pleasing to find in Mr. Clarke that wide liberality, without profusion or extravagance, which leads him to make so beneficent use of the wealth Providence has entrusted to his care.

76

Tuesday October 14th

Packed up and left Rupertswood at 9.30. We started in the buggy. Sir William Clarke drove Sir Henry, Lady Loch and Master Douglas in his coach and four horses to the station. Reached home about 12 midday. Unpacked and packed up for Warrnambool.

ON THE LOCHS' return from Rupertswood, Emma at once began packing for their next journey which was to begin early next morning, for the restful days in the country were followed by the longest and busiest visit that the Governor had yet undertaken. It was necessary to leave Government House soon after 7 a.m. to allow time for travelling into Spencer Street behind horses and then seeing their luggage safely stowed away on the train before it departed punctually at 8 o'clock. The first halt was at Geelong where a deputation waited on Sir Henry to ask him to open their show the following month. The second stop was Colac, where they were greeted not only by the customary group of officials, but by what the paper described as 'a lubra of the almost extinct race of aborigines'. She gave a demonstration of boomerang throwing, a word that was obviously new and unknown to Emma who was forced to leave a space in her diary, though she appreciated the skill shown in the exhibition of its use. The diary continues with her account of the endless round of activities.

October 15th

Left Government House at 7.15 for Spencer Street Station with Lady Loch in brougham. Sir Henry went in his phaeton and Capt. Traill. Mr Hughes and Lord Castlerosse in another conveyance. Started in special train at 8 a.m. Had a good nap on the way. At one place there were some Aborigines at the station to receive Sir Henry and, after a long chat about the country and that it all belonged to them before the white men came, they showed Sir Henry a wonderful knack of throwing a piece of wood in such a way that it will kill a bird and come back to them. It's called an ____ [boomerang].

We had a good luncheon in the train. Turkey, ham, tongue, salad, pastry, cream, jelly, wine all served as the train was flying along to its destination. We reached Camperdown about 12. Here the school children were drawn up and a great crowd of people. The children strewed the pathway with flowers and sang the National Anthem, and after many addresses, Sir Henry and Lady Loch, the Mayor and Mr Deakin drove off in a carriage and four horses. The staff went in another open conveyance and four horses. There were five conveyances, each with four horses. We started in the last on the box with the driver, a very nice man, Mr Howard, we had fine weather, a splendid road, and went at full gallop for some miles when our coach had to pull up as the carriage wheel, in which Sir Henry and Lady Loch drove, became heated and they had to wait till it cooled.

We changed horses at Terang, and again refreshments were provided free of cost, champagne, etc. Mr Howard knows this country so well, we had a most delightful drive, he describing every house the whole way 40 miles thro' the bush. He is gentlemanly, and has told us a great deal of his life and the different trades he has tried since he came to this country. Several triumphal arches have been erected on the road, and houses decorated in honour of Sir Henry's visit.

Warrnambool was reached about 5 p.m. We were both rather stiff and glad to get down at Airlee, a nice house lent to the Governor so that they might be quiet and rest better after their long drive, as the hotel is all noisy at these times. The day is a general holiday, hundreds of people strolling about trying to get a sight of the vice-regal party. There was fireworks and illuminations at night. We all went to bed early, tired and to get a good rest for tomorrow when there is a long programme to go thro'.

Warrnambool October 16th

A fine bright morning. All up early to breakfast. Sir Henry and Lady Loch went off, and the staff, to see a beautiful place 10 miles off. Mr Lovegrove and me went to see if we could get some papers. The

Warrnambool.

town is en fete, flags flying and people dressed to death. At 12 the party returned and dressed for the agricultural show where a banquet will be given and much speech making. We went to see what it was like, and really the people are quite a sight, thousands in the field where the show took place. There was a splendid show of cart horses, ponies, cobs, and all classes; implements for farming purposes, flowers, vegetables, butter, bread, fat sheep, wool, pigs, carts, phaetons, etc., etc.

After the banquet the Governor and party occupied a tent and the horses that had taken prizes filed past them. Then some good riding and jumping took place. At 4 o'clock we had to return to Airlee to prepare for the ball and reached home just in time to receive them. Lady Loch had a rest till 6 p.m. then dressed for the ball in amber and black trimmed with black Spanish lace and amber feathers in her hair, ornaments: rubies and diamonds. The ball commenced at 9.30 and went off well. Lady Loch and Sir Henry returned home about 12.30. Some of the gentlemen did not return till 3 a.m., others later still, so we, who might have rested, did not get much sleep. The noise seemed to be going on all night.

We got up at 6 and left Warrnambool soon after 8. All seemed sorry we were going as this visit seems to have cheered them up. The drive back was dreadfully dusty, my clothes were perfectly white, eyes and mouth full of it. We changed horses at Terang, and brushed up a bit and when the carriage was starting with some of the gentlemen of the staff and some of the members, they had a very narrow escape from one of the front horses having been wrongly harnessed. The horse, instead of going forward, turned round sharp and almost upset the carriage, broke the pole, and made the other horses restive. The gentlemen jumped out and luckily escaped. They packed in with some of the other members and were soon after Sir Henry, who knew nothing about the accident, they having gone on to get a fine view of the coast and a picnic under the trees. We reached Camperdown soon after 12 noon and had time to get rid of some of the dirt before the ladies and gentlemen arrived. The special train left about 1 p.m. and we reached home about 6 p.m., rather tired out tho' much pleased with all we had seen.

IN HIS SPEECH in reply to the many royal toasts that were honoured, at the Warrnambool banquet, Sir Henry had again reminded his audience of the astounding progress that the district had made since he had first seen it in 1853, and he foretold that with the completion of the new breakwater, Warrnambool would prosper as never before. He had been astonished, he said, to see highly cultivated farms and rich pastures where, before, there had been nothing but forest and scrub. He also congratulated the audience on the excellent condition of their roads, which were in marked contrast to those in the immediate neighbourhood of Government House, this remark being greeted with both laughter and cheers.

The return journey to Melbourne was broken by a pleasant halt at Camperdown. After driving the forty miles from Warrnambool, during which time they were smothered with dust (despite Sir Henry's complimentary remarks about their roads!), they had barely time to dust their clothes before they were taken to the park and publicly entertained at a banquet there. The town's usual population of about a thousand had swelled considerably for this enjoyable event, and Sir Henry expressed his great pleasure not only at the warm welcome but at the superb view of the lakes that they obtained from Park Hill, to which they had been driven.

Spring Racing Carnival and Christmas Festivities

23 October–31 December 1884

TOWARDS THE END of October the Lochs' guests began to arrive for the spring racing carnival. As other visitors to Marvellous Melbourne at the time observed, the year was measured not from one Christmas to another, but from one Cup week to the next.

October 23rd

Sir William and Miss Robinson arrived. We found they had come on our return from church. Miss Markwell and Mr Hawkins, valet, seem to be very nice and sociable.

The first guest to arrive was Sir William Robinson, who, after serving a successful term as Governor of Western Australia, was now installed in Adelaide's Government House. As his wife did not care for racing, perhaps because she had grown up as a bishop's daughter, Sir William was accompanied by the oldest of his three daughters, and she, of course, was accompanied by her personal maid.

Although Sir William had held a number of important diplomatic posts in various parts of the world, he was always rather overshadowed by his more famous brother, Sir Hercules Robinson; but in one sphere, at least, his superiority went unchallenged, and that was music. As well as possessing a beautiful singing voice, he was an accomplished pianist and played the violin, often playing his own compositions. Some people, admittedly, found his manner somewhat intimidating, but he was a man with many interests, and a brilliant conversationalist, the centre of attention in any gathering.

Another governor to join the house party was Sir George Strahan, who had been the Lochs' host in Hobart when they had first arrived in Australia, and there were overseas visitors as well. One of these was the Duke of Manchester, who already had extensive mining interests, and hoped to spend some months in the colonies looking at mining prospects here. As each guest usually brought a valet or secretary, Government House's accommodation rapidly filled up as Cup week approached.

The Lochs, of course, had planned their entertainments long beforehand and elegant invitations for the various functions at Government House had been sent out prior to their country tours in September and October.

Though the actual Cup was not run until early November, the round of festivities began on 28 October, with the Government House garden party, which was blessed, as usual, with sunny skies. Emma's diary shows, a darker side of this event, although the newspapers wrote enthusiastically about the Lochs' lavish hospitality, and gave glowing accounts of the day.

October 28th

Garden party. Lovely day and, for the first, I suppose it was managed pretty well, but we felt if there had been more hands we might have done better. Miss Robinson's maid and Mam'selle Meyster helped us, but we were overwhelmed. All rushed in at once and many must have gone away without getting what they wanted. We had a detective on the premises who acted as waiter, and we were all deceived. He seemed quite up to his work. Mr O'Donnell went by the name of Smith and was told many things by one and other who would be glad enough to recall their words. One man on the premises asked him to watch whilst he helped himself out of the tea caddy, so soon as he had his hand in the tin he shouted out 'Here he comes', meaning Mr Hawkins, so he did not gain much tea, and we have learnt a lesson. Several things have gone astray lately, and no wonder. Mr O'Donnell had not been in the house many hours before he saw a man, who is employed on the premises, that had only been out of prison a few months. Mr O'Donnell had his photograph and knew there was no doubt about the matter. Next morning Mr Wilson did not put in an appearance, which looked bad. Two days later he turned up and made some excuse about illness being the cause of his not coming to work. He was shown the report and photograph and hurried off the premises. He was well known as a burglar and petty thief and might have caused much trouble in the house had he remained, so we are thankful Mr O'Donnell was here, though we thought it strange at first.

THE GOVERNMENT HOUSE ENTERTAINMENTS
THE GARDEN PARTY

Our representative of royalty in Victoria enjoyed on October 28 that charmingly fine weather which it is the fashion to call "Queen's weather", for their first large entertainment. With a hospitality which well deserves the title of "unbounded", Sir Henry and Lady Loch had invited about 2,000 ladies and gentlemen to share in the pleasant festivity, which took the form of a garden party. From 3 until nearly 5 a steady stream of people passed through the marquee erected on the spacious lawn near the main entrance, each in turn receiving a cordial welcome from Lady Loch, who, accompanied by her little daughters, selected that place to receive her guests. Her ladyship looked very charming in a white costume of some soft silken material, dotted with raised silk dots, and elegantly trimmed with white silk embroidery and lace. A light mantelet of the same material was worn, semi-dolman in character, which was almost hidden beneath lace and embroidery. The small "Pierrot" bonnet was of maize-coloured velvet and lace, the small crown having upon it a black lace butterfly as its sole ornament. In the front was a feather curling over the brim, which had folds of maize or amber velvet. A white tulle veil and full string of the same material were worn. Lady Loch carried a beautiful bunch of crimson and yellow roses, over which hovered and trembled tiny humming birds mounted on wire, which had a very pretty and realistic effect. The Misses Loch wore dresses of cream silk, Indian muslin, trimmed with white lace, and straw hats.

The ball-room, the state drawingroom, and the conservatories were thrown open to the visitors, besides the grassy lawns which formed such a delightful promenade, and from which, if one chose to contrast the delightful with the disagreeable, the dusty streets of Melbourne could be seen, with the dust fiend in full possession. But, to the credit of the authorities in these matters, it must be admitted that the St. Kilda road was en fête and entirely free from dust; the watering had evidently been of the thoroughly good kind.

Two DAYS LATER came Lady Clarke's Fancy Ball, one of the most colourful functions ever held in Melbourne. Are such elaborate decorations seen nowadays, one wonders. Of this brilliant social event 'Humming Bee' wrote in the *Australasian*:

LADY CLARKE'S FANCY BALL

The fancy ball given by Lady Clarke on Thursday night, Oct. 30, at the Town-hall was a splendid episode in what it has become the fashion to call the Melbourne carnival season. As a social event it was worthy of the well-known hospitality of Sir William and Lady Clarke, and as a festive gathering it was, in point of completeness, comfort, brilliancy of total effect, and all that goes to make up the enjoyability of a ball, the most distinguished success we have ever had in Melbourne. Several fastidious social critics, whose memory ranges over a much longer vista of fancy balls than I can recall, agreed in assuring me that the Clarke ball of 1884 was the most brilliant ever held in this city. That so great a success was attained on every side implied much careful preparation and wise forethought, and in some remarks which he made at the supper table, in reply to the toast of "The Host and Hostess", Sir William Clarke indicated where the credit was due. It was all due, he said to the good generalship and watchful care of Lady Clarke, and the result was a magnificent success. The bare Town-hall was transformed into a bower of beauty almost beyond recognition. Underneath the balconies of either side were miniature drawingrooms, completely furnished with mirrors, tête-à-tête, and occasional chairs, and fancy tables of all kinds. Here, too, forming these sweet retreats into something more than drawingrooms, blossomed and bloomed huge azaleas of all known colours, and magnificent rhododendrons added their wealth of foliage and colour; from pillar to pillar were festooned long ropes of pittosporums, in the centre of whose half arches hung fairy-like baskets of flowers, the foundations sometimes being roses or azaleas, while delicate fern fronds and drooping coloured plumes filled up the top part. And the perfect groves of fern trees, which gave a look of cool verdure to the balcony and the orchestra gallery, the great hall was at once a ballroom, drawingroom and conservatory. In the front of the south gallery was arranged on a raised dais a drawingroom, matching in harmony the smaller ones before referred to, but sufficiently large to form a pleasant rendezvous for the hostess and her friends. Here Lady Clarke, attired as "Marie Antoinette", received her guests, accompanied by Sir William, who wore the dark uniform of the old Victorian Yeoman Cavalry.

The dress of Lady Clarke was of pink brocaded silk, the flowers being deeper in tint than the foundation shade. The design was of the usual poudré costume of the period, having the large sacque pleat at the back. In the petticoat front, pale blue merveilleuse silk was used, but was nearly hidden with quantities of pale pink roses, which were laid on in close rows, and beneath them fell flounces of white lace. On the one side

Fashions at the 1884 Melbourne Cup. (National Library of Australia, Canberra)

of the powdered wig was worn a spray of pink roses and a small feather. Many diamonds were also worn in the hair, and looking down upon Lady Clarke from the balcony, the diamond gleams met you at every turn. Lady Loch, who with Sir Henry Loch, Sir William Robinson, Miss Robinson, and Sir George Strahan, were among Lady Clarke's guests, wore a full evening costume of pale blue brocade trimmed with mushroom lace. The three governors were among those who came in their own characters, and as Sir William Robinson remarked at supper, this placed them rather at an advantage. Indeed, he had evidently noticed the many people who, feeling very much out of their usual every-day costume, persistently kept seated in the side lounging places, or else showed a marked preference for the balcony. As the evening wore on courage came to most of those present, and, helped by supper, very few were found avoiding the responsibilities they had brought on themselves by adopting the part of some hero or heroine of the past. As a rule, I think the gentlemen looked best. They bore their honours more bravely than their sisters and wives, and if they felt any of their tremours they avoided showing them.

WHEN CUP DAY came round, the Governor and his guests drove to Flemington in great style to join the thousands who thronged the course to see Malus win. But for the ladies of the colony, the dresses were far more important than the horses. Lady Loch's gowns were always of special interest; not only were they beautiful, and beautifully displayed on her elegant figure, but they gave Melbourne residents a glimpse of the latest Paris fashions. Lady Loch's sister was the wife of a senior British diplomat in Paris, so she was able to have her gowns made there, to fit her sister, and then posted to Australia. As the sisters were identical twins, the gowns were always a perfect fit. From babyhood it had been difficult to tell the two girls apart, and after looking at them very closely, one of their aunts had written to their father: 'Edith is perhaps the prettiest, but Lizzie [Lady Loch] is the finest child'.

Racegoers watch the Melbourne Cup from the Members Stand.

We know that both lived to 90, and celebrated their birthdays with a great party in London.

For the ladies in distant parts of the colony, who were unable to get to Flemington to see the fashions for themselves, the *Argus* gave a full description of the smartest gowns, and it was followed next day by an account of the glittering State Ball, at which, for a change, the gentlemen apparently outshone the ladies.

 From a feminine point of view, the improvement in everything seemed marvellous. Refined taste in apparel was everywhere visible, and there was an utter absence of that competition in dress which was the bane of former years. That wonderful feminine desire to "beggar my neighbour" at any cost, which was at one time a sort of mania on Cup Day, is dead and gone with many another faded glory of the past. But although the desire to "dress to death" has vanished, still womankind loves her race day as much as ever. The stand was ludicrously inadequate to accommodate the visitors; indeed, there was barely room to seat half the ladies present, that is, under shelter. Just imagine for a moment what the effect would have been on those handsome toilettes had a heavy shower of rain passed over. Not one of them but would have been utterly ruined, and Mr. Moore would certainly have been one of the best-abused men in Victoria.

As we promenade the lawn we have ample opportunity of noting well the various styles adopted, and we at once come to the conclusion that the only place to witness a full display of the spring fashions is at Flemington on Cup Day. Here we get the combined effects of all the large spring drapery shows, with the advantage of living models. The bright sunshine, too, is a great help. It is difficult to judge of many materials heaped up on shop counters, in not always the best of lights. But if one had to select a gown or bonnet now, as the wearers pass and repass, we could do so with very little difficulty, be our styles subdued or smart. Here we can see exactly how the costume would look "on", how it should be made up, the materials that combine best on it, the size of the pattern that would best suit our complexions and figures, and many more points of detail that it is needless to mention. Notice how white still holds its own, and what today looks fresher or prettier? Lace is everywhere in quantities. Black, coffee, drab and ficelle predominate. Many costumes are completely shrouded in it. Although an old favourite, it was never used so lavishly as it is at present. Everyone seems to have discovered that there is nothing so becoming. Many parasols are entirely composed of it, and it flutters in tiers on others. Nothing gives a more charming framing to a pretty face than a cleverly-used parasol, and in matters of flirtation it is on an equality with the ballroom fan. Anyone who cares to notice can see there is as much spooning carried on under cover of a parasol on the lawn as there is behind a feather fan in the fern recesses of the conservatory. Although such a quantity of brown and ficelle lace are worn, yet there are no two gowns alike in every detail. There is always visible the artistic touch of the costumier, who has taken care to vary each frock in some way or other so as to prevent anything like sameness. To illustrate the foregoing remarks, notice the group that is standing by the judge's box. One fair girl wears a pale blue satin covered with ficelle lace, her dark companion wears cream lace over cardinal satin, a third has a gown of bronze draped with coffee lace, cream lace over gold forms the costume of a fourth. Each of these gowns is individualised quite as much as the faces of the wearers. As a contrast to these costumes, note a lovely French grey satin covered with pearls, that dance in the sunlight like bubbles on the bosom of a lake. Next to coloured comes the black lace. It also is worn over every imaginable colour, draped and arranged in graceful folds. How stylish that black dress looks with its bodice and back drape of merveilliex, cardinal de Lyon front draped over with point lace caught up with pompoms, and how exquisitely the cardinal waistcoat covered with lace gives the finishing touch to the whole model. Lady Loch wore a superbly made gown of grey broché satin, with elegant cashmere draperies, bodice trimmed with point lace and India muslin. The general effect and style of this dress was quite admirable. Lady Clarke was attired in cream Valenciennes lace dress over satin, ornamented with gold pompoms. One of her daughters wore an India embroidered muslin dress over blue satin, trimmed with brown point lace.

November 5th

First ball at Government House. We had a busy day putting up fruit and cakes, then comes the dressing, then to attend the buffet tea and coffee. The Governor and Lady Loch and the Governor of Adelaide, Sir Wm. Robinson, Miss Robinson, Sir George Strahan Governor of Tasmania, Lord Wm. Neville, Mr and Mrs Howard Vincent, Hon. Mr Wallop, Mr Manning and the staff took their places in the Ballroom at 9.30 when the band played the National Anthem and the company came streaming in and promenaded around the Ballroom. About 10 p.m. the first quadrille was danced by the House

*party, then dancing was kept up with great spirit and enjoyment till
3.30 a.m. when the programme was finished and by 4 a.m. all had
vanished, as rapidly as they arrived. I think the ball was a great
success from beginning to end. Plenty of everything, and all seemed
happy and contented. The ladies were, most of them, beautifully
dressed, only a few were badly got up. We retired about 4.30, very
tired after twenty-one hours of hard work. I was up at 6 a.m.*

THE STATE BALL

The first ball given at Government house since the arrival of
Sir Henry and Lady Loch was held on November 5. The ballroom was tastefully decorated with flags, foliage, and flowers.
On the walls were stars formed of swords and wreaths of
evergreens over the archways. At the head of the room was the
Union Jack. The dais and orchestra gallery were embowered in
pot plants and ferns. The drawingroom tables were laden with
choice bouquets, and the passages leading to them were conservatories in bloom. The guests began to arrive at half-past 9
o'clock . . . Captain Thomas, of the Victorian Naval Forces,
and the officers of H.M.S. Diamond, were present, and con-
trasting with the British naval uniforms were those of Com-
mander Bossu and Captain La Porte, of the French steamer
Havre, and his officers. Colonel Disney and members of the
Headquarters Staff also accepted invitations, of which 1,200
were issued. At a quarter to 10 the vice regal-party entered the
ball-room and proceeded to the dais. Lady and Sir Henry
Loch were accompanied by the Misses and Master Douglas
Loch, Sir William Robinson, Sir George Strahan, Governor
of Tasmania, Captain Traill, private secretary to Sir H.B.
Loch, Lord Castlerosse, and Captain [sic] Hughes, A.D.C.'S,
Mr. Sturgess, Mdlle. Heyman, Lord William Neville, Mr.
and Mrs. Howard Vincent, who are guests at Government
house. The band having played the National Anthem, the
company passed before the dais and dancing then commenced. The first set was composed as follows: Sir H.B. Loch
and Lady Stawell, Sir W. Robinson and Lady Loch, Sir

George Strahan and Miss Robinson, Sir William Clarke and Mrs. Howard Vincent, the mayor of Melbourne (Councillor Smith) and Lady O'Loghlan, Mr. Deakin and Mrs. Disney, Colonel Brownrigg and Miss Smith, Mr. Howard Vincent and Lady Clarke. In the intervals of dancing the cool evening was enjoyed on the lawn by many of the guests. Refreshments were served before and after supper, in the right wing of the ballroom, and at half-past 11 the company proceeded to the diningroom, where tables were sumptuously laid. The only toast proposed was that of "The Queen", and dancing was then resumed until two o'clock.

These balls were followed by the concert, where Sir William Robinson's song 'Remember me no more' brought rapturous applause.

November 6th

Concert. Went to bed about noon and had a rest to get ready for another night's work. At 9 p.m. the company began to arrive for the concert. Altogether about 600 assembled in the Ballroom to hear the Metropolitan Liedertafel. We had some chairs at the door and enjoyed the music very much, especially the song composed by Sir William Robinson. It was beautifully sung by Mrs Palmer. We had to serve tea and coffee in the dining room. There was a great crowd afterwards in the refreshment room, but I hope all were served and well satisfied. Much is expected out here. Unfortunately all rush into the room at the same time. It is impossible to serve them as one would like. We had cleaned up soon after 1 a.m.

THE CONCERT

The musical "at home" held at Government-house on November 6 by Lady Loch was a brilliant gathering, the attendance numbering fully 500 ladies and gentlemen. The evening's proceedings consisted chiefly of a concert of vocal and instrumental music given by the members of the Metropolitan Liedertafel, who were invited to be present in honour of Sir William Robinson, Governor of South Australia, who, together with Sir George Strahan, Governor of Tasmania, is the guest of Sir Henry Loch. The ballroom was tastefully decorated with evergreens, and draped with flags, and when the visitors were seated it presented a very bright and pleasing aspect. As their Excellencies, accompanied by Lady Loch and Miss Robinson, entered the room, the Liedertafel sang the National Anthem. The concert which followed was very enjoyable. It included the following part songs, which, as will be seen, represented some of the choicest selections of the repertory of the society:- "Hymn to the Night" (Beethoven), "Hunter's Joy" (Astholz), double chorus from "Oedipus", "Thou comest here to the land" (F. Mendelssohn-Bartholdy), "Loreley" (Silcher), "The Image of the Rose" (Leichardt), Bacchus chorus from "Antigone" (Mendelssohn-Bartholdy), "A May Night" (Abt) with tenor solo by Mr. Kendall; and "Margaretha" (Chadwick). All these pieces were rendered with grace and expression, the singers being thoroughly under the command of their conductor, Mr. Julius Herz. "The Image of the Rose", in which Mr. Armes Beaumont sang the solo, was partially repeated at the request of His Excellency, and the number was loudly applauded. Mr. Beaumont also con- tributed Beethoven's "Adelaide", and Mrs. Palmer rendered Sir W. Robinson's song, "Remember me no more", both vocalists giving a sympathetic interpretation of the music . . . On the termination of the concert Lady Loch held a reception in the drawingroom, where supper was laid. The proceedings throughout the evening were of a highly pleasurable character, being divested of unnecessary formality, and it was after mid- night when the last of the visitors departed.

Friday November 7th

Went to the paddock to see some buck jumping. Very dangerous work.

Saturday November 8th

Sir Wm. and Miss Robinson left for Adelaide at 11.30. Sir Henry and Lady Loch, Sir George Strahan, Lord Wm. Neville and the gentlemen in waiting left at the same time for the race course, Flemington. A glorious day. Such fine brilliant weather has never been before, not one bad day during the festivities.

Saturday November 15th

The Duke of Manchester arrived on a visit.

Sunday November 16th

A bright, hot summer's day. Went to Christ Church, South Yarra and found the heat oppressive. Heard that our men had quarrelled and fought last night. One is not presentable today—John. William had been struck with a riding whip on his head and lay on the floor insensible for some time, then Charles came in and renewed the quarrel with John, blacked both eyes. All have been reviewed and got their leave: 'tis terrible to think what might have happened in the heat of passion. We are very sorry, but hope it will be a lesson to each one of them. They all look ashamed of themselves.

Monday November 17th

Sir G. Strahan left for Tasmania at 2 p.m. and his Private Secretary, Mr Wallop.

[Tuesday November 18th]

At 7.30 a.m. we left Government House for Spencer Street Station by special train for Portland where a Jubilee is to be held in honour of Mr E. Henty, who landed at Portland in 1834 and planted in Victorian soil the seed of civilisation which has spread so rapidly. It was thought a fitting occasion to invite Sir Henry and Lady Loch to

The Portland Jubilee. (National Library of Australia, Canberra)

that part of Victoria, and the Duke of Manchester also. It was a lovely bright morning and we started at 10 minutes to 8 a.m. The engine was gaily decorated and all very nice. I had my comfortable armchair and had a nice nap before we reached Ballarat where luncheon was served, and a crowd of people to see the start. Another stoppage at Ararat where the school children sang and presented a bouquet to Lady Loch—and also strawberries and cream. It was very hot and we were glad to get away from the station. The next stopping place was Hamilton where we had a cup of tea. After a short stay and much speech making and cheering from the crowd the train went off and reached Portland at a few minutes to 6—nearly 10 hours journey. Mr Jordan, the Duke's valet, Mr Thornley's man, Mr Lovegrove and myself went with the luggage to Mac's Hotel, where one part of the hotel had been reserved for the whole party. A nice view of the bay from the windows. The streets are all decorated with flags and arches for the Jubilee, and if it was possible to remove a show stationed right opposite, where two wonderful dwarfs are to

95

be seen and tie up the showman's jaws, also his drum, it would be a great relief to one's ears and nerves at the same time.

[Wednesday November 19th]

The weather is lovely, so bright and warm. The procession from the hotel at 11 was a long one, with troopers, Aborigines, school children, Foresters, Mayor, Vice-Regal party and staff in carriages. A general holiday, thousands of people in the street. Lady Loch came in about 1 p.m. to rest. At 3 p.m. a banquet was given and much speech making, and at 4 p.m. Lady Loch held a reception. Many came, and at 7 they dined at the hotel. After dinner all the party went around the town to see the illuminations and fireworks. At 10.30 all went to bed.

Thursday November 20th

All up early. Started from Portland at 8.50 a.m. for home. So hot, the warmest day we have had. Dinner at Ararat, and had some time at Geelong. Reached Melbourne at 6.30, rather tired but not quite used up.

AFTER THE LONG journey from Portland Emma was obviously too 'used up' to recount in detail the events of the last few days. On a previous country visit she had seen her first Aborigine, the woman at Colac, who had demonstrated her skills with the boomerang. At Portland, in contrast to the noise of the Foundry Band which serenaded the Governor, the flags and the bunting, the triumphal arch with its Latin mottoes, the milling crowds and the long procession honouring the Henty brothers, a simple ceremony took place. This was when Albert White, 'representing his fellow blacks of the Lake Condah mission station, presented an address to His Excellency, after reading it in capital style. In their address the aborigines desired to thank the Government for the care and attention bestowed upon their temporal and spiritual welfare. As survivors of a once large and numerous tribe, the subscribers hoped that His Excellency's stay in Victoria would be accompanied by peace and happiness and prosperity to himself and to all who were under the rule of Her Majesty's Government'. Needless to say, Sir Henry made a very kind reply to this address. One wonders if Albert White's descendants still survive in the Portland district.

Sunday November 23rd

Lovely hot, bright day. Went to Christ Church, South Yarra, in the morning. When we returned we found Mrs Macpherson had arrived. She used to live with Sir Henry's father (when Sir Henry was a boy) as laundry maid. She has been out here 35 years and says she could not live in Scotland now—too cold. She belongs to Golspie near Dunrobin Castle. Seems a very cheery old party, is a widow and has one daughter married out here.

December 5th

Lady Loch and two young ladies and Lucy have gone to a place called Macedon, about ____ miles from Melbourne. They stay till Tuesday. I shall get a nice quiet time for three days.

December 9th

Lord Castlerosse got a nasty fall from his horse today. He was trying to make it jump and he struck the pony a blow. It bolted, and carried him like the wind to the back premises where he either fell or threw himself off. His elbow and hip are both badly grazed. He is dreadfully stiff and much shaken. He might have been killed.

As 25 DECEMBER approached, the Lochs did all in their power to make this first summer-time Christmas a particularly happy occasion for their staff. With their usual generosity they planned a lavish Christmas dinner, to which their staff could invite their Melbourne friends, so lavish indeed that there were good things left over to share with friends who could not join in the meal. The Lochs themselves spent the day quietly; a simple Christmas was part of the Scottish way of life, where Easter and Christmas festivities fade into insignificance before the merrymaking at New Year.

December 25th

A beautiful hot summer's day. Went off to 11 a.m. service at Christ Church, South Yarra, with Lucy. Nice musical service. The church was prettily decorated and the choir came in procession singing 'Hark the Herald Angles Sing'. It is difficult to realize that Christmas has really come again. We stayed for Communion and had to hurry home to get things put up. We dressed as we have Mr Hayes and children, Mr and Mrs Martin, Mr and Mrs Loyd, Mr Coffee—the gardener, David, and we mustered eighty-three to dinner without Mrs Calla or three kitchen maids. We had a capital dinner, sat down at 2 p.m. and it was nearly 4 when we finished. Toasts, songs.

Mrs Martin, Lucy and me went to see Mrs Cotterell's little boy who is paralysed and took him some pudding, mince pies and pastry. It is a sad sight. He is fourteen years of age and does not look more than six or seven. He has fits daily and it must be a trial to the poor mother as there is no hope of his ever being any better. Death alone will give them rest from this terrible affliction. Mr Cotterell suffers acutely from homerage [haemorrhage] of the lungs. He is a clever little man, and has built an organ entirely by himself. Mrs Cotterell played to us. We thought the music sounded very soft and sweet.

We reached home soon after 5 p.m. and had tea, after which Mr and Mrs Martin went as they had arranged to go to the Town Hall to hear the Messiah. *Sir Henry, Lady Loch and the children went. The young people put the tables aside and had a dance. Mr Hayes played the violin for them and they danced till 10, then had supper and the company dispersed. We all felt tired, but glad our first Christmas in Australia was so agreeable and evidently a pleasant day to all that were invited.*

The great organ in the Melbourne Town Hall where the Lochs went to hear the Messiah.

December 26th

Boxing Day. Went to see Mr and Mrs Wise in the Botanical Gardens after breakfast to take the children some cards and plum pudding and wish them a merry Christmas. We then went on to see Mrs Cotterell's little boy, who was lying in a perambulator outside to get some fresh air. His poor face was blistered from some cause—I think the sun must have caught him. Poor child, he seemed very restless.

Tuesday December 30th

Went to Melbourne in the morning and saw an immense shark that had been caught near the coast. The intestines were taken out and a waistcoat with a silver watch, ten shillings in silver, a man's hand

and two hundred weight of small fish, was found. The watch belonged to a young gentleman who was drowned from a yacht a short time previous. The shark's teeth were stolen during the time it was left on the beach—one can imagine what strength a fish this size must possess. To bolt a man whole would be very easy work.

FOR THE PEOPLE who were unable to go into the city to shudder at the sight of the shark, as Emma had done, the papers provided all the grizzly details they had missed. First they described the yachting accident on 13 December in which two brothers, Hugh and William Browne, were lost, as was their companion a sailor named Murray. Only William's body had been found. On Boxing Day, a huge shark was seen and subsequently shot near the jetty at Frankston. When the monster was hauled ashore, Mr. Coxall cut the fish open and found:

 . . . the lower part of a human arm (the right), with a hand complete; a coat, with a wooden pipe and meerschaum stem in the pocket; a vest, having a gold watch attached to it by a chain, and pair of trousers, wanting one leg, with a bunch of keys and 10s. 6d. in silver in the pocket. The watch was old-fashioned, and had numerals instead of letters on the dial. Mr. Thomas Browne, brother of the deceased young gentlemen, on hearing of the discovery, went to Frankston on Saturday night by the last train, and identified the clothes, watch, &c., as those of Hugh Browne. The hand was not recognisable. It may be that of William Browne, whose body, when found off Picnic Point, was without the right arm . . . All the clothing was more or less torn. The internal parts of the watch were loose and much rusted; the hands were standing at 9 o'clock.

[Evening. December 30th]

In the evening there was a dinner party for eighteen. All was going well till the mince pies were served, when a small lamp used for burnt brandy, which Mr Hawkins was carrying, exploded, and the flame from the spirit flew into his face. Mr Hughes placed a table napkin over his head and smothered the flames, but he is sadly burnt and the pain was terrible. Doctor Ford was dining and ordered oil to be applied at once and sent him to bed. Then the orderly was sent off to Melbourne for lime water and lint linseed oil. Dr Ford kindly left the guests and dressed his face. Gave him a draught to soothe the nerves and we hope he won't be much scarred, tho' Dr Ford seems to think he will not be presentable for 10 days.

This disastrous dinner party was the last function of the year at Government House.

December 31st

Mr Hawkins has had a very restless night. He is in good spirits and bears the pain well. His face is entirely covered up, with only two peepholes for his eyes. Someone said he looked like Father Christmas. They were right, he looks as if he has been out in the snow. We are dreadfully sorry for him—he is very jolly and we miss his merry face at table and everywhere about the house. He is very patient, and bears it so well. Everybody seems sorry for him.

A Place Called Macedon

4 January–1 March 1885

THE YEAR OF 1885 began with Mr Hawkins on the road to recovery, and was to see the Lochs continuing their travels in country Victoria. Their first expedition was quite an adventurous one—a tour with a group of the colony's leading citizens who felt that the Governor should be shown some of the beauties of the Australian Alps, and Emma's diary gives the whole picture. It only remains to add that the district, which is now largely a national park, is as beautiful as ever, and Bright's Empire Hotel still stands, now with a new name and with the addition of a motel built round a courtyard, where, its owner assures me, the guests can sleep completely undisturbed. In the Lochs' day it was a narrow two-storeyed inn, its centrally placed door opening directly into the bar, and having a window each side, and an outside staircase up which the guests climbed to reach their upstairs bedrooms. And the New Hotel, where the Lochs' sought refuge on their homeward journey, is also still standing, though greatly enlarged and modernized.

January 4th

Mr Hawkins is making good progress towards recovery. He is up and mooching about the house. He only complains of slight weakness in the eyes, which we hope may vanish in a few days. His face is going on famously. We don't think he will be scarred at all if he is careful and keeps the sun and wind off till the new skin is thick enough to bear exposure.

January 13th

We started for the Australian Alps. Mr Lovegrove and I left Government House at 8.40 with three cab loads of baggage, bedding, etc. for Spencer Street Station. All was ready and in waiting. The special train left at 9.10. The heat was very great. The party, Sir Henry and Lady Loch, Master Douglas, Capt. Traill, Lord Castlerosse, Mr Sturgess, Mr Wallace MHR, Mr Kerford (Attorney General), Mr Campbell (Postmaster General), and two reporters, are all I can recognize. Others joined the party at Myrtleford. Mr Brown MLC, and Mr Billson MLA from Beechworth.

We reached Benalla about noon and had luncheon there, which only seemed to make one hotter, the effort of eating chicken and ham. The thermometer was 98½ degrees in the shade—115 degrees in the sun. The heat actually drew great blisters in the paint on the carriage.

We reached Myrtleford about 4 p.m. A great crowd at the station. The dust and flies are indeed a pest—they seem ready to eat one up. After some little time Sir Henry and Lady Loch, Master Douglas, Hon. G. B. Kerford (Attorney General), Mr P. B. Wallace MLA and my little self started in a dray with four grey horses and went at a splendid pace thro' a beautiful valley. The air was sultry and it rained, but only a few heat drops fell occasionally. Several vivid flashes of forked lightning fell, and the thunder seemed to get nearer and nearer, but luckily it kept off, and such a cavalcade of ladies and gentlemen met us on the road and formed an escort till Bright was reached. Here the school's children were drawn up in line and sang the National Anthem: Sir Henry thanked them and asked the master for a holiday for the children. They seemed pleased and wished it to be Friday.

The carriage then moved on and such a crowd with it—the band in front playing 'Rule Britannia'. The large rain drops now began to fall in earnest. We only had time, and hardly that, to scramble out of the wagonette when the deluge fell. Lucky we escaped it—such torrents I never saw—the water seemed to fall in sheets and after half an hour it cleared off, and we had a beautiful fine evening. The band played a selection of music opposite the Empire Hotel, and all seemed refreshed from the storm. There was incessant lightning all the evening, a long distance off. All went to bed early, except the gentlemen, who were entertained at a banquet. Such a hot night, the small rooms seem almost suffocating and the partitions are so thin I can hear Lord Castlerosse turn in bed. 'Tis impossible to sleep, so was up and down all night.

[January 14th]

Got up at 6 a.m. and found Lady Loch had hardly slept at all. The bed, tho' it looked clean, was infested with bugs. Poor Master Douglas' legs are completely bunged up. Capt. Traill has been disturbed with them and Mr Sturgess, so there can be no mistake. We breakfasted and left at 8.30 for Harrietville. Sir Henry, Lady Loch, Mr Kerford, Mr Wallace, Master Douglas and me. It was a splendid drive, the dust well laid. The coachman drove thro' the Chinese quarter and the Chinamen saluted Sir Henry.

[January 16th]

Allen, the Hotel proprietor [at Harrietville], *had decorated his doorway and collected all the people in the place to salute the travellers. It was lucky we started early. The heat was very great, and the dust and flies enough to devour one. We had a good luncheon, and at 1 p.m. started. Sir Henry, Master Douglas, Mr Wallace, Capt. Traill, Lord Castlerosse, Mr Sturgess and an orderly on horseback. Lady Loch, Hon. G. Kerford and the Postmaster General and me in the dray and four grey horses, then a Royal Mail Coach with Mr Billson, Mr Brown and two reporters; they had four brown horses.*

We began to ascend the hill directly. It was very steep and the curves so sharp the front horses had to go quite close to the edge of the precipice to turn. It looked so dangerous. Our coachman was won-

derfully steady or I should have felt nervous. The view as we rose higher and higher was truly grand. The flowers looked so pretty. The banks are covered with ferns, wild myrtle, red gum trees with such lovely foliage, the masses of timber all bleached and whitened— either killed with cold or heat—not a leaf or branch to be seen in some places. Some thought the snow had killed them, others the fires that so often happen in the bush. We saw several fires, but far, far away. We had some water at the tunnel about half-way up the mountains. It tasted rather like snow: and we found out afterwards that our thirst increased very much. Oh, how we longed to get a cup of nice tea.

About 5 we reached the Hospice Mount St Bernard, kept by Sailor Bill. Mr Braststear and his wife had a cup of tea and some delicious scones ready in a short time, to which all did full justice. The hospice is 500031 [sic] feet above sea level. We left about 5.30 for the camp and after another hour and half struggle the poor horses had reached their journey's end, 6000500 [sic] feet. It all looked very comfortable. A large tent for dining, another for Sir Henry and Lady Loch with the Union Jack flying, a small one for Master Douglas and me, and another small one as a retiring room. They had fenced this part off and put a thick hedge of scrub all round. There were two other tents for food. After all had dined, large fires were lit and most of the party collected round the blazing pile in easy fashion, some on their knees, others lying on their backs, some on their stomachs, some sketching. At 10 most of the party retired to rest, tho' we did not get much. So many loose horses, with bells round their necks, kept up a constant jingle, then a wind got up a little and our tent seemed inclined to topple over. So I was up and down ready for anything that should occur.

[January 17th]

Daylight came at last. What joy to think one could see the sun rising in all its beauty 6000 feet above the sea. Soon all were stirring and most of the young people went to the valley to have a wash as there was only one basin available for thirty people. Washing is not a part

Mount Feathertop.

of camp life it seems. At 9.30 Sir Henry, Master Douglas, Capt. Traill, Mr Sturgess, Lord Castlerosse, Mr Wallace, Mr Campbell, Mr Stirling and others who I don't know, started on horseback for Feathertop. We packed up mattresses, blankets, sheets, etc., and after all was ready for the baggage wagon we picked flowers for those at home. Then the orderly arrived with papers and some letters for Lady Loch. Dinner time arrived and it all seemed so good under the shade of a red gum tree. We had cold chicken and ham, pastry, tartlets and a nice cup of tea.

At 4 p.m. the gentlemen returned, all much sunburnt and tired. They had tea and after seeing a few people who called to pay their respects, the whole party started for the St Bernard Hospice. It is a little place to hold twenty-one people. We arrived about 5.30 and all are to be accommodated. It's a lovely spot at this time of year. Mrs Braststear tells me that for six months of the year they are snowed up and see no-one but the postman, who comes twice a week. I had to share a tiny room with Eliza, the servant. She is a clean looking girl, so I don't mind. The whole party had a good plain dinner and retired about 10 p.m., all tired out. Every noise is heard thro' these wooden partitions—'tis almost like being in the same room.

[January 18th]

All got up early and left the hospice about 10.30 for Harrietville: the road seems steeper going down than coming up. We had a good driver who seems to feel the responsibility of driving four horses down a steep mountain road. Reached Harrietville at lunch time. Had a good rest till 4 p.m., when all were ready to start. The whole party were photographed by a local artist. I hope it will be a good picture. I went inside the coach to Bright and missed much dust. Mr Brown and Mr Campbell were my fellow travellers. Reached Bright about 6 p.m., and had nice quarters at the New Hotel. Everything so clean and nice and the food all much better than at the Empire. After a good supper all went to their rooms and slept well.

[January 19th]

After breakfast (Saturday) all started for a drive to a place called ____ [Wandiligong], where Lady Loch had many bouquets given to her by the school children. It commenced raining soon after they started and continued coming down hard up to the time we left Bright at 1.30 for Myrtleford. The rain fell in torrents. I had a cloak lent me to keep me dry, but as Mr Wallace told me to get a seat inside the coach I did not get wet. Lady Loch went on the box of [the] wagonette and kept free from damp with her new macintosh and umbrella. The weather cleared before we got to the station, where a lot of people had assembled to see them off. We left about 4 p.m. by special train for Melbourne. It was 10.40 p.m. when we arrived at Flinders Street Station. I never felt more utterly used up in all my life. We reached Government House soon after 11 p.m., then all to unpack and a house full of company. Admiral Tryon, Lord Macdonald, Lord Elphinstone, Lord Wm. Neville and two other gentlemen and one valet. Lucy went to Rupertswood (Sir Wm. Clarke's) last Wednesday with the young ladies, so no one here to talk to and tell all we have done. Had some C. and soup and got to bed between 12 and 1 a.m. Oh, the joy of a room to oneself and a good bath.

FROM THE BEGINNING of 1885, the mountain retreat of Mount Macedon was to play an increasingly important part in the Lochs' life, and in after years, some of the family's happiest memories were of the carefree days they had spent there. To Sir Henry, and to most of the British Army officers who had served in India, the exodus to the hill stations in that country was the greatest event of the year. Once they arrived there they were able to enjoy not only cool nights, but at large hill stations such as Simla, to enjoy an endless round of tennis parties, polo matches, race meetings and garden parties, while at night dances and amateur theatricals awaited them—and perhaps romance. In fact, English girls who feared they were becoming wallflowers, had only to secure an invitation to visit Simla, and their future happiness was assured.

The journey from Melbourne to the heights of Macedon was relatively simple: fast trains steaming out of Spencer Street at regular intervals, and Mr Cogger, whose livery stables were famous, meeting every train with a suitable conveyance. The Lochs' first holiday in Macedon was spent in a house rented from Mr David Syme, an enterprising Scotsman who was the owner of the Melbourne *Age* and who had been one of the first to recognize the beauty of Mount Macedon and to build there. His house was in a magnificent position on the hillside, and although quite large enough for a family, had hardly rooms enough for the Governor, his official staff and his servants (not to mention his guests), and its wonderful views hardly compensated for the paper-thin walls which made privacy impossible. However, Sir Henry's enthusiasm for the spot was such that the Government was persuaded to purchase the property and to make plans for the erection of a more suitable residence there.

Sunday February 1st

A lovely day [at Macedon]. *Sat on the mount at the back of the house all day. The grass has been cut, and we piled it up and made a nice couch. The children were happy. We shelled peas, read, wrote and played like so many children and had tea up there. Did not fear the snakes or anything. We sat out till it was too cold to stay any longer. Lady Loch and the young ladies went to afternoon service, a small church close by. Mr Froude and son, and Lord Elphinstone are here. I can't see anything remarkable in Mr Froude, the great historian. He looks like other mortals, and occupies himself reading, writing and sketching.*

JAMES ANTHONY FROUDE was such a controversial figure, and so much the centre of every gathering, that Emma had evidently grown tired of hearing his praises sung to her—he was just one more visitor to be looked after! He was one of three brilliant brothers, one a cleric, a close friend of Newman, and the other a marine engineer who had worked with Brunel on the Thames tunnel, but it was J. A. Froude who always stole the limelight. His first book, on religion, was so controversial that in one diocese in England it had been publicly burned. At that time he had just been offered a high post in Tasmania, but when the news of the notoriety of this book reached the colony, the offer was withdrawn. But he went from strength to strength in the fields of journalism and modern history and had come to Australia to look at the question of federation, which was uppermost in politicians' minds. Even Sir Henry, who prided himself on his impartiality, mentioned the subject in almost every speech, and hoped that the colonies would achieve it within the next ten years.

Most people in Australia, and certainly everyone in Victoria, took it for granted that the capital of the new federation would be Marvellous Melbourne—their optimism at this time was unbounded. The Victorian premier, Mr Service, for instance, assured Froude that in the next fifty years, that is, by the 1930s, the population of Australia would have reached fifty million! Wherever Froude moved, men gathered round anxious to hear his impressions and he always reassured them. 'The colony, and Melbourne as its capital, have evidently a brilliant future before them. They cannot miss it', he declared. The Government provided him with a special train whenever he wanted to travel, and one function followed another, so that the peaceful days on Macedon's shady hillsides made a welcome break for him.

Lady Loch, too, probably enjoyed having someone to join her in her sketching expeditions. She had considerable skill, and six of her watercolours were to be displayed at the great Centennial Exhibition of 1888, but her work had always been overshadowed by that of her older sister, Teresa. This older sister studied art under some of London's foremost teachers, and achieved considerable success, but her skill as an artist was forgotten when, at the age of sixty, she suddenly became famous as an author. Her first book, a rambling account of her adventures in her garden called *Pot Pourri from a Surrey Garden* was an instant success (still being reprinted today), to be followed by a series of similar volumes.

These early weeks of 1885 gave Emma her first glimpse of Macedon. She does not dwell on its beauties but we can turn for a fuller description to that given by Froude, who obviously enjoyed his days of sketching and walking there.

 At this time of year [the Australian dog days] Melbourne, generally cool and pleasant, becomes oppressive, especially to children . . . Sir Henry Loch, had removed with his family to a cottage in the mountains, 3,000 feet above the sea, forty miles only from Melbourne, and . . . had kindly requested us to rejoin him. It was called Mount Macedon from the hill on which it stood . . . We made our way from the station in a post-cart to the mountain which we saw rising before us, clothed from foot to crest with gigantic gum-trees. There was forest all about us as far as eye could reach . . .

After ascending four hundred feet we found a level plateau, laid out prettily with cottages, a good-looking house or two, and an English-looking village church. A short descent again, and then an equal rise, brought us to the gate of the summer residence of the Governor, a long, low, one storied building with a deep verandah round it clustered over with

Dryden's Rock, Mount Macedon. J. A. Froude thought the landscape 'was perfection'.

creepers. As at Madeira, where the climate changes with the elevation, and an hours' ride will take you from sugar-canes into snow, so here we found the flora of temperate regions in full vigour, which refuse to grow at all at the lower levels. We still had the gum-trees about us, shooting up freely, two hundred feet or more; some magnificent, in full foliage; others naked, bare, and skeleton-like, having been killed by bush fires; but round the house, oaks and elms, cypress and deodara seemed at home and happy; filbert-trees were bending with fruit too abundant for them to ripen, while the grounds were blazing with roses and geraniums and gladiolus. The Australian plain spread out far below our feet, the horizon forty miles away; the reddish-green of the near eucalyptus softening off into the transparent blue of distance. Behind the house the mountain rose for another thousand feet, inviting a climb which might be dangerous, for it swarms with snakes—black snakes and tiger snakes—both venomous, and the latter deadly . . .

The landscape surrounding was perfection; and in this delightful situation and in the doubly delightful society of the Governor's family, we lingered day after day. He himself was called frequently to Melbourne on business, but he could go and return in the same day. We walked, sketched, lounged, and botanised, perhaps best employed when doing nothing except wandering in the shade of the wood. One night upon the terrace I can never forget. The moon rose with unnatural brightness over the shoulder of the mountain; the gorges below were in black shadow; the foliage of the gum-trees shone pale as if the leaves were silver, and they rustled crisply in the light night-breeze. The stillness was only broken by the far-off bark of some wandering dog, who was perhaps on the scent of an opossum.

Monday February 2nd

Such a nice fresh breeze outside. Sat on the mount all the morning. Two men have erected a pole and put the Union Jack up. Had tea outdoors again, but it was almost too cold. There are several bush-fires in the distance. The sky was lighted up for miles with the reflection. 'Tis a grand sight.

Tuesday February 3rd

At 9.30 Sir Henry, Lord Elphinstone, Mr Froude and his son, Lord Castlerosse and Mr Hughes left for Lilydale. A warm day it was too. Lucy and me walked to the post office. The dust was terrible and the sun so hot.

Wednesday February 4th

Very hot sun and wind. Dreadfully oppressed all day with the heat. The wind has brought the bushfire so close that the trees at the top of the Mount are on fire. No doubt this accounts for much of the heat.

One fire is calculated to be at least 8 miles in extent, and the house is full of smoke. We were rather nervous at 2 p.m. The wind increased and blew the flames into the paddock where many valuable horses and cows are kept. We packed up everything of any value, so as to be ready for any emergency. Mrs Ryan, who lives near, came and assured Lady Loch there was no immediate danger, but the men who are beating the flames back declare that if the wind rises, in a quarter of an hour the fire would reach this little house, which is built entirely of wood and would blaze like a band box. We kept going to see if the fire increased all the morning. The roaring and crackling of the flames sounded horrible, and now and again a large tree would fall with a heavy thud. Joseph, William and Jack, one of the stable boys, sat up to give us warning of any danger, so we retired and slept with one eye open till 1 a.m., when Lucy got up as the wind seemed to be increasing. She came in satisfied that there was no need to run at present, though I had a great mind to put on some clothes, the roaring of the fire unnerves one.

February 5th

A very hot day, over 90 degrees in the shade, 116 degrees outside. We all feel ready to drop, and the flies are a perfect pest. The fire is raging on our left. Seems to have run along the top of the Mount and across the valley. Volumes of flames and smoke rising in the air. At 3.30 p.m. Sir Henry arrived, Lord Elphinstone and Mr Hughes, by special train, expecting to find Lady Loch in a great state of anxiety, but all have calmed down today. The view from the front of the house is grand. Hundreds of trees, one mass of fire from top to bottom. Now and again one falls with a crash like a cannonball, and the sparks fly in the air like so many rockets. A finer sight could not be seen. The fire is still at the top of Mount Macedon and tho' much nearer than last night, as the wind carries the flame the other way, the men say there is no danger. Lucy went down after supper to see the paddock. Mary, Kate and Joseph went too. I went to bed as I felt done up with the heat of the day.

February 6th

All up to 8 a.m. Breakfast. Sir Henry left at 8.30 for Melbourne, Mr Hughes accompanied him. Sir Henry returned about 6 p.m. in a heavy shower of rain, which is much needed, for vegetation, everything, is dried up. At 8 p.m. we had a sharp thunderstorm. The lightning kept ringing the telephone bell which is 'conveniently' placed in our bedroom. The storm was over soon at 9, tho' the lightning lit up the country round for sometime after. The air is fresh, and we all feel the benefit of the rain, tho' the changes are very sudden.

February 7th

Fresh cold morning. Thermometer only 34 degrees in Lady Loch's bedroom. We all need an extra garment this morning. Such a shrieking in the stable at 2 a.m. Murray, the horse that goes in the phaeton, got on his back and couldn't turn himself; the stable men, Henry and Jack, got up and helped him to rise. Sir Henry got up too. There is only a thin partition between our room and their's. These are the funniest little shanties. 'Tis almost like living in one large room. You can hear all that is going on in every part of the house— kitchen, pantry, bathroom, drawing room, dining room and bedrooms all on one floor, with thin partitions only between each.

Afternoon February 7th

Frequent hail showers, extremely cold all day and a thunderstorm between 7 and 8 p.m., the lightning very vivid. The telephone wires (which are fixed in our little room) made such a noise.

Sunday February 8th

Very cold and winter-like. Lucy and I took a walk soon after 9 to get warm. There is no morning service at the little church. It is used for Presbyterian Service in the morning and Church of England afternoon—a nice plain service. Mrs Ryan plays the harmonium.

During the Lochs' first summer at Macedon, a stream of visitors arrived to stay with them. The names appear, one after the other, in the diary: Mr Froude and his son and Lord Elphinstone were soon followed by Admiral Tryon, by friends from the Isle of Man, and by other overseas guests. Government House, of course, had numerous rooms for their guests, and smaller attic rooms for their valets, but how did these guests fit into the smaller house at Macedon—and where was their baggage put? No one could 'travel light' last century, especially if they moved in viceregal circles. Even the most casual traveller must have taken large trunks with him, for a guide book of the 1880s gives the following list of 'the articles that may be considered as constituting a traveller's serviceable kit'. No wonder each gentleman brought his valet to pack and unpack the mountain of clothing.

Three sleeping suits, ½ dozen white shirts, ½ dozen regatta shirts, ½ dozen soft shirts (mixed silk and wool); have all stud holes in shirts, no buttons; 2 dozen white collars, ½ dozen white dress ties, ½ dozen black ties, 2 dozen pairs of socks, 3 dozen pairs of dress socks, 2 dozen pocket handkerchiefs: suit of clothes—light texture, medium, heavy, evening dress, flannel (for cricket etc. on board); black silk coat for wearing at dinner; overcoat, heavy and warm; waterproof coat; railway rug; warm soft travelling cap; warm soft woollen comforter; soft French felt hat; black silk shell hat; black skull cap; hat box (leather); walking boots; dress shoes; boot tree; smooth bottomed India rubber-soled shoes, for wearing on wet or damp decks; slippers; cork soles for wearing inside of walking boots; braces; warm gloves; kid gloves; umbrella; walking cane; field glass; opera glass; haversack for carrying important papers, guide books etc.; hassif (furnished); air pillow (if necessary can also be used as lifebuoy); tidy (for your brushes in cabin); brushes—hair, clothes, hat, tooth and nail . . . smoke-glass goggles to relieve the eyes of dust and flies and the glare of sun, sea and towns built of limestone . . . cardigan jacket (knitted wool) to put on over waistcoat and under greatcoat in sudden lowering of temperature.

Monday February 9th

Started for Melbourne at 8.30. Sir Henry, Lady Loch, Lord Elphinstone, Mr Hughes, Capt. Traill, Mary, Mr Lovegrove, Emily, William and myself reached Government House soon after 11 a.m. and found all well (except Mr Hawkins, who looks very poorly).

Tuesday February 10th

Melbourne to do some shopping. Had a pretty warm walk and felt the heat terribly. At 2 p.m. Commodore Erskine arrived, and Miss Constable, who are on their way to England. Mr A. Froude and son, and Lord Elphinstone.

Wednesday February 11th

Hot wind again. Unfortunately had to go and finish shopping. Reached home quite exhausted. Fourteen to dinner. Sir Henry and Lady de Voux, and amongst the rest is Mr Pender's youngest daughter, who was in the schoolroom when we stayed at their Lodge in Scotland. She has now three children and looks older than she is, twenty-eight only.

Thursday February 12th

At 5.30 I woke in such a fright. A crash, the like of which I never heard before! and could not make out, but felt the house must be falling. Flew out of bed to the door and met Mrs Calla, who seemed even more alarmed than I was. It was a clap of thunder that awoke us. I went to bed again, but not to sleep. Mrs Calla went to Mary in her room. Packed up and left Government House at 3.15 for Macedon. Only one conveyance ordered. We were waiting about more than half an hour, then another conveyance was sent for. Quite cold when we reached Macedon at 6.30. No bushfires to be seen anywhere. The heavy rain and fog has at any rate effectually put an end to them.

Shopping was one of Emma's favourite pastimes.

February 22nd

Very hot day. Lucy and me walked to the road that leads to Sir George Verdon's. We did not go far. The road seemed alive with lizards and grasshoppers. Creeping things of all sorts have come out to bask in the hot sunshine and we felt half afraid there might be some snakes. On our way down we met Sir Henry Loch, Mr Ryan and Mr Sturgess. Did not go to church. Had a nice tea on the Mount, Lucy, Mary, Kate and myself. It all tasted so good in the open air. Such a lovely evening, so clear and warm.

IT IS NOT to be wondered at that Emma and Lucy gave up the idea of walking up to the Verdon's house that hot afternoon, for it was situated nearly a thousand feet above the Governor's residence. Sir George Verdon's impressive house, built in what they chose to call 'the Venetian Gothic Style', was one of the first built on the Mount, and although the Governor's choice of Macedon for his holiday house had encouraged other people to build there, the Verdon's house, Alton, remained the largest. And it still stands today, having survived all the bushfires that have destroyed so many of the mountain's houses. With its large reception rooms, library, billiard rooms and numerous bedrooms, it is set on twenty-five acres of hillside, which Sir George planted with trees from all over the world. Its wide variety of trees and shrubs have made it a gardener's paradise; some of the trees, in fact, have grown too vigorously, and when a recent owner offered it to some of his friends for their holidays he waved aside the subject of rent, but said, 'I am going to ask every one of you to pull up ten sycamore seedlings every day'.

Another Macedon house with a wonderful collection of trees was that belonging to the Charles Ryans. In its sheltered valleys he was able to grow tender flowers and shrubs from many different countries, and some of these shrubs still survive in the different gardens into which the original huge estate was later divided. The Ryans are often mentioned in Emma's diary. They were great supporters of the Mount's tiny church, used for Presbyterian services in the morning, and Anglican ones in the afternoon, with Mrs Ryan or one of her daughters usually presiding at the organ. One daughter, in particular, inherited her father's passion for flowers, and her paintings of Australian wildflowers have made her name, Ellis Rowan, well known both here and abroad.

Monday February 23rd

Left Mount Macedon at 8.30 for Melbourne. Sir Henry, Lady Loch, Lord Castlerosse, Mary, Mr Lovegrove and myself. Very warm in the train. Reached Government House at 11.30 a.m. Mr Moore

Sir George Verdon's house on Mount Macedon.

(from Craithbourne?), Isle of Man, is here. He came out in the s.s. Rome for his health. Lady Loch took him all thro' the house and grounds, and all the house party had early dinner. Sir Wm. and Lady de Voux, Lord William Trebitt, Mr Moore and the staff all went to a grand concert at the Town Hall.

February 24th

Lady Loch, Mr Moore and Mr Hughes left for Macedon at 11.30. Mary also returned. I went with them in the cab to Melbourne to do some shopping. Christine goes today, and Jane returns to Government House. I packed up clothes for early start tomorrow.

February 25th

Left Government House at 10.15 for Ercildoun. Left by special train at 11.30 from Spencer Street Station and reached Burrumbeet about 4 p.m. Mr Fiskin met Sir Henry at the station and Sir Henry sat on the box seat of the buggy. Lady Loch, Lord Castlerosse, young Mr

Fiskin and me inside. The horses (four greys) were rather fresh, particularly the leaders. They were good at shieing, and I was nearly off my balance once—all but thrown into Lady Loch's lap. The road was a very rough one. Reached Ercildoun soon after 5 p.m. Such a fine station belonging to Sir Samuel Wilson, who is away (in England). We had some tea. There is a nice little English woman here, a Mrs Vicars, as nurse, and the gardener's wife (Mrs Hale) has come in to help make all go smooth. She lived at Lord Gerard's as kitchen maid before marriage. Mr Hale lived under Mr Skene as foreman. Mrs Hale knows several people that I do—we were soon chatting away as if we had known each other for years.

February 26th Ercildoun

Lovely hot day. The gentlemen went off about 10 a.m. deer shooting. Mr Hale took us round the garden, which is a very nice one, such quantities of fruit, but the parrots are very destructive. Bushels of fruit lying on the ground half eaten away, and on the trees too. There are hundreds of parrots of all colours. I never saw so many in all my life. I should think at the least fifty flew off one tree. The rosellas and galahs are lovely. Mrs Vicars took me to see her little boy, who is staying at the blacksmith's. Returned at 12.30 to dinner, then the gentlemen returned. Sir Henry shot a fine stag, weighs nearly three hundredweight. At 2.30 me, Mrs Vicars, two young gentlemen, Mr Lovegrove, went to see the prize sheep, and the house where six gentlemen rough it and learn farming and this Australian bush life. One old man to do everything for them—cleaning, cooking, washing and all they require. After tea Mr Lovegrove went into the kitchen garden to shoot parrots, and the two little boys went too. He managed to shoot four rosellas. Beautifully marked, red, green, blue, mauve, they are very gay. All colours. Packed up after dressing.

THIS SEEMS to have been the first time that the Lochs actually stayed on a sheep station, although they had visited so many country towns. Coming straight from England where household

Ercildoun station.

staff were so numerous and young gentlemen so well looked after, Emma was obviously surprised that the jackeroos, those six young men who had come to learn farming, had to depend for everything on the services of one old man. And at Ercildoun the jackeroos' quarters were probably palatial when compared with those in the 'real' outback. Ercildoun, in the Ballarat district, was one of Victoria's richest properties, and fortunately there is a full description of it as it was at this time, once again from the pen of Mr Froude.

 We came at last to a gate, which needed only a lodge to be like the entrance to a great English domain.

The park-like character was more marked when we drove through—short grass, eucalyptus trees, and blackwood trees scattered over it like the oaks at Richmond . . . The only exotic features were the parrots, small and large, which were flying like cuckoos from one tree to another, flashing with blue and crimson.

After passing a second gate we found more variety. There were plantations which had been skilfully made. English trees were mixed with the indigenous, eucalypti still preponderating however, some towering into the sky, some, as before, fantastically gnarled; here and there a dead one stretching up its gaunt arms as perches for the hawks and crows. High hills stood out all round us, covered with forest. The drive was broad, level, and excellently kept. The plantation gradually became thicker. A third gate and we were between high trimmed hedges of evergreen, catching a sight at intervals of a sheet of water overhung with weeping willows; a moment more, and we were at the door of what might have been an ancient Scottish manor house, solidly built of rough-hewn granite, the walls overrun with ivy, climbing roses, and other multitudinous creepers, which formed a border to the diamond-paned, old-fashioned windows. On the north side was a clean-mown and carefully-watered lawn, with tennis-ground and croquet-ground, flower-beds bright with scarlet geraniums, heliotropes, verbenas, fuchsias—we had arrived, in fact, at an English aristocrat's country house reproduced in another hemisphere, and shone upon at night by other constellations. Inside, the illusion was even more complete. The estate belonged to a millionaire who resided in England. Ercildoun, so the place was called, was occupied by his friends. We found a high-bred English family—English in everything except that they were Australian-born, and cultivated perhaps above the English average—bright young ladies, well, but not over-dressed; their tall, handsome brother; our host, their father, polite, gracious, dignified; our hostess with the ease of a grande dame . . . Good pictures hung round the rooms. Books, reviews, newspapers—all English—and 'the latest publications' were strewed about the tables—the 'Saturday', the 'Spectator', and the rest of them. The contrast between the scene which I had expected and the scene which I found took my breath away.

February 27th

Left Ercildoun at 10.30 in the same buggy and four greys. The two Miss Fiskins came with us in the special [train] to Melbourne— Lady Loch went on by next train to Macedon. Sir Henry and Lord Castlerosse went to Government House. I took luggage and packed away visiting dresses as we have no conveniences for them at Macedon.

Saturday February 28th

Packed up and left Government House at 2.40 p.m. Train very full. Reached at 6 p.m. Dear little girls so pleased, and wanted me to get down at the gate as the road was very slippery and the horse could hardly get any foothold and the hill is so steep. Mr Cogger said, 'It wouldn't be the first time if the horse did fall' and he knew 'how to get up again'. Very consoling when one would like to spring out. Found all so nipped up with cold.

Sunday March 1st

Still very cold and some rain falling. It cleared at 10.30 and I went for a turn to warm myself. At 12 noon Lucy and I went off again and only returned in time to find them all at dinner. Went to afternoon service—rather late. Sir George Verdon read the first part of the service very nicely, then we had a good plain sermon from Mr Hall, who is very earnest. After service Mary, Lucy, Mr Lovegrove and me walked up Mount Macedon at the back of the house. We had such a nice view. It's very clear and cold—feels quite autumnal.

A carriage pulling up outside Scots Church, Collins Street, Melbourne.

AUTUMN 1885

24 March–26 May 1885

A UTUMN IS CONSIDERED the most beautiful time of the year at Macedon, but the Lochs' first autumn there was marred by Lady Loch's attack of that painful illness, quinsy. However, with a very attentive doctor, and an equally attentive family and staff, she was soon nursed back to health, and this meant that Sir Henry felt able to leave for a day to fulfil his promise of reviewing the combined defence forces at Frankston.

The defence of the colony was a burning question at that time; for Britain had her hands full with the long drawn out war in the Sudan and might not always be able to spring to the defence if Australian colonies were threatened. Sir Henry was anxious to see a confederation of the various governments here, so that they could co-ordinate their land and sea defences, and Froude, too, was a valuable advocate of this policy. Admiral Tryon had also come to Australia with the express purpose of reorganising the embryonic navy, and Sir Peter Scratchley was about to go to Papua as Britain's special commissioner there to deter any foreign power from using it as a base for some possible attack. The newspapers of the day were clamouring for concerted action on defence, a typical leading article in 1885 beginning:

Having escaped a Russian attack when we were imperfectly prepared for it, we should have only ourselves to blame if there should be a recurrence of the late score. It will be our own fault if we should not close the entrance to Port Phillip against any naval force likely to visit us.

March 24th

Left Macedon at 1.30 to prepare for Lady Loch, who comes tomorrow for a marriage, Hon. C. Cavendish to a Miss Bailey. He is a brother of Lord Chesham of Latimer. She is a squatter's daughter. They are reported rich.

March 25th

A fine day for the wedding. After I had dressed Lady Loch I started out to see the wedding at the Scots Church, Collins Street. I arrived in time to see the bride and bridegroom leave the church. He is a fine, tall, fair young man of twenty-three years. She is a blonde with very yellow hair—and a very bright colour. She will be twenty-seven next birthday. There was a great crowd of gazers, and a number of people as wedding guests dressed in the first fashion, with every colour well represented. Returned to Macedon at 3.40 with Lady Loch. Sir Henry remains in Melbourne, and Lord Castlerosse. It was raining when we reached Macedon Station and a thick mist. Lady Loch had a covered buggy. Mr Cogger drove and when about half way he showed me a snake his son had killed. Mr Cogger says he had killed hundreds at different times on his way to the station and that they are very harmless and soon done for. One stroke with a stick generally kills them, though we are told once and once again that they never die until sundown. Lady Loch has got cold and feels very chilly.

March 26th

Very busy packing all day. Unfortunately our last day at Macedon is wet. Lady Loch no better, talks of going early tomorrow morning, leaving us to follow.

March 28th

*Got up at 6 a.m. Lit the kitchen fire for Lady Loch to bathe her face.
She has decided to go by early train to Melbourne for medical advice.
Mam'selle Heyman left with Lady Loch at 8.30. We had a busy day.
Left Macedon at 2 p.m. Miss Edith and Miss Evelyn, Lucy, Mary,
Kate, Mr Sturgess, Master Douglas, Mr Cogger and me all in one
buggy. It was a squash. All travelled together in the Saloon
Carriage, lucky for us, as we had so many small packages. Reached
Melbourne at 4.30 and Government House just before 5. Lady Loch
had to go to bed at once. Very sore quinsy throat. Dr Turner has
ordered linseed poultices made with poppy head and camomile
flower decoctions. Dr Turner has been twice and given many orders
as to treatment.*

Saturday March 28th

*Lady Loch had a most restless night. Sir Henry up and down all
night. The throat and tongue looked very bad.*

Sunday March 29th

*Another bad night. Dr Turner came three times during the day. We
change the poultices every two hours, and give either chicken broth
or milk every hour. Sir Henry is so attentive and seems so very
anxious.*

Monday March 30th

*Lady Loch very depressed and suffering. About midday there was
some discharge and the throat was easier almost at once, tho' it looks
quite scarlet. It is less difficult to swallow and great improvement
since morning. I felt quite anxious this morning before the ulcer
broke. Now all looks better, I am thankful to say.*

'*Sir Henry and Master Douglas went to Frankston to a review.*'

April 4th

Lady Loch was allowed to take a carriage drive. Sir Henry and Master Douglas went to Frankston to a review. Were very tired and worn out. They started at 9 a.m. and were on horseback 9 hours. They returned about 10.30 p.m.

SIR HENRY and Master Douglas may have felt worn out when they arrived home late on Saturday night, after their long hours in the saddle going to Frankston, but they were able to relax in the lovely autumn days that lay ahead. Melbourne was looking its best, the grounds of Government House and the neighbouring Botanic Gardens were at the peak of their beauty, and a succession of admiring visitors came and went. The newly-weds, the Cavendish couple whose wedding the Lochs had attended at Scots

Church, spent part of their honeymoon at Government House, and other newly-weds, the Lymingtons, arrived from England. Emma evidently felt that a long sea voyage in the small and stuffy cabins of the day entailed a difficult start to married life, and in this she echoed the warning that Victorian etiquette books gave to brides. These books stressed that it was often a shock for the new husband, who had only seen his wife when she was complete with her curled transformation, to suddenly see her stripped of this useful addition to her outfit, and they advised brides to have a becoming frilled boudoir cap made to match each of her frilled nightgowns to minimise the shock. Possibly Lady Lymington, a Quaker, had a mind above such frivolities. At this date Emma barely mentions the bride's maid, Miss Homes, but they obviously became friends during this visit, and when the Lochs went up to Sydney, Emma at once called on her and they went sightseeing together.

April 9th

Mr Hughes left Melbourne by the P. & O. m.s.s. Pekin for England. He left in good spirits. I expect he will meet with a cold reception at Kinmel. He hopes to return and claim his beautiful fiancée Miss Stevens, very soon. We doubt if he will ever be allowed to return, so opposed are his parents to the match. Mr Lawyer has gone with him—he is very fragile, but we trust he may live to see his poor mother again.

April 12th

Lord and Lady Lymington arrived. He is a brother of Mr Wallop, secretary to Sir George Strahan (in Tasmania). Lord Lymington only married a week before they started for the colony. This is a very long and tedious journey to make during the honeymoon. Miss Pease belongs to a Quaker family. Has no father or mother. Plenty of the needful. Miss Homes, Lady Lymington's maid, is a very nice gentle little woman. I fear very delicate.

April 20th

Lord and Lady Lymington left Government House at 1.30 p.m. for Tasmania. They expect to return here in two or three weeks.

April 21st

A great demonstration to celebrate the Eight Hours [Day] anniversary. Sir Henry and Lady Loch went to the Treasury to see the procession pass. All trades are represented by large banners and cars. It is the largest gathering I have yet seen in Australia. After going to see poor Mr Cotterell in the Botanical Gardens, we walked by the Yarra and saw the procession file along towards the Friendly Societies' Gardens, where they assemble and spend the day. Various amusements are provided for them. Racing bicycles, music, etc., etc. All seem bent on the one thing: a holiday. May it last (but war preparation's going on apace). Our dear old England will be stamped out with all this trouble and fighting.

No WONDER the newcomers were impressed by the way that Eight Hours Day was celebrated in Victoria. The *Argus* devoted two columns to an enthusiastic description of it, though a few short paragraphs are enough to give some idea of the preparations that went into the grand display.

 Yesterday the thirtieth anniversary of the inauguration of the eight hour system in Victoria was celebrated in the usual manner in various parts of the colony. The chief event was, of course, the procession of the trades unions through the city to the Friendly Societies' Gardens, where the customary fête took place. There is no doubt that this is the greatest procession of the year, so far as the metropolis is concerned, and that the 21st of April is observed as a holiday in this colony more and more jealously and by a larger number of persons in each succeeding year . . .

The procession of yesterday was the largest ever seen in Melbourne, and it attracted an immense number of spectators.

It is estimated that the procession and the spectators of it in the streets comprised about one-sixth of the total metropolitan population. Many persons who observed the day as a holiday did not go to the fête, but went to Brighton or other places usually resorted to on such occasions. In the evening the theatres and other places of amusement were well attended. The day's proceedings were carried out in so orderly a manner that His Excellency the Governor commented, during the remarks which he found occasion to deliver, upon this satisfactory feature. Large masses of the population, he pointed out, had thronged the streets, and assembled at the Friendly Societies' Ground, at which the sports were held, without a suspicion of disorder . . .

All along the route of the procession windows were filled with sight-seers, who clambered upon verandahs, the Post-office and Town-hall steps, and every place where a good view of the sight could be obtained. His Excellency the Governor, Lady Loch, and family, attended by Captain Traill, private secretary, the Premier (Mr. Gillies), and the Chief Secretary (Mr. A. Deakin) occupied the steps of the Parliament houses. As the procession passed by, the leading band halted and played the National Anthem, and cheers were heartily given, which were acknowledged by the vice-regal party. The line then resumed its march, and at intervals other societies took up the cheering—the greeting accorded to His Excellency and the heads of the Ministry being of an enthusiastic character. The procession occupied 50 minutes in passing the Parliament-houses . . .

By the courtesy of the Tramway Company the tram-cars stopped running in Flinders-street while the procession was passing across the intersection of Flinders and Swanston-streets, so that the march was uninterrupted and there was no confusion . . .

The start was made with commendable punctuality at 10 o'clock. The route taken was from the Trades-hall to Lonsdale-street by Russell-street, and thence by way of

The Eight Hours Day anniversary procession.

Swanston-street, along Spring-street into Bourke-street, and thence by way of Swanston-street to the Friendly Societies' Gardens. The numerous bands enlivened the march with inspiring airs, and the display was very imposing and picturesque. The high wind that was blowing unfortunately tore some of the banners of the older eight-hour trades, giving them a sort of battle-scarred appearance, but there were several new and very handsome banners exhibited for the first time by some of the nine handicrafts who have joined the associated trades since last Eight Hours Day . . .

The brickmakers splashed puddled clay all over the spectators, who bore with good humour the vigour with which the representatives of the guild gave a practical lesson in brick moulding. The process of bottling aerated waters was exemplified by the Aerated Waters and Cordial Makers' Society, whose workman was grotesquely attired, for safety sake, something like "the man in the iron mask". The felt hatters had quite a workshop on wheels, including fires and hot irons, and a gorgeous display of every kind of head covering. Besides the active work done en route by handicraftsmen, other features, such as six differently apparelled horses of the saddlers', tinsmiths' knights in armour, and the cooper's tiers of barrels and hogsheads, displayed the fruits of their skills.

Sir Henry evidently faced the wind and dust of the Gardens with his usual good humour, for the newspaper report goes on to speak of his attending the banquet there after the procession. In his speech he once again congratulated the company on 'the evident prosperity of the industrial classes' and, as always, referred hopefully to the prospects of inter-colonial federation. These Gardens, then known as the 'Friendly Societies' Gardens', were on the north bank of the Yarra, near the site of the present Olympic Pool.

May 6th

Mr and Mrs Cavendish came to stay. They seem to be very devoted at present. I only hope it may last till death doth separate them.

May 9th

Lady Robinson and Miss Robinson—from Adelaide—arrived, and the secretary. Quite a large party in the house just now.

May 18th

Lady Robinson left for Tasmania.

May 19th

Dramatic entertainment in the State Saloon by the dramatic company. About two hundred ladies and gentlemen. We served light refreshments in the State Dining Room and finished up about 12 p.m.

May 22nd

*A grand Torchlight Procession by the members of the Fire Brigade.
At Government House fireworks were let off and coloured lights
burnt. The effect was grand. The men numbered more than 1000,
and went thro' a series of evolutions—first rate—and presented
Lady Loch with a special bouquet of violets as large as a small table
and a solid silver bouquet holder with her name engraved thereon.
The whole thing was so well carried out we shall never see a prettier
sight. So very effective.*

CLOSE ON THE HEELS of the Eight Hours Day procession came
this display by the Fire Brigades, which was perhaps even more
spectacular. The celebrations commenced in the afternoon, when,
as the papers reported:

> There was a large gathering in the Exhibition Building this
> afternoon to witness the demonstration under the auspices of
> the Metropolitan Fire Brigades' Association. The proceedings
> were under the patronage of Lady Loch, and Mr. Graham
> Berry was also in attendance during the afternoon. Shortly
> before 4 o'clock Lady Loch and suite put in an appearance, the
> firemen being drawn up as a bodyguard on her entrance.
> Having been accommodated on a seat, her Ladyship stayed
> during a rendition of a musical entertainment, and was after-
> wards introduced to the chief officers of the brigades.

May 25th

*Sir Henry held a levee in honour of Queen's Birthday from 11 to 12.
A continual rush of gentlemen; Military in their uniform, and the
Navy well represented. Clergy and bishops in their gowns of many
colours. We had a capital view of all from the gallery at the end of
the Ballroom, Miss Homes (Lady Lymington's maid), Lucy and me.
We sat behind the ferns and saw all without being seen. All was over
by 12, then early luncheon and the ladies and gentlemen went to a
Review at Albert Park.*

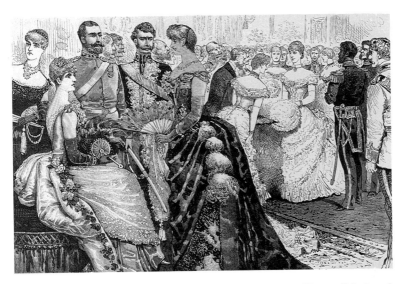

The Lochs entertained on a lavish scale at Government House. (National Library of Australia, Canberra)

May 26th

Dinner for the Queen's Birthday. Seventy to dinner and 800 invited for a reception or At Home afterwards. Miss Cross came to have a peep at the gay dresses and pretty girls. She was delighted, and went off about 11 p.m. All over by 12 p.m. A band of music in the gallery made the time pass quickly. We retired to our beds as the clock was striking 1 a.m.

MELBOURNE PEOPLE were again very impressed by the lavish scale on which the Lochs entertained, and on this occasion the papers reported that:

> When the presentations were over, the company adjourned to the ball-room, and about 10 o'clock this very fine room was a most brilliant picture. The walls were beautifully decorated with trophies of gay flags, whose resplendent colours shone under the brilliant lights placed at short intervals along the walls. At one end of the room a green alcove had been formed,

and here tall waving palm trees and noble-looking tree ferns towered high above the heads of those beneath. Around the room were arranged cosy lounges, where pleasant moments were spent watching the brilliant throng, which, ever changing, each moment presented some new harmony, some delicious juxtaposition of colour and effect which gratified the eye and interested the observer. The brilliant costumes of the ladies, charming as many of them were, did not stand out in such strong and bright relief as is sometimes noticeable, for the very obvious reason that a large number of the gentlemen present were in uniform, and in uniform so attractive-looking that they equally divided attention with the ladies. I never noticed before such a large proportion of officers, and presume the recent war scare has something to do with this marvellously rapid increase of bold warriors.

I cannot do justice to the gowns. These frequent visits to Europe, in which so many of our prominent leaders of fashion indulge themselves, have one charming result as far as those who have to stay at home are concerned, it gives them an opportunity of seeing in an Australian drawingroom the masterpieces of Worth, and Pingat, and Felix . . .

Lady Loch's gown was of white satin, artistically draped with rich old lace of a deep tawny tint. As is usual on all occasions of full dress, Lady Loch wore a low, short-sleeved bodice, and it is only fair that her ladyship's example of full evening dress should be followed by those whom she so hospitably entertains. Lady Stawell wore a sweet dress fashioned of soft dove-coloured satin, with ample draperies of black lace . . .

Of course there were some terrible frocks, generally worn by those to whom nature has been redundant in her gifts. Why will not stout ladies wear quiet tints, and cease to endeavour to dress in a way only suitable for sylphs of sweet seventeen? Why should multitudinous charms be amplified by draperies, by puffings, and pleatings, till the eye is wearied and the mind on the rack by the too-too muchness of the whole?

SYDNEY

1 June–20 July 1885

IN JUNE, the Governor and Lady Loch travelled to Sydney, and this was, for the Lochs, probably one of the pleasantest visits they were to make in Australia. It was certainly the happiest as far as Emma was concerned. She had the wonders of the city to explore in her free time, and she already had a friend there, Miss Homes, the lady's maid who had accompanied the Lymingtons when they came to Government House on their honeymoon. She and Emma soon discovered that they had many tastes in common.

What helped to make the visit to Sydney so enjoyable for the Lochs was that it was to be a private visit, Sir Henry being accompanied by only his ADC, Lord Castlerosse, and his valet. He looked forward to staying with Lord Loftus, and being able to discuss with him in private the questions of federation and of defence, and with the Lochs' growing interest in the poor of Australia's great cities he was anxious to visit the training ship, the *Vernon*.

Emma barely mentions the Governor of New South Wales or Lady Loftus in her journal entries. Perhaps she thought Lady Loftus intimidating, as so many people did. The outspoken Mr Froude wrote of her:

 The share in the official duties which fell to Lady Augustus was, perhaps, heavier than her husband's . . . On her fell the obligation of giving balls and dinners, of entertaining the miscellaneous multitude which constitutes Sydney society; and there are some women, and those perhaps of the finest quality, to whom the presiding in public ceremonies of this kind, in any sphere and among any kind of guests, is naturally uncongenial. Lady Augustus was (and is) a woman whose intellectual powers have been cultivated into unusual excellence . . . In her youth she must have been strikingly handsome. Now she has sons grown to manhood, and out in the world in various professions. She had delicate health, and it was late in life for her to take up with a new round of interests. She was admired and respected in the Colony, but her stately manners alarmed more than they attracted, and I could easily believe when I was told that she was not generally popular . . . In her own house and to her private guests Lady Augustus was a most charming hostess.

June 1st

Left Spencer Street Station at 2.50 p.m. for Sydney in special train. Reached Albury about 8 p.m. and changed into the Pullman or sleeping car on the New South Wales Line—very luxurious carriage. Berths for ladies and gentlemen, with sheets, pillows and every convenience: lavatories, brushes, combs, towels, sponge, dressing room. Saloon—smoking and dining room and kitchen attached. Two waiters in attendance. We had a nice hot dinner, turkey, chicken, new potatoes, salad, green peas, jelly, dessert, wines of all kinds. Went to bed about 10.30. Lady Loch and me occupied one cabin with four berths and slept pretty well, considering how the car swayed to and fro. That, no doubt, is owing to the length.

June 2nd

Got up at 6.30. Dressed Lady Loch and had a good breakfast. Packed up our traps and reached Sydney at 9 a.m. The Volunteers were drawn up at the station. Two aides-de-camp were in waiting,

Changing trains at Albury.

dressed in their uniform, to conduct Sir Henry and Lady Loch to Government House. We were welcomed by Miss Reeves, Lady Loftus' maid, and after a cup of tea, unpacked and had a wash and change of raiment. Had a turn with Miss Reeves in the afternoon to see the shops. The streets are not so wide as Melbourne. Plenty of traffic and dust. There has been no rain for months. The trees and flowers are parched for want of moisture. Jolly comfortable party. Mr Hickey, the steward, is quite irresistible, a thorough Irishman full of wit and funny sayings. He keeps us in a continual roar of laughter, Mrs Fraser (cook) and Miss Chaplin are the party in the rooms.

1. MUSEUM.
2. POST OFFICE.
3. ST. ANDREW'S CATHEDRAL.
4. TOWN HALL.
5. COLONIAL SECRETARY'S OFFICE.

Public buildings of Sydney.

THIS SYDNEY VISIT had no advance publicity, and the Sydney papers did not even give the time of their arrival, so that the Lochs were able to enjoy two leisurely free days before the first notice appeared in the *Herald*.

 It was omitted to be stated yesterday that on his arrival at Redfern Station, Sir Henry Loch, Governor of Victoria was met by the acting Commandant and the Brigade Major. A guard of honour, consisting of fifty men of the Volunteer Infantry, under two officers, was drawn up on the platform and an escort of Light Horse attended His Excellency to Government House. His Excellency paid a visit of courtesy to the Honourable Alexander Stuart at that gentleman's office yesterday. It is the intention of His Excellency during his present stay, to visit several of the public institutions in and around the city.

June 3rd

Lovely day again. Went out with Miss Homes in the morning to the P. & O. agency for Lady Lymington's ulster that was left on the Syria. Then we had a peep at the shops and bought a few things. Came home to dinner. Went at 3 p.m. for Miss Homes to P____ [Pfahlert's] Hotel. We took a hansom to the museum and saw a beautiful collection of birds, beasts and fishes, fossils, skeletons, precious stones, and every sort of curious weapon that were used in times past by the inhabitants of this side the Globe. A dinner party at Government House for twenty-five. Band playing in the corridor made the house merry.

WITH WARM sunny days, everyone enjoyed Sydney to the full. Miss Homes took Emma under her wing. She was with the Lymingtons at Pfahlert's, one of Sydney's leading hotels—no wonder Emma at first left a blank in her diary for this name, for it would seem bizarre to Anglo-Saxons. On the day of their arrival Miss Reeves had shown Emma some of the big shops, only a few minutes walk from Government House, and with Miss Homes she now explored the Botanic Gardens, fascinating even in a time of drought, and the museum, as well as parts of the coastline from Cook's landing site at Botany Bay to Watsons Bay.

June 4th

Miss Homes called for me at 11 a.m. to go thro' the Botanical Gardens. They are beautiful. Alas, alas, everything shows a great want of moisture. We admired the lovely coral plant with its bright new pendants and the Australian fig is marvellous. Another dinner party for twenty. Miss Homes came for supper and had a good laugh. Mr Hickey is so funny. We got to bed very late.

June 5th

Lovely day. Went off at 11, called at Pharlert's [Pfahlert's] Hotel for Miss Homes. Found she was out. Met her in the principal street, George Street. Did more shopping and arranged to meet at the Bridge Street Tram office at 2 p.m. and go to Botany Bay. Before I reached home the rain, which is so sorely wanted, came down in torrents. Our trip was out of the question. It rained on slowly but surely all night. Everyone seems so thankful as they have had no rain for months and everything 'tis dried up. Lady Loch and Sir Henry went to the Grand Opera.

Government House Sydney June 6th

Lovely bright morning. Nature looks so refreshed from yesterday's downpour. I went to Pharlert's Hotel to see Miss Homes. She starts with Lord and Lady Lymington for the Blue Mountains at 1.30 p.m. Mr Hickey and Mr Lovegrove went to the races. Sir Henry, Lady Loch, Lady Augustus, Lord Loftus, Lord Castlerosse also went. Miss Reeves, Mrs Fraser, Miss Chaplin and myself started at 2 p.m. for a trip round the Harbour. It was most enjoyable. Had a fine view of the Nelson and many other fine war boats. We landed

The Nelson, *with Sydney's Government House in the background.*

*for about 10 minutes at the end of Watson's Harbour and brought
home some oysters. Reached Government House about 5.30 and
had a peep at the Bazaar held in the Ballroom for some charitable
purpose. We saw nothing we wanted, so did not purchase. After tea,
which we all enjoyed very much, dressed Lady Loch, who dined with
Admiral Tryon on board the* Nelson. *Supped at 8—and started at
8.30 for 'Paddy's Fair'. Mr Hickey, Mr Lovegrove, Miss Reeves,
Miss Chaplin, Mrs Fraser and self. What an uproar. Every sort of
goods for sale, meat, fowl, fish, cheese, wearing apparel of all kinds,
old and new—a second Whitechapel. Whirligigs and merry go
rounds doing a fine trade. The rough element well represented—they
did not interfere with us. We walked thro' all three arcades. Sometimes you cannot get thro'. Had we been an hour later it would have
been too much to wade thro'. Such a crowd of unwashed. Called on a
friend of Miss Reeves, Mrs Little, a fine woman, but sad to say they
are selling their business—for reasons best known to themselves. She
has had D. T. and laid up for six weeks. Reached Government House
just as the carriage swept up to the door.*

THIS BAZAAR, held during the Lochs' visit, was one of the occasions when Lady Augustus Loftus was seen at her most charming. She had offered to lend the huge ballroom for a two-day fête to raise money for a hostel for the Girls' Friendly Society, a place where girls in need could live very economically. The papers reported that 'The opening ceremony was performed by Lady Augustus Loftus who was accompanied by Lady Loch and the Primate of Australia.'

The goods consist of a variety of articles of a very choice character. Among these articles are a valuable collection from the Kensington School of Art. The verandah of the ballroom has been screened off and has been converted into an entertainment room. Another temporary room created in the verandah and decorated by Mr Quong Tart is allotted to the enterprising caterer. In it are supplied refreshments so excellent in kind that they have helped to gain Mr Tart a certain amount of fame. The gardens attached to Government House have been opened to visitors, who will have the privilege of strolling through them. In the afternoon the band of H.M.S. "Nelson" contributed an excellent selection of music, and a series of vocal and instrumental entertainment was also carried out.

Though Quong Tart's name is virtually forgotten today, he was a legend in his own time, and recipes for Quong Tart's scones can be found in many old Australian cookery books. Coming as a child from China, with relatives who were indented to work on the goldfields, he was befriended by a family on the fields, who taught him English and arranged for him to attend the local school. By the time he was twenty-one he was himself a successful mining investor. Selling his mining interests and moving to Sydney, he became a tea-importer with a stall in a fashionable arcade, where he not only sold packets of tea but invited weary shoppers to taste a cup of the delicious beverage. Soon he opened a cafe upstairs where people could enjoy his tea and his famous scones, in a series of tastefully decorated rooms, one for 'Ladies Only'.

Although Quong Tart's establishments perhaps lacked the prestige of Melbourne's Gunsler's, on 'the Block', his tearooms had a tremendous popular appeal and were one of Sydney's favourite meeting places.

While Lady Loch was assisting at the fête and sampling Quong Tart's scones, Sir Henry was carried off by some of the members of the Government to the *Vernon*, where he 'made a most careful inspection of the installation'.

Upon arrival the Governor was received with the usual vice-regal honours, a salute of 17 guns being fired, and a guard of honour being drawn up in the quarter deck. The library and boys' reading room, which contained twelve hundred volumes and is decorated with a large number of pictures including "England for Ever". The schoolroom then claimed the Governor's attention and over half an hour was occupied therein. All hands were piped to fall in, which enabled His Excellency to examine each boy individually, and not one case of sickness was found to exist among the large ship's company of 231 boys and 15 officers. Sir Henry, who is an old experienced artillery officer, expressed his approbation of the way in which the guns were manned. A call to fire quarters, and manning the yards brought the visit to a close after His Excellency had read some letters from ex-Vernon boys, taken at random from a pile of many hundreds, and made the following note in the visitors' book: "Had the greatest pleasure in visiting this most admirably conducted institution."

HIS EXCELLENCY also had an opportunity of seeing the raw material with which the Vernon has to deal, as two new recruits arrived during his visit, both deplorably dirty and one a 'most pronounced type of the genus larrikin'. As there had been considerable discussion in Victoria about the merits of the Vernon system, Sir Henry had been determined to make a careful assessment of it, and he also found time to visit the Girls' Reformatory at Biloela, which again won his approval. And on the last day before his return to Melbourne, Sir Henry made another visit of inspection, this time to Parramatta to see the Asylum for the

Infirm and Destitute, a depressing name for any institution. He and his ADC travelled to Parramatta by train, and also had time to see St John's Church and the wonderful orchard planted by James Pye, before lunching with Sir Henry Parkes, that staunch advocate of federation, and returning to Sydney by river.

Sydney June 7th

Another fine frosty morning. Went off at 10.30 by tram with Miss Chaplin to the cathedral. Such a capital sermon, so earnest. The singing was very good and the congregation fairly attentive. We had a hansom to Government House as it was rather late. After dinner Mr and Mrs Buckle called and took Miss Reeves and me for a drive. Nice easy buggy and a good pair of horses. Took us to the Heads. Such a splendid drive—every turn a view of the Harbour seemed more and more beautiful. The place where the Dunbar *went down was pointed out, and where the convicts were kept, but they used to swim ashore and escape. Woolloomooloo is a pretty place, bears a bad reputation tho'. We reached home at 5.30. Mr and Mrs Buckle stayed for tea and supper. We all laughed at Mr Hickey's wit and humour till we could laugh no more. Retired at 11 and slept like a top until morning.*

ALL VISITORS were taken to The Gap to shudder as they looked down and thought of the *Dunbar* being dashed against the rocks in a violent midnight storm thirty years before, and to imagine the agony of the sole survivor who had clung perilously to a rock for thirty-six hours before being rescued.

Sydney June 8th

Bright, fresh, sunny morn. Went with Lady Loch to some shops in the morning, and at 2 started for Botany Bay with Miss Reeves. We took a top seat in the tram, so had a fine view of Sydney and the suburbs. Reached Botany and went to see a Mrs Smith at the hotel. Walked thro' the grounds which are very extensive, and dancing

Service in St Andrew's Cathedral, Sydney.

pavilion. The spot where Captain Cook landed was pointed out. And after a little time on the beach we returned by tram, reaching Sydney at 6 p.m. all the better for our trip.

Tuesday June 9th

Our last day, I am sorry to say. Went off at 11 with Miss Reeves to get some house shoes. Called at Pharford's [Pfahlert's] *Hotel to see Miss Homes, and to say goodbye to Mrs Buckle, who gave us some beautiful pearl oyster shells as a remembrance of our visit to Sydney. All are certainly most kind to us.*

Got back about 1.40 after a good dinner. Packed up all our traps. Miss Homes came in the evening, also Mr and Mrs Buckle to supper. The latter brought me another pair of lovely smoked pearl oyster shells. Mr Hickey gave me a Tasmanian shell necklace—such a merry party. I am quite sorry our pleasant visit is over.

June 10th

Got up at 6. Packed up and left Government House at 8.30 for the station. The special left Sydney at 9—dining saloon, kitchen, smoking room, lavatory, dressing room and beds with sheets if we like to rest, writing paper and ink and every convenience in the sitting room. I used the dressing room and had a nice nap to freshen me up. At 11 a.m. they fetched me to have some oysters and bread and butter, which I enjoyed immensely, they were so fresh. At 1.30 a capital luncheon of chicken, green peas, new potatoes, dessert, bread and butter. At 4 a nice hot cup of tea, so refreshing to get as one flies through the country. Things are done well in New South Wales. At 7.30 we dined. Soup, turkey, dressed cauliflower, new potatoes, roll, butter, cheese, dessert, claret. At 10 we changed on to the Victorian line. Tho' it was a saloon carriage it all seemed cold and dull after the luxurious Pullman. It was a bitter cold night. We were nearly frozen [even] *with all our wraps. Reached Melbourne at 3.30 and Government House 3.55. Had some hot soup and a good warm, then turned into bed till 8. Felt very stiff, but glad to have seen Sydney under such pleasant circumstances.*

June 11th

Very tired all day. Lady Robinson and Miss Robinson and Mr Howard arrived from Tasmania about 12. Also Sir Geo. Strahan and Mr Smith (valet). Lady Loch held a reception, not many luckily as we had made no provision. Lucy went to Gunston [Gunsler's] in the morning and secured a few cakes. Mr Westlake called.

AFTER LEAVING their cold carriage to step on to a cold windy Melbourne platform in the small hours of the morning, the Lochs finally reached Government House, and must have been very glad of those few hours in bed before they were called on to give their proverbial warm welcome to their next round of guests. These were Lady Robinson and her daughter, on their way home after their holiday in Tasmania, and they were accompanied by Tasmanian governor, Sir George Strahan. No doubt they were just as weary as the Lochs, for the passage from Hobart is a notoriously rough one.

But the next day was Thursday, and in the afternoon Lady Loch was always At Home to callers, so one of the maids was at once despatched to the city to bring back a selection of Gunsler's delicious cakes. Gunsler's must have been a godsend to Lady Loch and to many other Melbourne hostesses when unexpected guests arrived, or when cook was pressed for time; they could always produce one of Gunsler's elaborate cakes or desserts, which would not only make an attractive centrepiece for the table but provide a memorable sweets course.

The firm had been established in Melbourne for a number of years and had recently moved to Collins Street, to spacious new premises on The Block. It bore the name 'Café Gunsler', and stood between Mullen's Library and Mr Fletcher's Art Gallery, a site later to be occupied by the Hotel Australia. On the ground floor was an elegant restaurant with a bar serving oysters and coffee 'for those whose time is too limited to seat themselves at tables'. The stairs, again described as 'elegant', led to two large luncheon rooms, one open to both ladies and gentlemen and the other one, as in Quong Tart's famous tearooms in Sydney, open to

'Ladies Only'. Each floor was provided with retiring rooms, which no doubt again could be described as elegant, and which were furnished with patent tip-up lavatory basins and finished with white glazed tile wall linings. On the second floor was a lofty banqueting room, nearly seventy feet long, which, as well as serving for formal banquets, could be used for meetings, such as those of the Melbourne Liederfelden.

June 13th

Lord and Lady Lymington arrived. Mr Wallop. We are glad to see a little more of Miss Homes.

June 14th

Went to St Paul's in the morning with Miss Homes. Mr Westlake sat just in front of us.

June 15th

Opening of Parliament. Sir Henry started about 2 p.m., with orderlies and troopers, for the Parliament Houses, top of Collins Street. Lady Loch also went. I went in a cab with Lucy and the children, but there was nothing to see but a crowd of people at the Treasury buildings, so came away as it rained. The guns are firing and the town is quite gay. All seemed anxious to catch a sight of the Governor in his uniform and the staff looked quite gay in their helmets and scarlet and gold uniform.

AFTER ONLY a few days since their return from Sydney the usual round of official engagements had begun in earnest for the Lochs, with Sir Henry opening Parliament and the following day taking the chair at the tea meeting and display by the YMCA members at the Town Hall. The papers reported that:

. . . notwithstanding the weather was so inclement, there was a large assembly of spectators both inside and outside Parliament House. His Excellency was received at the foot of the steps leading up to the Grand Hall by a guard of honour from the No. 2 Battalion. The council Chamber was crowded, amongst the spectators Lady Loch, Sir George Strahan, Governor of Tasmania, the naval and military officers and the consuls of Japan, France and Austria.

June 23rd

Sir G. Strahan left—also Mr Wallop and Mr Smith—for Hobart. We are sorry to lose Mr Smith. He is such a perfect gentleman in every way.

June 24th

Mr and Miss Costello arrive to stay. Dinner for sixteen.

July 3rd

At 2.50 a.m. a shock of earthquake. Supposed to be the worst for some time. Mam'selle got up and was much alarmed. Sir Henry heard the shaking of doors and windows. The girls upstairs were all awakened. Something woke me up, but I did not know what till after all was quiet.

July 19th

Bad cold and cough. Could not go to St Paul's for the last service before it's pulled down for the cathedral. Seems a pity to pull a church down only fifty years old, in good condition too. Canon Chase gave a most excellent sermon. The Ven. Dean Macartney in the evening. Mr Dion Bouciaouh [Don Boucciacoult], *his son and daughter, came to luncheon.*

THE RAIN WHICH descended on the crowd of onlookers when Sir Henry opened Parliament had left Emma with a bad cough, preventing her from attending the last service in St Paul's before it was demolished. It was hard to convince people that Melbourne really needed a bigger and better cathedral for so many had glowing memories of St Paul's in the old days, of church parades with the glittering uniforms of the 40th Regiment of Foot and the 23rd Fusiliers with their bands. It was a particularly sad day for the people who had worked so hard when it was being built in the early 1850s, for the church was barely half finished when the gold fever broke out, and every able bodied man rushed off to make his fortune. The contractor was left with only one workman, and although he tried desperately to get replacements, he was unsuccessful. Finally the ingenuity of Canon Chase succeeded where he had failed. Chase put up large posters round the site, appealing to all Christian men not to let their church stand roofless and unusable, but to come and lend a hand. He promised them the current wage for all they did, and his scheme was so successful that the church was ready, at the promised date, for Bishop Perry to take his first service there. And now all this was to go!

On this same Sunday, Don Boucciacoult, the famous Irish dramatist and actor, brought his son and daughter to luncheon at Government House. During their short season in Melbourne the theatre was packed every night, for it was the first time he had come to Australia. His fame had preceded him, and he had won all hearts when he had come on the stage of the Theatre Royal to say:

> Seven weeks ago we met here for the first time, not as strangers—for I have visited in the spirit many times when my pieces were presented here. We had passed many evenings together and that they were very pleasant ones, I am assured by the hearty reception you gave me and mine. You came with both hands extended to give an old friend welcome. I was handicapped by the favours heaped on the author.

It must also have been gratifying for him to learn from the management that the receipts from the theatre would exceed any receipts taken in the colonies during a similar season: however he warned other companies against coming to Australia, pointing out that counting the weeks of voyage out, that it would take thirty-four weeks for them to earn twenty-two weeks box office receipts, and declaring it was only because of phenomenally high bookings that he had made any profit. From the shelter of New Zealand, Don Boucciacoult went on to tell the press what he really thought of Melbourne—it was 'bleak, raw and wet', and the hotels 'are not worthy of the city. The rooms are small and dingy, the bedrooms poorly furnished, food is displeasing. We found the Theatre Royal a large dusty primitive building with poor accommodation for the audience and still more wretched arrangements for the actors behind the scenes'. The best he had to say of us was that we were 'an independent and republican community—clean, bright and saucy'.

July 20th

A busy morning. Linen to send into the laundry, and then to Melbourne to see about dessert cakes etc. for the 22nd. Got back about 1.40. Lucy sent to St Kilda about some shoes for the young ladies. I had a great fright. Nearly lost Mrs Calla's cheque for £20 5s 8d. A cab driver kindly drew my attention to it—he saw me drop it on the footway. At 2.40 Miss Cross came to see us, and Johann Strus [Krause] the great violinist played his violin so beautifully in the Drawing Room. We had the pleasure of hearing one of the best musicians the world has ever known. So soft and sweet. 'Tis indeed a great treat.

COULD EMMA BE growing a little deaf? She had obviously heard so much said in praise of the musician who was coming to play at Government House that she was convinced that she was hearing Strauss himself. Admittedly, the name of the violinist who was captivating audiences in Melbourne, Krause, sounded very similar. It is strange that we should have forgotten his name today, for he was perhaps our very first Australian-born musician to have achieved worldwide recognition. His parents were German settlers and the young Krause went to Berlin to study the violin under the great master Joachim. The Lochs were so impressed by his playing that they asked him to give a recital at Government House, and several hundred of their friends were able to enjoy, in lovely surroundings, his programme of Handel, Mendelssohn and Chopin.

The newspapers reported this recital by the gifted young Victorian violinist, and reminded its readers that the last Melbourne appearance of Herr Krause would take place at the Town Hall that evening. They did not announce, however, that another young Victorian artist would also appear on that programme, Nellie Armstrong. Ten years later they would again appear on the same programme, at one of the famous Albert Hall concerts, he as Professor Krause, leader of the orchestra, and she as Madam Melba.

A Second Spring

22 July–4 November 1885

THE LOCHS had now been in Melbourne for a full year, and as spring approached, heralding the racing carnival with its round of lavish entertainments, the staff of Government House felt far more confident of their ability to handle these enormous gatherings. They now knew just how many extra helpers would be needed at each function, and they had evidently built up a good relationship with the temporary staff who came in to help at such times.

The festivities commenced as they had the previous year, with the two large Parliamentary dinners, each followed by a reception where the guests danced to the strains of Herr Platt's orchestra until the small hours.

July 22nd

Parliamentary dinner for seventy. Several were unable to attend thro' illness or bereavement. The dinner went off well and Lady Loch held an At Home after at 9. They commenced arriving and streamed into the Ballroom till after 10. Considerably over 1000 people attended and dancing was kept up with great spirit till after 12, then the company began to leave. The ladies were nicely dressed and a great many wore full dress. We got to bed about 2 a.m., very tired.

July 29th

Another dinner party for sixty—Parliamentary. Again several were unable to come thro' this terrible bronchitis. So many peoples are laid up with it. About 1500 ladies and gentlemen came after dinner. All went off well. Herr ____ [Platt's] Band played in the Ballroom and dancing was indulged in for two or three hours by the youthful. Miss Kirby and Miss Cross helped us with the refreshments and were highly delighted to get a sight of the company. Miss Kirby went home with Mrs Mallison. Miss Cross remained here for the night. Dear little Miss Evelyn's ninth birthday. Some nice presents have been sent for her. She is so excited

August 7th

Admiral Tryon arrived from Sydney on a visit.

August 10th

Admiral Tryon left for Sydney, N.S.W.

August 12th

Sir Wm., Lady Clark and Miss Shannon came for one night. Miss Shannon was in great form.

August 13th

The Bishop of Ballarat came to stay. We had the pleasure of seeing him. He read prayers in Lady Loch's boudoir this morning. He looks very learned and reads so clearly and distinctly.

August 16th

Mr Hawkins, Mary and I went to Christ Church, South Yarra, this morning. About 3 p.m. Miss Kirby arrived. Miss Edith is not very well, a feverish cold, high temperature. She has not been down since Thursday.

Brighton Beach.

cAugust 20th

Sir Henry and Lady Loch opened the agricultural show this morning. Were entertained at luncheon, speech making, champagne, etc., etc. Lucy, Mr Hawkins and me went off directly after dinner to South Yarra station for Brighton. Very warm and pleasant on the beach. We sat on the sands till a few minutes to 5, when the train brought us back just in time to get a cup of tea and ready for early dinner, 6.40.

IT IS SURPRISING to hear of people sitting on the beach till dusk in August, for this is a notoriously cold month in Victoria. But 1885 must have been an exceptional year, for the papers, in their accounts of the Show, commented on the strong north wind, a warm wind.

The attendance at the National Agricultural Show today was very large, notwithstanding the strong northerly wind and close atmosphere, which rendered out-door exertion so decidedly unpleasant. His Excellency the Governor visited the grounds, and made a minute inspection of the chief objects of interest, Sir Henry Loch expressing himself pleased with the highly satisfactory results obtained . . . A half-holiday having been proclaimed, and this being the most interesting day of the Show, led to the great attendance, and the trains and vehicles running to the grounds were well patronised during the day. Sir Henry and Lady Loch and suite arrived punctually at noon, and were formally welcomed at the entrance gate by Dr. Plummer, the President, and members of the Committee. As the party alighted the Brass Band played the National Anthem, and formal introductions followed, after which an inspection of the exhibits took place. At half-past one o'clock a luncheon was held, at which members of the Ministry were present, and the usual toasts honoured.

Sunday August 23rd

Mrs MacMillan came to stay during her husband's absence at Adelaide.

August 25th

Mr Lovegrove not well. A rash has come out all over him. It looks like nettle rash.

August 31st

Mr Cask and servant arrived from England. He is a very clever young man. Head boy at Eton for two years. He had a fall from his horse and is subject to fainting fits. Has been advised to take this voyage, which has so far succeeded (Mr Morey tells us).

September 4th

Mr and Mrs G. Anderson had luncheon. They leave by the Orient *tonight for England. Mrs Lorimer, the nurse, has taken some necklaces home for Alice and Floss. It was a capital opportunity.*

September 18th

Had a nice lot of letters today, Sunday. One from Tom, two from Ted, two from Mrs Holloway, one from Mary Cavote, one from Turner Cavote, one from Mrs Cavote.

September 15th

Lady Loch's birthday. Master Douglas not well. Sir Henry had neuralgia, not able to attend the bazaar at Geelong.

September 16th

Primate and Mrs Barry arrived from N.S.W. Master Douglas in bed with cold and enlarged glands.

September 17th

Reception. Dinner for twenty-six. Evening party for two hundred.

September 18th

Master Douglas no better. Temperature 100 degrees. Bishop and Mrs Barry left.

THROUGHOUT the spring the Lochs' visitors came and went, some from overseas, getting their first glimpse of Marvellous Melbourne, and some from other parts of Australia. A number of these guests were bishops.

In the nineteenth century, all Australia's bishops came from Britain, as did all our governors, so it is only natural that they had much in common. Sometimes both governor and bishop were from the same college at Oxford or Cambridge, or from the same county where they were sure to have mutual friends. Bishop Thornton, who had been appointed the first Bishop of Ballarat ten years before, was the first of the Governor's ecclesiastical guests that year, his arrival noted by Emma in her journal entry for 13 August. He and the Governor had many interests in common. Thornton was a man of vision who had great plans for the future of his diocese. His first task had been to raise the funds to purchase a suitable home for its bishop, for his furniture and books had to remain in their packing cases until this house was found; and now he felt it was time to proceed with his plans for a vast new cathedral that would be worthy of the rich area of Victoria which it served. Sir Henry was obviously impressed by his visitor and he agreed to make another visit to Ballarat where he would preside at a public meeting to launch a building fund for the new cathedral.

In September another of those outstanding early bishops, with his wife, stayed at Government House. Bishop Barry, from Sydney, was a son of Sir Charles Barry, the architect who was chosen to design the Houses of Parliament at Westminster.

After his ordination, Barry had held a number of educational posts, and while he was head of Cheltenham College he had been so impressed by the high achievements of the sister school, under its remarkable principal, Miss Beale, that he remained for ever after a strong supporter of wider educational openings for girls. As both Sir Henry and Lady Loch were keenly interested in the provision of training for both boys and girls, the poor as well as the wealthy, this was a strong mutual interest. In the matter of federation, the bishops of the various colonies were a step ahead of the politicians, for the bishops had already agreed to accept that one of their number, Bishop Barry, be authorised, as Primate of Australia, to speak for them all as head of the Anglican church here.

September 19th

Lady Loch attended a concert in the evening.

September 20th

Did not go to church today, so tired. Started in the rain for Botanical Gardens and had to wait at Mrs Cotterell's till a heavy shower had passed. We both got a good drenching.

September 23rd

Lady and Miss Stawell came to stay. All went to the Mayor's Ball in the evening at the Melbourne Town Hall. Master Douglas very

Botanic Gardens, Melbourne.

unwell. His glands are very painful and it is very disappointing to see him no better. We think he must have got a chill last time he was up in the schoolroom.

As THE END of September drew near, notices in the press reminded the citizens of the approaching Mayor's Ball. They were warned that Swanston Street and Collins Street would be closed to general traffic all the evening, so that the guests' carriages could roll up freely to the portico of the Town Hall, and as a final caution, all the invited guests were reminded that they must carry their invitation cards with them. The ball was voted a great success, and the *Age* was able to report the next day:

 Probably the two most poignant sarcasms ever levelled against the Anglo-Saxon race by foreign critics are that they are a nation of shopkeepers, and that they take their pleasure sadly.

The author of the first expiated his offence after finding that the shopkeeper was a stronger man than he who sought to spoil his goods by exile and death at St. Helena, and if any answer to the second was needed it would be supplied by the brilliant ball given last evening at the Town Hall, which glorified the setting splendour of Cr. Carter's Chief Magistracy. The civic bodies of Melbourne and the vicinity were assembled, as duty bound, in great force, and no part of the community was left unrepresented, the beauty and splendour of the scene being enhanced by the great number and variety of the uniforms and the toilettes of the ladies. The opening quadrille was danced by his Excellency the Governor and Mrs. Carter, The Mayor and Lady Loch, Sir W. J. Clarke, Bart., and Lady Stawell, Sir H. B. Nicholson, Bart., and Lady Clarke, Alderman Stewart and Miss McKenzie, and Captain Barker (United States man-of-war Enterprise) and Mrs Stewart. Major-General Downes, Col. Walker, of the Imperial Staff were also present; the Ministry, the officers of the Garrison and Field Artillery, the Victorian Rifles, the Naval Brigade, the consular body and the members of both Houses of Assembly were represented, the festive throng being completed by members of all the society of Melbourne, quos nuc describere longum est. The hall was most beautifully decorated and illuminated, and dancing was kept up till an early hour this morning. The comfort of the guests was provided for in the most thoughtful manner, the Mayor's parlour, the library, the committee rooms and other resources of the Town Hall being devoted to smoking, card rooms and other addenda to a ball which are frequented by non-dancers. The material wants of the Mayor's guests were ministered to by buffets loaded with creature comforts in the annexes of the great hall.

For the many Scotsmen who were present at the ball, the highlight of the evening was undoubtedly the Governor's entrance, for he was accompanied by three pipers, selected by the Caledonian Society, who played 'The Campbells are Coming', and as soon as the pipers ceased the band struck up the National Anthem.

September 28th

Lady Loch, Miss Edith and Miss Evelyn and myself went to Queenscliff at 4 p.m. Had tea at Geelong and reached Queenscliff about 7.40. Such a lot of people at the station to see Lady Loch. We had nice rooms facing the sea at the Hotel Baillieu. Mrs Baillieu is a nice homely English-woman, very anxious and attentive. Unfortunately the hotel is very draughty. I am afraid we have all taken cold. 'Tis a little too early, and the weather too fickle for enjoyment. The seaweed is lovely, all colours from white to deep red—and the shells are so pearly and beautifully marked from Swan Island.

Saturday October 2nd

Left Queenscliff at 12 for Melbourne. Miss Evey far from well.

Lady Loch had evidently felt that a breath of sea air was what was needed to cure the family's succession of colds and sore throats, and decided to go down to Queenscliff. This was their first visit to Baillieu's Hotel, which, despite Emma's complaints about its draughts, was to become a favourite retreat of theirs.

This grand hotel, with its eighty bedrooms, its tower, and its wide balconies with their elaborate cast iron decoration, had been built by the Baillieus only a few years previously, and was a conspicuous landmark along the shore. It adjoined Lathamstowe, a splendid mansion with a similar tower, whose main room bore a gilded inscription saying 'These buildings are dedicated by Edward Latham of the Carlton Brewery for the use and benefit of the clergy of the Church of England in the diocese of Melbourne'.

These two families, the Baillieus and the Lathams, were soon to become connected, with the Baillieu's son William, marrying Latham's daughter Bertha, and seven years later, after his wife's death, Latham himself marrying William's sister, Emma Elizabeth.

Both these fine buildings still stand as landmarks in Gellibrand Street today. Lathamstowe sheltered the clergy for over 100 years, and the hotel, now renamed the 'Ozone', still opening its elegant doors to a constant stream of visitors.

October 8th

Sir Henry and the young ladies left for Ballarat. Lady Loch was too unwell with sore throat. Dr Turner applied a leech under the left ear, which has taken the inflammation down considerably.

October 9th

Lady Loch was much better this morning and decided to join Sir Henry at Ballarat and go on with him to Carngham, Mr Russells' station 20 miles drive from Ballarat. Master Douglas is the only one at home except Mr Sturgess and Mr Thomas Stawell, who has kindly come to keep Master Douglas from feeling lonely. I am having a nice quiet time but expect poor Nelly will find her hands full with three ladies to wait upon.

CLEARLY THE sea breezes of Queenscliff did not cure Lady Loch's painful throat and initially she was too ill to go with her husband on the promised visit to the Russells at Carngham. But the leeches applied by Dr Turner appear to have worked wonders, and by the next day Lady Loch felt well enough to join the others. Emma had naturally stayed on at Government House with her mistress and now that Lady Loch was able to travel, Emma was able to relax for a few days. Her only worry appears to have been her concern that Nelly—presumably one of the junior maids—might not be able to manage having to wait on 'three ladies', strange as it seems to us that little girls of nine and ten should require any waiting on.

Christ Church, South Yarra. Emma went to services here as often as she could.

Sunday October 11th

Got ready for church, but the rain fell in torrents as we were starting, so gave it up and only went to see Mr Cotterell at 4 p.m.

October 12th

Mr Hale called this morning and brought me some parrots' wings which he promised to cure for me at Ercildoun. He is anxious to get work in Melbourne on account of Mrs Hale, who is delicate. A dance in the Hall. About fifty invited guests. Neither Mrs Calla or myself showed up.

October 13th

Miss Cross arrived early in the forenoon to help me. Miss Knight came in after dinner. Mr Hawkins went to the races and only returned in time for supper.

October 14th

Mr Tyler called—from the s.s. John Elder. *He had tea with us and kindly offered to take any little thing home for me.*

October 15th

Miss Cunningham's wedding day. Very bright and clear. Lady Loch, Sir Henry and the young ladies returned home from Carngham about 6.30 p.m. They all looked tired, have enjoyed themselves very much.

THE LOCHS apparently returned in very good spirits. Sir Henry and Philip Russell, fellow Scots, would have had much in common, and Russell, as one of the colony's leading breeders of fine merinos, would have had a wealth of interesting information for the visitors. Carngham had been the home of the family since the 1840s, and in this time had grown, as so many homesteads had, from a small cottage to a large and comfortable house, surrounded by splendid banks of shelter trees.

Now that the Lochs had returned, preparations began in earnest for the festivities of Cup week.

October 30th

Garden Party. Very Warm. Bad dust storm in afternoon. About 2000 people. All very exhausted from heat.

As THE SPRING racing season approached, the weather became hotter and hotter, the Observatory reporting one record temperature after another. The day of the first big function, Lady Loch's garden party, was one of the days of abnormally high temperatures with storm clouds on the horizon. No wonder that Emma's entry in her diary is brief and to the point—'very exhausted from heat'. However, the *Age* was able to report that:

> The grounds and reception rooms at Government House were thronged yesterday afternoon by the elite of Melbourne who attended Lady Loch's At Home for the purpose of paying their respects to her Ladyship and the Governor. Sir William Robinson, the Governor of South Australia, was present, Sir Frederick Napier-Broome, the Governor of Western Australia being unavoidably absent through indisposition. The commandant and other officers of the local forces in undress uniform and a brilliant show of morning toilettes imparted brightness and freshness to the scene. Lady Loch received her visitors in a large marquee, and owing to the atmospheric disturbances prevailing during the afternoon, the company did not stray far from the shelter afforded by the residency, but happily the threatened downpour did not occur during the afternoon. Altogether fully three thousand persons were present during the course of the reception.

Other papers informed their readers that selections of music were played alternately by the military band and the orchestra under the baton of Herr Zelman, and gave details of the costumes of the ladies 'which were more notable as a rule for simplicity and good taste than for display, pure white trimmed with blue or buttercup predominating'.

November 3rd

Cup Day. Lovely day.

IN CONTRAST to the stormy conditions that made the garden party so tiring, it was a perfect day for the Cup. As the *Australasian Sketcher* correspondent commented:

No prophecy is more anxiously scanned on the morning of the eventful day than is that of the Government astronomer, and with all due respects to the experts of the turf, it may be said that no other prophet is so trustworthy. A fine day was promised, and the pledge was kept. A little too much heat was turned on, however. About 3 o'clock the ladies who were crowded out of the shade were forced to complain . . .

The sight of the hill and of the grand-stand, and the lawn and the saddling paddock, made sure that the Victoria Racing Club would net its heaviest return. The secretary reports a substantial advance upon last year's takings, and so much was expected. The rush quickly set in. The moderately early bird, who made sure of having the pick of the grand-stand, found that there were even earlier birds than himself . . .

The vehicles came rolling up, and still the trains discharged their throngs, until at 1 o'clock there was the maximum throng. By that time you have taken your hat off as the National Anthem is played to welcome the Governor and Lady Loch and their party. You have made any provision you can for the softer sex, and you are free to mingle with and observe the crowd. Melbourne sends its tens of thousands. You meet your doctor, your lawyer, your draper, your sharebroker, your editor, if you only know him, and, if you are lucky, you may meet your clergyman. One or two junior members of the Protestant cloth are there, and not only a priest or two, but also a popular dignitary of the Church of Rome. And if the clergy are to study human nature, where could they better be? Perhaps the reverend visitors will condemn what they witnessed, but they will know what they are talking about, and even in the pulpit that is a recommendation. But apart from the Melbourne throng, the attendance grows more and more Australasian in character each year . . .

The squatter is there from the Barcoo and Warrego, the pioneer from Port Darwin, and the old identity from Tasmania. Some are from "the never never" country and the "land where the pelican builds," spending money because they cannot be worse off; and others come from the Riverina and Hamilton plains because their prospects were never so good before. Perth, in the far, far west, sends representatives, and Brisbane legislators linger, although in Queensland a crisis is at hand. You can pick out the "pioneers" generally because their faces are tanned, and their attire from their polished hats to their fancy boots is eloquent of a visit the previous day to Collins-street or Bourke-street emporiums. A great deal is to be said about the Cup as a federating agency. Rome was saved by cackling geese. Australia may be built up by the fraternal racehorse . . . The rapid growth of wealth in Melbourne is visible from the stone steps at Flemington. The four-in-hand drag, unknown a few years ago, is now an institution. Three-hundred-guinea landaus are as common as apple carts at Whitechapel. A man who drives a single horse must expect to be cut by his friends, unless he can plead in mitigation the presence of a fashionable trap and a blood mare. Here the drivers display their skill in the final turn, and in bringing up sharp and clean before handing the ribbons to groom or coachman. Here also is caught the first sight of those toilettes of toilettes which have been whispered about in society for a month past.

These toilettes that were seen on the lawns of Flemington on the day that Sheet Anchor won the Cup were obviously much more elaborate than the cool white costumes that had predominated at the garden party for 'Queen Bee' reported in the *Australasian*:

When the morning broke gloriously beautiful, there was no doubt or uncertainty as to what should be worn, and the smartest gowns were at once looked out, and everything got ready with enthusiasm for a display of Summer fashions: It is an old story to tell of the magnificent display of dress on the lawn: but this year the well-worn phrase is true and more applicable than ever. Not, let it be understood, that there was anything like overdressing or gorgeousness about it, quite the reverse; everything was fresh, airy, harmonious and in good keeping. Poppies and other field flowers were a good deal worn as favourite trimmings on sailor hats and if they are irrelevant, one forgives the irrelevance when the dainty headgear is seen on a charming head.

A few outré gowns were, of course, about. No race meeting would be perfect without them, no more than without the little dog who takes his mad canter down the course just before the starting of the Cup.

BY THE DAY after the Cup the heatwave had returned and Emma's diary entry is of the briefest.

November 4th

Ball for 1500. Very hot night.

THE PAPERS, however, give us more detail, reporting that:

 The festivities at Government House last night formed the climax of what may be not ineptly termed the Melbourne Carnival.

Lady Loch commenced to receive her visitors at 9 o'clock and it was way past 10 when the last carriage had deposited the invitees who contributed to the brilliant reunion which assembled within the ballroom. Sir Henry Loch's distinguished guests were present, and the splendour of the scene was specially enhanced by the uniforms, the naval display fairly distancing the staff and local forces, prominent as usual on such occasions. This was mainly due to the presence of Admiral Tryon and the officers from the 'Nelson', who thoroughly entered into the spirit of the occasion and danced the different events on the programme with a verve which the heat of the evening did not appear to dampen.

GIPPSLAND

10 November–24 December 1885

WHEN CUP WEEK was over, one by one the Lochs' guests departed; Sir William Robinson returned to Adelaide with a promise that the Lochs would visit him in the coming months, and Sir Frederich Napier-Broome sailed for Western Australia. Emma does not mention him in her diary, but the press recorded his presence at Government House and he must surely have been one of the Lochs' most interesting guests. He had an unusual background for a Governor, being the son of a missionary and having worked as a journalist for *The Times* before joining the Colonial Service, and when he was appointed Governor of Western Australia he was instrumental in helping it to achieve responsible government. His name is familiar to all Australians from the town of Broome, which was named after him, and his wife, too, is remembered, as an authoress. When they married, in 1864, she was the widow of Sir Richard Barker, and as Broome at that time had not been knighted, she retained her title of Lady Barker. One of her books, *Station Life in New Zealand*, describing her life with Broome on the Canterbury Plains, ran into many editions and is still in print today.

Sir George Strahan, who had, as usual, been one of the Lochs' guests for Cup week, had applied for leave of absence to make a quick trip to Britain, and sailed in the *Massilia*. He set off from Government House in some style, escorted to the ship by a guard of honour, a detachment of the Victorian Permanent Forces.

And as the carriage of the last of the Cup guests rolled away, there were fresh arrivals: Lord Augustus Loftus and his wife on their way to Britain at the end of his term at Sydney's Government House. His time in Sydney was not particularly happy for he was troubled by increasing deafness, and spent more and more time in Sydney's 'hill station' retreat, the house near Moss Vale, which he had persuaded the Government to purchase. He was now going home to face a series of financial disasters and was to spend the rest of his life very quietly in Surrey, working on his memoirs.

November 10th

Lord Augustus Loftus and Lady arrived on their way to England.

November 11th

Poor Mr Cotterell died in the afternoon, soon after we had left. He died in a fit in his chair. The poor soul has suffered more or less for years. Has done nothing since Christmas.

December 3rd

Went to Sandridge [Port Melbourne] *to see the French steamer* Caledonia.

December 5th

Lord and Lady Augustus Loftus left today by French steamer Caledonia *for Marseilles. Mr Hickey and Miss Reeve started at 10.30. I hope they have enjoyed themselves. We have done our best to make their visit a pleasant one.*

The landing of Lord and Lady Carrington in Melbourne.

December 6th

A quiet day. First quiet Sunday we have had for weeks. Mr Wise came in at tea time. Only stayed a little time.

December 7th

A very busy day. Lord and Lady Carrington arrived from England. Miss Harbord, three gentlemen in suite, three children, two nurses, two maids, two valets. Every room occupied. Forty-seven to dinner in State dining room, and 500 in the evening. All went off capitally. We got to bed soon after 2 a.m.

BEFORE SIR AUGUSTUS and Lady Loftus sailed for Marseilles in the *Caledonia*, some of the Government House staff, presumably with the amusing Mr Hickey, went down to Port Melbourne to inspect the ship at the dockside. Emma had done everything she

could to make the brief stay of Mr Hickey and the rest of the staff
as enjoyable as her stay in Sydney had been. One of the treats for
visitors was to take them to see the panoramic view of Melbourne
from the top of the Government House tower, a feat which
entailed climbing such precipitous stairs that it was usually
likened to climbing the Arc de Triomphe.

The staff had only Sunday to relax before what Emma
rightly describes as the 'very busy day' of the Carringtons' arrival
from England.

Melbourne's Government House had often been described
as unnecessarily large and ostentatious, but on occasions such as
the arrival of the Carringtons, their family and their staff, every
one of those rooms was needed, for there were fifteen in the
group. While Emma and her colleagues were helping the
Carringtons' staff to feel at home, showing them where to find
kitchens and pantries, and arranging the children's meal times, the
Carringtons themselves had a full day of engagements, culmi-
nating in the State dinner followed by one of Lady Loch's popular
receptions.

From the moment the Carringtons' ship had berthed everything had gone smoothly.

[The vessel was boarded by Lord Castlerosse and Captain
Traill] who welcomed Lord Carrington to the colony, and
escorted him and Lady Carrington to the special train
awaiting them, by which they were conveyed to Spencer-
street, where a guard of honour, consisting of a company of the
Permanent Artillery, under Lieutenant Howard, was drawn
up to receive them, and the party proceeded to Government
House. The travellers looked remarkably well, and are stated
to have enjoyed a singularly pleasant passage . . . During the
course of the afternoon his lordship was driven to see several
of the more interesting spots in the city, but no extended
excursion was made owing to the great heat which prevailed.
In the evening Lady Loch's dinner party included several of
the Ministers and others invited to meet his Excellency the

✠ Governor of New South Wales and Lady Carrington, and a
reception was held after its close.

It was no wonder that Lady Loch's reception was thronged, despite the oppressively hot night, for everyone was anxious to catch a glimpse of the new Governor of New South Wales and his wife. His fame had already reached Australia. From the moment that his appointment had been announced, the papers had spoken of his remarkable popularity, declaring that 'he is rich in the gifts and graces which peers sometimes lack', and informing readers that he was a close friend of the Prince of Wales! Carrington had, indeed, accompanied the Prince as aide-de-camp on his State Tour of India, and no less than ten members of the Royal Family had been present at Carrington's marriage in the Chapel Royal— so now perhaps the Prince would come out to Australia to visit his friend. (This was not to be. About six months later, in July 1886, an important cable came from London. The papers informed the public that although the Prince had been formally invited to pay a visit to the Australian colonies the following year, he had replied to the effect that however much gratification it might afford him to accept the invitation, it was quite impossible for him to do so.)

The *Australasian Sketcher* had presented its readers with portraits of the Carringtons, and predicted that 'the social qualities of Lord and Lady Carrington will lend life and grace to that important, but often little considered part, of a Governor's activity—his social duties'. And details were cabled to Australia of the vast crowds that had thronged Victoria Station to wish them well as they boarded the boat train for their long journey.

December 8th

A very hot day, too hot to do much. After dinner the maids went up the tower and to the Botanical Gardens in the evening. They seem delighted with everything at present.

WHILE EMMA and the Carringtons' maids strolled in the cool avenues at the Botanical Gardens, their mistresses were braving the heat of the city to attend the huge concert held in the Town Hall to raise funds to endow a Chair of Music in Melbourne. This concert, we read, raised the sum of £667 14s 6d.

December 9th

Lord and Lady Carrington left at 10.30 for Sydney, New South Wales. He is to have a public reception on Saturday next.

December 19th

Left Government House at 8.30 for the station. Left at 9.30 for Sale. Sir Henry and Lady Loch, Capt. Traill, Lord Castlerosse, Mr Wallace, reporter for the Argus, *and others. Reached Sale at 3 p.m. Fearfully hot. Luckily a storm came on between W____, which cooled the air considerably. A large concourse of people at the station, and troopers to escort the Governor to Kilmany Park. Mr Pearson is the owner. Reached the house about 4 and felt better after a cup of tea and change of raiment. Mr Pearson treated the troopers to champagne, sent it out in buckets. A house of plenty. He, Mr Pearson, has a fine stock of race horses. Frying Pan is here, who won the Derby in ____. Mr Geary and Mr Chrysty are here—seems like home to see some of the waiters who are often at Government House.*

For Emma, and the Lochs, the year had begun with the strenuous tour, during a heatwave, to the Australian Alps, and it was to end with an even more strenuous one, this time to Gippsland.

This tour entailed six days of constant travelling, and again the temperatures were abnormally high. To Sir Henry, a survivor of hazardous military campaigns, not to mention the conditions he endured in the Chinese prisons, the Gippsland tour must have seemed one continuous picnic, but for the womenfolk it was very different. For Emma, in fact, it was slightly less strenuous than for Lady Loch, for Emma was sometimes able to remain in the background while her mistress attended lengthy receptions and

Flinders Street railway station, Melbourne.

banquets. But it fell to Emma's lot, of course, to pack and unpack the elaborate costumes and bonnets of the day, and to sponge and brush the travel-stained garments each evening.

The Lochs' route seems to have taken in nearly every town in the district: some of these still remain the quiet townships that they saw, while others have become large, sprawling cities, served by frequent electric trains and now forming part of Melbourne's commuter belt.

Their special train made its first halt at Drouin, a tiny community of about four hundred people, but boasting its own newspaper, the *Gippsland Independent*, and able to assemble a large group of farmers, their wives and their daughters, to welcome His Excellency and to chat about their crops to the reporters.

At each stop, Warragul, Traralgon and Rosedale, the crowds grew larger, and there was always an illuminated address to present, to which Sir Henry responded in a very cordial manner. As the train sped along, the drought was temporarily broken by a downpour so heavy that at Traralgon the presentation had to be made inside the State Carriage to avoid a soaking.

Their host for the weekend, William Pearson, was waiting for them at Sale, and they drove out to Kilmany Park in great style escorted by a corps of mounted troopers. The *Age* reported that the men 'were well mounted and dressed in the now well known Kahkee uniform and Alpine hat, and were fully armed with the regulation carbine and cartridge belt,' and that 'they maintained a steady line and solidity of countenance that would have done credit to regular troops'.

Well might Mr Pearson dispense his champagne by the bucketful, for he was one of the colony's richest men. As well as his income from his huge pastoral interests and his racehorse stud, he was a lucky mining speculator, his £5 shares in the Walhalla gold mine each rising in value to £212, and each bringing him £512 in dividends during the lifetime of the mine. Everyone seems to have enjoyed the weekend at Kilmeny Park, although the weather was too wet for sight-seeing.

No doubt Sir Henry enjoyed the company of this fellow Scot, with his wide experience in politics as well as of life on the land, and Emma also found herself among friends. This was because two of the waiters brought in to augment Mr Pearson's staff during the viceregal visit, were men who had often helped to cater for large functions at Government House.

December 20th

A quiet day. None of the ladies or gentlemen could get out till the afternoon, then several went for a long ride, and were drenched to the skin. Very sultry. Tho' a quantity of rain has fallen, glad of a quiet day.

December 21st

Started from Kilmany soon after 8, and left Sale at 9 by the Omeo, *a nice little steamer, chartered and painted up for the occasion. The lakes are very fine. Plenty of wild duck and black swans, but they*

Lake King, near Bairnsdale, Victoria.

keep a good distance of the steamer. Reached Bairnsdale about 5 p.m. Miss Knight and her mother were there to receive us and Vera, who I think such a nice little girl. We could only say a word to them, then rushed off to the hotel with luggage, and after getting our rooms and unpacked, who should turn up but the orderly, with something for Sir Henry.

IT IS TO BE hoped that the beds at Peterson's Club Hotel were very comfortable ones, for the visitors had had a long and tiring day, and knew they would have to be up very early to carry out the programme that had been arranged.

The day's journey down the lakes in the little *Omeo*, 'painted up for the occasion', had been full of incidents. As the viceregal party boarded the vessel, the reporters asserted that:

The visitors could not fail to be pleased with the appearance of the country, with its wealth of verdure of every shade and description. The length of the journey to Lakes Entrance [Bairnsdale was the destination] was pleasantly curtailed by an excellent dejeuner provided by Messrs. Boddinton and Smith, provedores to the Gippsland Steam Navigation Company. Whilst the steamer was passing from Lake Wellington to Lake Victoria, through McMillan's Straits [McLennan Strait], a sharp thud astounded the captain, who stated that there was sufficient water to accommodate a vessel with double the draught of the Omeo; but as the latter immediately slowed down, it was surmised, as afterwards proved correct, that one of the propeller blades had broken. To make up for the deficiency, an extra notch was given to the steam valve, and the vessel attained her former speed. After passing through Lake Victoria, and gaining the narrow passage [McMillan Strait] leading into Lake King, a second thud proclaimed the fact that another propeller blade had broken, and as 60 more miles had to be traversed before the steamer would reach the township of Bairnsdale, the question arose as to whether the remaining blades would hold out. Fortunately they did, though the task of steering the steamer was rendered unusually difficult . . .

On the down trip the vice regal party passed the steamers Tambo and Ethel Jackson, the excursionists on which gave hearty cheers for Sir Henry and Lady Loch, the welcome on the latter steamer being supplemented by a volley fired by a number of riflemen. The Omeo, still labouring under the loss of two propeller blades, made an excellent run across Lake King and entered the Mitchell River, the banks of which are dotted for several miles with hop gardens. The most humble cottage contributed, in one shape or other, to the welcome accorded to the visitors. Shortly before six o'clock the Omeo drew abreast of the Bairnsdale wharf, which was crowded by the residents of the thriving township. On alighting from the steamer the Governor and Lady Loch were greeted with loud cheers, followed by the National Anthem, played by the Bairnsdale brass band.

On the Tambo River, near Bruthen.

December 22nd

Up at 5 a.m. Went to Lady Loch at 6, as they start for ____ [Bruthen] at 8 a.m. Such an early start. After they left we cleaned up and started in Mr Knight's buggy for Barwon. Ivy Young, Mr Hawkins' aunt. They were good to us, and showed us a little of bush life and gave me a nice little rosella and shells, feathers and bear skin. Mr Lovegrove and I enjoyed our day out very much—reached Bairnsdale just in time to receive Sir Henry and party who returned very tired.

FOR THE LOCHS' visit to Bruthen there was a clear, azure sky but once again the *Omeo* was in trouble. The *Age* reported that,

 . . . after going about 7 miles the third propeller blade broke, two having been broken on the previous day during the journey from Sale to the lakes' entrance [Bairnsdale]. Only one blade and the stumps of three others were now left to do a

distance of 17 miles ... The wind had risen considerably, causing a heavy swell in Lake King, through which the Omeo struggled valiantly with its one propeller blade. This, the most difficult part of the trip, was accomplished without any mishap, and the steamer entered the Tambo River, notwithstanding her crippled condition, fully ten minutes in advance of the Bogong. The trip up the river, without doubt one of the most magnificent streams in Victoria, was exceedingly pleasant. The wide expanse of water, the ever changing appearance of the scenery on each side, together with the balmy weather, and the many evidences of the presence of a prosperous yeomanry, lent a charm to the scene, which could not fail to commend the warm admiration of the visitors ... It was half past one o'clock when the Omeo reached Batten's landing, beyond which the river is not navigable. The party was accordingly transferred to the little tug steamer Yarra, and a start was made for Mossiface. After getting stuck across the stream at Humbug-reach Point ... the Yarra drew alongside the Mossiface wharf, where his Excellency and Lady Loch were greeted by hearty cheers from a goodly assemblage of residents of Bruthen, and by the National Anthem, played by the Bairnsdale brass band, which had proceeded to Bruthen earlier in the day.

Bruthen may have had to borrow a neighbouring town's brass band, but, although it had a population of only two hundred, it already had its own newspaper, the *Times*.

It was seven o'clock when the travellers at last reached the shelter of the Club Hotel, and Sir Henry at once had to hurry off to a large banquet given by the shire councillors. But for Lady Loch, at least, the twelve hours of travel, sometimes very rough travel, were over and she was able to sink into bed. For Emma, and Lovegrove, the valet, it had been a comparatively free day, and Mr Hawkins, the Government House butler, had thoughtfully arranged for his aunt to show them some of the lesser attractions of the district.

December 23rd

Left Club Hotel, Bairnsdale, at 8 a.m. for Sale—rained almost all time. The lake looked very pretty, if the weather had been favourable for the trip. It poured when we reached Sale and my face was like a full blown peony, with sun and wind together. The hotel was gaily decked with evergreens, and a crowd of people round the door. Lady Loch held a reception in the afternoon and Sir Henry and staff were entertained at a banquet. The school children were drawn up in line and serenaded Lady Loch during the evening. Crowds of people collected to hear the children sing.

TIRED AND wind burnt, Emma's diary is very short. The volume of Gippsland photographs presented to Lady Loch that day, a large leather-bound volume embossed with her initials 'E.L.', is now one of the treasures in Melbourne's La Trobe Library.

When the travellers woke next morning, their first thought was probably 'It's Christmas Eve'. But they were still a long way from home, however, and for the men of the party, there was a full programme of events to be carried out before they caught the special train that was to take them back to Melbourne.

At seven o'clock in the morning his Excellency, in company with Master Loch, Mr. Cust, Captain Traill, Messrs. M. Lean and P. B. Wallace, M.L.A.'s, and Mr. Wise, Mayor of Sale, departed in vehicles from the Club Hotel and arrived at Ramabyuck at nine o'clock. On crossing the river by means of a boat the Governor was received by the superintendent, the Rev. Mr. Haganeur, and about 120 blacks, who signified their pleasure by hearty cheers. The party, under the guidance of the superintendent, made a thorough inspection of the hop gardens and maize fields, cultivated with a great deal of skill by the blacks, as well as their dwellings, a series of 17 detached cottages, the interiors of which were so clean and orderly as to command the warm appreciation of his Excellency. Before the party left the blacks were assembled in the church and sung a hymn. The eldest son of the late chief of the Sale tribe then presented an address of welcome to his Excellency. After expressing the great pleasure the blacks felt at the visit of the Governor, the address referred in touching terms to the fact that the small community of blacks was the last of a fast expiring race, which had been treated with every kindness and consideration by the various Governments of the colony. His Excellency made a suitable reply, after which the blacks sung the national anthem and the party then departed amidst the cheers of the sable settlement.

For Sir Henry this was probably the most interesting day of the whole trip. Although he had been impressed by the skills of the Aborigines he had met on his earlier tours, this was the first time he had seen a whole settlement. Emma's diary entry is very brief.

December 24th

Left Sale at 1 p.m. for Melbourne. Very glad to give up this touring during this hot weather. Reached Melbourne about 4, and home by 5 p.m. Christmas Eve.

A Very Hot Summer

Christmas 1885–18 May 1886

THIS SECOND SUMMER that the Lochs spent in Australia was an exceptionally hot one, and before the days of air conditioning, or of electric fans, the family found the heat very trying: they did not even have the big palm-leaf punkahs, worked day and night by servants, that helped their friends in India to survive the summers.

December 25th

Christmas day. Did not go to church—found plenty to do at home, and almost done up. Forty to dinner in Servants' Hall, most of which left by 4 p.m. Only Mr and Mrs Martin stayed to tea and supper.

As in the previous December, the Lochs spent Christmas Day very quietly, enjoying a day with their children, quite free from engagements of any kind, and this meant that most of their staff had a free day, too, when they could invite their friends to join in the festivities in the servants' hall.

December 28th

Sir William and Lady Clarke came to stay for the night. Also Miss Shannon.

Beechworth.

December 29th

Sir Henry, Lady Loch and the young ladies left Government House for Beechworth at 10.30 a.m.

As THE ONLY guests at Government House this week were the Clarkes, from Rupertswood, spending a few days in Melbourne before embarking on a trip to Britain, the Lochs decided to take the whole family up to the Australian Alps for a few days. They had been much attracted by Beechworth when they had passed through it on their New Year camping trip, and now returned to enjoy it at their leisure. As Emma was still feeling 'almost done up' after the oppressive heat and the constant travelling in Gippsland, it was presumably the younger maid, Lucy, who helped the ladies on their holiday.

If the Lochs thought they were about to enjoy a few leisurely days in the hills they were certainly mistaken, for the day they reached Beechworth, its paper, the *Ovens and Murray Advertiser* informed its readers that:

 Beechworth will this afternoon have the honour and pleasure of welcoming to the district on a short visit of a few days His Excellency Sir Henry B. Loch, K.C.B., Governor of Victoria, and his amiable wife, Lady Loch. We only hope their stay will be as great a pleasure to them as it will be to the people of

Beechworth and the surrounding country, and, in order to make it so, it has been resolved that they and their party shall enjoy as much privacy as is compatible with such an occasion. The distinguished visitors will be accompanied by a son and two daughters, with Captain Traill as A.D.C. and His Honor Mr. Justice Kerferd will also be one of the party, and several other well-known persons. They will arrive at Beechworth terminus by special train at 5 p.m., where they will be received by the president and members of the Beechworth United Shire Council. A number of Chinese from various parts of the district will be present in full costume, and receive His Excellency in a manner which he, no doubt, will be quite able to appreciate, as he understands the customs of our Chinese fellow-colonists. Mrs. Fletcher, the wife of the president will here present a bouquet to Lady Loch on behalf of the ladies of the town, and the visitors will then be escorted to Tanswell's Commercial Hotel, where everything has been prepared for their comfort, and where they will be allowed to spend their evening without any intrusion whatever. Next morning they will be driven to Mt. Stanley where an al fresco luncheon will await them, before proceeding on foot to the cairn from which, as our readers are aware, there is one of the most extensive and picturesque views in Australia. Lady Loch has been requested to hold a reception on her return from this trip, either in the Town Hall or at her hotel, and she will no doubt comply with so reasonable a desire if not too much fatigued. At the reception there will be presented to her by Mrs. Fletcher, as a memento of Beechworth, a very beautiful photographic album, containing views of the town and neighbourhood, and bearing a suitable inscription. In the evening there will be a promenade concert in the Town hall and handsome garden adjoining, which will be brilliantly lighted with gas and Chinese lanterns, and where also there will be a display of fireworks. On Thursday morning it is proposed to accompany such of the party as desire to visit the public institutions of the town, and this will complete the proceedings, unless His Excellency and Lady Loch can be induced to remain for the race-meeting on the following day. We, in common, are sure, with everyone in the district, wish our distinguished guests a hearty welcome, and a pleasant visit.

December 31st

Sir Henry, Lady Loch and party returned from Beechworth. All suffered more or less from the heat, which has been very trying. Lord Castlerosse left in the Carthage *today for England, also Sir William and Lady Clarke and family. They expect to remain in England for about a year I am told.*

January 6th 1886

Sir Henry, Lady Loch and the children left Government House at 3 p.m. for Macedon. I am to remain a few days to clean up, look over linen and have a rest. Commenced raining, and rained hard all afternoon and all night.

January 7th

Pouring all day. I pity those who have gone to Macedon. It is a wretched place in wet weather. 'Twill do no end of good, and lay the terrible dust.

January 8th

Still raining hard. If we have much more there will be a flood. Poor Mr Geary is ill with bilious fever.

January 9th

Fine day at last. Went off to Melbourne early, shopping.

January 10th

Beautiful clear day. Too hot for much walking. Mr Hawkins went to Queenscliff and Mrs Calla to the Zoological Gardens with Mr and Mrs Martin. They asked me to join them, but I did not feel up to it.

January 11th

Fine, hot day. Looking thro' the linen all day. Went to see Mrs Wise in the Botanical Gardens after tea. She and the children walked thro' the Domain with me.

January 12th

Another lovely day. Only had a turn round the garden with Mrs Calla and Mr Hawkins after six o'clock tea. The fruit is very abundant. Apples and pears lying under the trees by hundreds. The Magnum Bourne plums heavy, like ropes of onions. I never saw trees so loaded with fruit. Cucumbers, tomatoes all grow apace. No frosts here to nip them.

January 13th

Hot wind. Miss Cross came to spend the day with me. After the evening meal we started for Prahran to see Mrs Vicars, who I met at Ercildoun. Got home about 9 p.m.

January 14th

Another hot, trying day. Miss Cross came about 5 p.m. to find Mr Hale at Hawthorne. We took the train at Prince's Bridge, and found Barkers Road without much trouble. They were glad to see us. Mr Hale kindly walked to the station with us. Reached Government House at 9.30.

Princes Bridge, allowing Government House residents access to Flinders Street Station on the north-western bank of the Yarra River.

January 15th

Very hot wind. Sir Henry came to luncheon and brought some friends with him. Mam'selle Heyman also came. [Sir Henry] Left about 5 p.m. for Macedon. I went to say goodbye to Mrs Wise and Mrs Geary. So glad to hear Mr Geary is better, tho' very weak and prostrate with the heat.

January 18th

Left Government House for Macedon soon after 11 a.m. Very hot journey. Found all well, and looking rosy from mountain air and bush life.

Mount Macedon January 31st

Very wet day thro'out—not able to get to church.

February 3rd

*Sir Henry kindly gave a picnic to his servants. Nearly all have gone
—except myself and Joseph. Mrs Parkins came in to cook potatoes,
keep up the fires, and clear the way. We managed fairly well. The
picnic party returned about 9, very merry and well pleased with
their outing. They were twenty-four in all, and drove to a place
near Gisborne called Plum Pudding Rocks. All have enjoyed themselves immensely. Sir Geo. Verdon's servants and Mr Ryan's joined
them.*

OLD MAPS of Gisborne have failed to show any spot named Plum
Pudding Rocks, but several people recalled brown boulders along
the creek which could be split open to reveal a surface that looked
very like a piece of plum pudding. These rocks were presumably
conglomerates, with a brown matrix binding together small darker
brown pebbles which looked rather like the fruit in a Christmas
pudding. One lady can remember her grandmother having a piece
of 'plum pudding rock' on her mantelpiece, a souvenir perhaps of
some family picnic, which was invariably shown to visitors and
which was marvelled at by the grandchildren.

Emma loved collecting curios—shells, feathers and coloured
seaweeds are mentioned among treasures of hers, and no doubt
she was able to add to these a piece of plum pudding rock.

February 8th

*Went to Melbourne to pay some bills and do a little shopping as
Master Douglas had to go. We left by 3.35 train for Macedon.
Mr Sturgess also returned by same train and drove the buggy. Had
a headache thro' the heat, and dragging about Melbourne.*

February 10th

A dance at the Hall, Upper Macedon. Most of the girls and men were invited, but it was not up to the mark. They were all more or less disappointed. The music was poor and the supper served in the ballroom wasted so much of the evening preparing and clearing away.

Wednesday February 24th

Lucy and I went off to Kyneton to see Mrs Blair, who gave us a very hearty welcome. We only stayed two hours. Returned by 5.15 train to Macedon. Mr Hayes met us with the wagonette. Miss Evey and Mary came to meet us.

February 26th

A theatrical performance at the Hall. The piece chosen was Box and Cox. *Mr Sturgess took part and Miss Mab Ryan was Mrs Bouncer. The whole party came to the cottage for supper.*

THE LOCHS certainly did all they could to make this holiday at Macedon a happy one for their staff, first the picnic to Gisborne, in which they were joined by some of their friends from the other large houses, the Verdons' and the Ryans', then the dance, and finally the performance of *Box and Cox*. This musical farce of Gilbert and Sullivan's had been making people laugh since it first opened at London's Adelphi twenty years before, sometimes being played as a curtain raiser for *Trial by Jury*, and sometimes being presented by itself. Full of unexpected turns, the story is of two men, one a hatter who worked all day, the other a printer who worked all night and, unbeknown to each other, occupied the same room in a lodging house.

Kyneton.

March 1st

I left Macedon at 8.30 with Mary for Melbourne. We unfortunately had to travel in one of those large carriages with Sir Geo. Verdon and son, Mr and Mrs Ryan, the Misses Frasers, and many others. The train was crowded. Found Mrs Calla looking out for me—all well, and glad I'm home.

March 2nd

Busy all day. Lucy, Emily, Kate, Mr Lovegrove, arrived at 4.30. Lady Loch had gone to Kyneton to open a Bazaar—returned about 7.40 p.m., hot, worn but merry.

As the Lochs had now been in Victoria for nearly two years, and had travelled constantly to new districts, most of the larger towns had now received a visit, but Kyneton, which was so close to Macedon, felt it had been overlooked. Its residents had several times seen the Governor's special train rush through its station on the way to townships further north, and now at last they were to receive a viceregal visit, for Lady Loch had consented to open their Grand Bazaar, and the town was in a great state of excitement.

As the bazaar was to raise funds for church repairs, the Rector and his wife were at the station to greet 'Lady Loch accompanied by her son and two daughters and her lady friends, and by Sir Henry's secretary' when they arrived by the afternoon train. They were taken for a drive round the township in Mr Booth's and Mr Mitchell's carriages, and escorted to the platform of the Mechanics Institute, where the church choir greeted them with the National Anthem.

The local paper was able to report that the weather was all that could be desired, and that there was an excellent attendance. Lady Loch, having wished the bazaar every success, helped to ensure the success by visiting every stall and making a purchase at each one, 'while the young people fished in the pond, dipped into lucky bags and shared in all the mild dissipations of the room'. What, one wonders, did she decide to purchase there, as one reads through the detailed descriptions of the goods on the six stalls. There were shelves of crewel-work drapes, brackets with drapes, and numerous embroidered mantel-drapes of rich fabrics, to be pinned round the large mantelpieces of the day. There were table covers of velvet with lace centres and falls, there were crazy patch-work tea-cosies, and 'an endless variety of articles of adornment and utility'. But on the Sunday School stall, we read 'utility had sovereignty over adornment; it was stocked with warm woollen underclothes and frocks and pinafores exhibiting graceful and elegant needlework, while in the centre of the stall, in a case of glass and cedar, stood a figure of Britannia, resplendent in Union Jack and crimson sateen skirt.' Other treasures on the stalls included 'painted mirrors and plaques, tastefully done, a model milking stool with dogs painted on the seat, and a model key rack in the form of pastry rollers with a landscape painted upon it'.

'Lady Loch charmed everyone with her pleasant affability, and having made purchases at the six stalls, Her Ladyship and party partook of tea prepared by Mrs Butters' refreshment rooms, and were escorted to the five o'clock train, pleased with their visit and having conferred pleasure in return.' She and her family had at least escaped before the even greater crowds in the evening sessions of the bazaar 'which were enlivened by the playing of the Phoenix Foundry Band'.

March 3rd

Dinner for the Bishop: thirty-six and reception after of 450. Very warm and the mosquitoes are ready to eat one up. Mr Geary was here for first time after his serious illness. He looks weak and fatigued.

The Lochs returned to Government House in time for the dinner and reception that they gave in honour of Bishop Moorhouse and his wife. Emma had returned to Melbourne a day before the rest of the party as there were so many details to be attended to in the Lochs' absence. She was pleased to see Mr Geary, the waiter, back again to augment the domestic staff during these functions, even though he was still suffering the effects of his illness.

The dinner at Government House was to be the first of many functions arranged to show Melbourne's appreciation of all that the Bishop had done in his nine years in the colony. Bishop Moorhouse was Melbourne's second bishop; he had been selected in England to follow the pioneering Bishop Perry, and he proved to be even more energetic than that remarkable man. His fame as an educationalist and a popular preacher had preceded him and when he reached Australia he found a special train waiting at Williamstown to convey him and his wife to the city where they were met by the carriage of the Governor of the day, Sir George Bowen, and taken to Government House. In his years in Melbourne he not only accomplished the building of St Paul's Cathedral and many new churches and Sunday Schools, but he soon became recognized as the intellectual leader of the colony. He was made chancellor of the University of Melbourne, and as well as influencing the academics of his day, he gave a series of weekday lectures on subjects of public interest for anyone who cared to walk into the cathedral, and as his audiences soon crammed every nook and cranny within, they were moved to the more spacious Town Hall. Although he avoided becoming involved in party politics, he was an outspoken advocate of irrigation schemes, and of federation, and at one Town Hall meeting on federation moved the audience to such a pitch of excitement that they rose to their feet and cheered. And even when confirming young men, he would stress on them their duty to use their vote to improve the condition of their country.

March 7th

Mr Wm. Neville and Miss Mary arrived at 11.30 by O.S.S. Cuzco on a visit to the colonies.

March 8th

A large meeting at the Town Hall to present Bishop Moorhouse with a sum of money, which is to be spent upon himself. He has given much to the church, and the Melbournites wish him to retain their present for his own special use. Sir Henry presided at the meeting.

March 9th

The Bishop and Mrs Moorhouse came to stay in the House till their departure for England.

March 10th

All up early. Lady Loch, Miss Greville, young ladies and Mam'selle went to eight o'clock service at Christ Church, South Yarra, with the Bishop and Mrs Moorhouse.

March 11th

Early Communion at St James's, to which all the family went, except the young ladies. About 500 communicants and friends of the Bishop's, who wished to see their Bishop for the last time and wish him Godspeed. The Bishop and Mrs Moorhouse left Government House at 11.30 for Williamstown, the s.s. Beaugat left at 1 p.m. If the Bishop is appreciated equally at Manchester as here, he need not regret the transfer.

March 18th

Left Government House for Tasmania at 2.30. Dr Turner thought Miss Evelyn might go, but would take no responsibility. Rather a rush at the last to get off. We sailed at 3 p.m. from Sandridge Pier in the Pateena. Miss Eve and me; Lady Loch and Miss Edith opposite; Miss Deverell and Mam'selle together; Sir Henry and Master Douglas; Mr Deverell and Mr Sturgess. Lucy in Ladys' cabin to get all the air possible. We all went to bed in good time. Had a most wretched night. All sick and utterly miserable. Such a rough sea, like a boiling pot. We reached Launceston about 1 p.m. Went to the Brisbane Hotel, got some good soup, which was a great support. Left by special train at 3 p.m. After much jolting reached Hobart at 7 p.m. and Government House at 7.30. Mr and Mrs Smith were very kind, and so glad to see us, tho' we are a large party of twelve. Hobart is very dull.

THE LOCHS, as usual, seem to have had a rough crossing, but as soon as they reached Launceston they were met by the Hon. J. Wallop, private secretary of the Governor's, who had travelled up to meet them. And as soon as the train reached Hobart that evening, they went straight to Government House. Emma found herself among the friends she had made when she first arrived from England, but although she was always complaining in Melbourne of being 'done up', we find her complaining that Hobart is dull.

March 19th

A lovely morning. Mrs Smith and me went to town to do shopping. The river looks quite lovely. The scenery much finer than Victoria.

March 20th

Started alone to St David's Cathedral to hear the Bishop of Tasmania, who preached a most excellent sermon. After dinner Mrs Fraser came, and a friend Mrs Wishart—a German. Lucy, Mrs Smith, Mrs Fraser and Mrs Wishart went thro' the gardens to the Botanical Gardens.

March 21st

Lucy and I went off to Hobart to have a look round for shell necklaces, photos, etc.

March 22nd

Mrs Smith, Lucy and me went off at 12 for Kangaroo Point. Missed the boat by a minute or two, so had a good look at the Museum, which is worth seeing. Left by steamer at 2 p.m. and returned at 5 as the whole party was going to the theatre. Saw the new fortifications and the lovely beach, so soft and sandy.

EMMA AND LUCY had another day's sightseeing, going to the Museum and for a ride on a ferry, but had to be back in good time to dress Lady Loch for the Governor's dinner party and the expedition to the theatre which followed.

 Theatre Royal. The Vice-Regal command night at the Theatre Royal was a great success. His Excellency Sir George Strahan was present in the central box with Lady Loch, and a large party of friends, and the house was crowded in every part. 'Ring of Iron' was again placed on the stage for that night only, and was as great a triumph as ever.

March 23rd

Went to town again as we could not go for a long excursion. Sir George Strahan and Mr Wallop have taken the whole party to Brighton on the coach and four horses.

Kangaroo Point, from Hobart.

March 24th

Mr and Mrs Smith, Mr Lovegrove and myself, started for Brown's River at 12 noon. Mrs Fraser and Miss Ward met us at the post office. Nice wagonette and pair of good horses took us a good pace for Brown's River. The time was too, too short. The beach is lovely, completely carpeted with shells of all sorts. Large pearl shells as large as your hand, only require cleaning. Lucy could not go at the last [minute] as Lady Loch, Miss Deverell and Mam'selle went up Mount Nelson. We reached home about 5.30. All the ladies and gentlemen went to a concert in the Town Hall.

March 25th

Lucy, Mrs Smith and self went off to town after the coach had started for New Norfolk. We called at Parliament House. Went to see

Brown's River Bay.

Mr St Leger, who kindly showed us the Council Chamber and where the prisoners are tried. We had a car home.

ALTHOUGH THE visit was essentially a private one, Sir Henry, as usual, visited some of the city's institutions to see how they compared with Melbourne's; but most of the time was spent in sightseeing. Probably the most enjoyable of their excursions was Friday's drive to New Norfolk with its attractive old inns, and to the picturesque Salmon Ponds a few miles away.

Emma and the other staff did not venture quite so far in their expeditions, but they visited Parliament House and the Museum, and travelled down to Brown's River, south of Hobart, with its prolific orchards and flower farms. And Emma, as usual, collected souvenirs from each place.

March 26th

Lovely hot, clear day. Not very well, have picked up a cold. Lucy and I had a nice turn in the garden—the violets are so fine and scent the air. Any amount of fruit: plums, pears, nectarines, apples, grapes, mulberries, cherrys, walnuts—a finer garden than at Melbourne. After dinner me, Lucy, Miss Evelyn and Master Douglas walked to the jetty to fish. Did not stay long, the wind blew so fresh off the water.

ON SATURDAY, while his family enjoyed the gardens of Government House, Sir Henry made one of his few official visits. A few lines in the newspaper commented on this, and reminded its readers that the Governor's visit to Tasmania was coming to an end.

 His Excellency Sir Henry Loch paid a visit to the batteries . . . under the guidance of the Minister for Defence (Mr. W. H. Burgess), the Hon. John Wallop, Captain Sturgess and Captain Mackenzie, of the New South Wales Defence Force being also present. The steamer Result had been chartered, and in her the party visited the Bluff and Alexandra Batteries. Sir Henry Loch and Lady Loch with their family leave Hobart by the express train for the North this morning, catching the Patina for Melbourne. The Marine Board tug has been placed at their disposal to take them to the steamer at Town Point.

March 27th

Such a hot day. Really a hot wind. So relaxing. Packed up as I dared not attempt church—my cough very troublesome. Mr Smith had a talk with Sir Geo. about leaving. They were both very upset.

March 28th

Woke at 5 a.m. Got up and called Miss Deverell at 6 p.m. Luggage ready by 7 a.m. We started at 7.30—the train leaves at 8 for Launceston. Sir George Strahan and Mr Wallop accompanied Sir Henry and party to _____. He is going for a trip. We reached

Launceston about 2 p.m. Went in a tug boat to get on the Pateena. *Lovely sail down the Tamar River. All tired. The Captain feared we might not clear the Heads before dark, and might have to lie in the river all night, but luckily it was managed. Poor little Miss Edie and Miss Evelyn were sick again, and I had to join them. Lucy kept well all night for a wonder.*

March 29th

Reached Melbourne about 1 p.m. and Government House 1.30. Unfortunately we were delayed by one of the traces breaking. The cabman got a piece of string and tied it. We felt rather alarmed for fear it might break again. Our horse had the staggers just as we got to the gate. Lucy and I got out and walked up. We don't want our limbs broken in the colonies.

March 30th

Very tired and busy putting straight. Miss Cross came. Lord Capel and Baron de Toille arrived from England. Lord Capel is not so handsome as his father, the late Lord Malden.

March 31st

Started off to Melbourne early to do shopping and had such a fright. We were in a buggy, crossing Prince's Bridge, and saw a runaway horse coming like a steam engine with a cart behind him and no driver. There was no room to get out of the way. He tried to pass and broke the splash board in two, and smashed both windows and fell just in front of us. A mercy we all escaped unhurt—the driver's wife and baby, Lucy and me.

April 4th

Miss Macintyre came to stay a few days.

April 5th

Sir Henry, Lady Loch, Lord Capel, Baron de Toille, Mr and Miss Deverell, started for Fernshaw at 8.40. Lucy and I went to town. Very hot and dusty.

WHEN THE LOCHS returned from Hobart they found that Melbourne was still hot and oppressive, and were no doubt delighted to escape for a few days to the cool, green heights of Fernshaw. This mountain district, to the north-east of Melbourne, had become one of their favourite haunts, and they enjoyed taking their English visitors there, to admire the enormous eucalypts and to explore the beautiful mountain paths. Most of these visitors, of course, knew tree ferns only from the ones they had seen in English conservatories, and they always exclaimed in wonder that here they could walk underneath their huge, arching fronds. Fernshaw's wineries, too, were another attraction. These dated from Governor La Trobe's day, for he had encouraged some of the Swiss settlers to experiment with vines, a move that had proved highly satisfactory.

April 6th

Started with Mr Hawkins and Lucy at 3 p.m. to see the Library and Pictures. We met Mr O'Donnell in Swanston Street. Got back about 5 p.m. as there is a cricket match between the household and outsiders.

April 8th

Sir Henry, Lady Loch and party returned from Fernshaw about 7 p.m., much pleased with their excursion. Mr Lovegrove and Mr Rigby have enjoyed themselves very much. Miss Macintyre left for England also, by R.M.S.S. Parramatta *today.*

April 16th

Mr and Miss Deverell left for Sydney at 4.35, also Lord Capel, Baron de Toille, Captain Harbord, Admiral Tryon. Lucy not well. Had to keep to her bed all day.

Palm Sunday

Wet morning, could not go to church.

April 19th

Went to see Mrs Cotterell at South Yarra. She seemed glad to see me. Her poor boy is no better. Someone has given her a perambulator, which enables her to move him from room to room.

April 21st

Anniversary of Eight Hours movement. Sir Henry, Lady Loch and the children went to the Treasury about 10.30 to see the procession. Lucy and me went to the ferry and met Mr and Mrs Martin, who crossed with us. The high wind and dust spoilt the effect very much. The banners could not be kept down. Some were much torn. Thousands of working men, women and children followed the procession into the Friendly Societies' Garden, where all kinds of sport are indulged in—till darkness comes and they disperse.

MELBOURNE'S EIGHT HOURS DAY celebrations were again held on a very windy day, with weather conditions that were even more unpleasant than they had been the previous year. The *Age* reported that, despite the blustery conditions:

 In the metropolis the display was the most imposing yet made on any similar occasion. The chief attraction, from a mere spectator's point of view, was the long procession which paraded many of the main thoroughfares of the city before reaching the Friendly Societies' Gardens . . . Thousands of spectators lined the streets along which the procession

The Eight Hours Day procession passing the Town Hall.

marched. Verandahs, balconies, windows, and in fact every
vantage point from which a glimpse of the pageant could be
obtained, was occupied by eager sightseers. The procession
itself was a magnificent display, and the largest of the kind
seen in Melbourne. The march past the Town Hall occupied

nearly an hour, a fact which gives some idea of the many hundreds who were included in the ranks. From ten o'clock in the morning until noon the city was thronged with people, and traffic was at a standstill. Music filled the air, and the flutter of the many banners displayed in the procession gave the city a holiday aspect.

And in its leader, the same paper sought to calm the tempers that had been ruffled when some people had been unable to reach the city in time to attend to business:

A procession such as that which yesterday wended its way through the busy streets of the city is a comparatively new thing in the history of the world, and there are many who misdoubt the wisdom of proceeding, and conceive that it is a custom which would be more honored in the breach than the observance. If there are to be public demonstrations, they conceive they should emanate from people in authority, who alone should be empowered to demand the closing of thoroughfares and interruption to traffic ... The people nowadays are making their own celebrations to commemorate the peaceful triumphs of labor, and not a few, slow to recognise the inception of a new social order, are disposed to cavil, and to question the propriety of interference with the ordinary routine of business for such an end. It is hardly necessary for us to say that we have no sympathy with these objections. A procession of the people organised by themselves in memory of a popular success is possibly the most completely justifiable display which could be given in a democratic community; and as the years roll by we may look to see them arranged on a grander scale, and with a more artistic taste, than any that have yet been witnessed.

At the same time there is no gainsaying the fact that exhibitions of this kind, while proving gratifying and satisfactory to vast sections of the public, do entail considerable temporary inconvenience, which it would be well to reduce to its lowest quantity.

The battery at Queenscliff.

Good Friday

Went to church in the morning. Sir Henry left for Queenscliff, and Master Douglas, to camp out for the Review, Easter Monday.

Easter Sunday

A lovely day. Went to Christ Church in the morning. Large congregation. Shortened service. Mr Tucker gave notice of his intended visit to England for a short time.

Easter Monday

Sir Henry returned from Queenscliff. All well. Sir Geo. Strahan and Mr Wallop arrived from Tasmania.

EASTER WAS a very busy time for Sir Henry, who took his son down to Queenscliff with him when he went to review the army manoeuvres that had been planned to take place there. The armed forces were under very close scrutiny at that time, for there was a feeling of uneasiness whether they would be capable of repulsing any threatened invasion of their land. Sir Peter Scratchley had come out here the previous year for the express purpose of co-ordinating the forces of the various colonies, but had been stricken with fever just before Christmas and had died at sea. This had been a profound shock to the governments of the colonies, and they felt there was an urgent need to adopt some plan of concerted action to ensure Australia's defence. Admiral Tryon had stayed at Melbourne's Government House several times, having long discussions with Sir Henry about the steps they should take, and now these great Easter manoeuvres had been arranged to give the forces some experience of working together.

Spending Easter under canvas cannot have been an inviting process, for the weather had suddenly turned very cold, as it so often does at the approach of the Easter holidays. It was reported that as the troops assembled at Spencer Street to board the special trains that were to convey them to the camp site, 'the cold weather was bleak, with a cold southerly wind blowing, and the rain at times came down in torrents. But the weather, while it dampened the men's uniforms, did not have a similar effect on their spirits, for their martial ardour was unmistakable.' When the troops reached Queenscliff they found that 'The camp arrangements were in a fair state of completeness'. No doubt Queenscliff's weather had been partly responsible for this, for there had been a violent dust storm from the north before the wind turned south-westerly and brought up heavy clouds and rain that continued without intermission. Next morning the difficulties continued. '. . . the parade was timed for nine o'clock, but the lateness of breakfast caused it to be postponed for an hour, and hardly had the march commenced when ominous clouds banked up from the South. A deluge of rain succeeded, and there was no alternative but to march back, sadder and wetter men.' This was Good Friday, the day which was to be spent rehearsing the great mock battle which was to take place, with one battalion taking up its position on the narrowest part of the Queenscliff peninsula, and then being attacked by the rest of the forces.

Saturday, however, dawned clear and fine at last, and we learn that 'His Excellency the Governor and Master Loch, attended by Captain Traill, left Baillieu's Hotel shortly after day break and rode to the camp'. From later newspaper reports we discover that: 'The sham engagement was a really fine spectacle,' and that the weather was delightful. In the evening, 'interesting experiments were made with electric light, in conjunction with Point Nepean, to determine whether an enemies torpedo boats might enter the Heads after dark. His Excellency and a numerous party of ladies and gentlemen watched the experiments from the ramparts of the fort on the cliff end of Swan island'.

On Sunday, with the weather still sunny, there was Church Parade, and next day the forces dispersed. As Sir Henry and Master Douglas had been protected from the worst of the weather, safely under the roof of Baillieu's Hotel, it was not surprising that Emma was able to record in her diary 'All well'.

May 6th

Lady Stawell and two daughters arrived on a visit.

May 8th

Sir Henry heard by telegram this morning (May 8th), that poor dear Mrs Loch died on the 3rd. No further particulars. This will be known by waiting six weeks. How long it seems.

May 10th

Sir Geo. Strahan and Mr Wallop left for Hobart, Tasmania. Very cold and stormy. They will have a rough passage.

May 11th

Went to the Exhibition to see a grand procession of Chinese, who have assembled from all parts: Ballarat, Geelong, etc., to help the fund now raising for the Women's Hospital. The building is large and with large fern trees in all directions and looks very gay. The

Chinese went thro' a piece of acting, but the crush was so great at one time we feared a panic. Someone called out 'Fire', and the crowd made for the door which of course was bolted. Luckily soon opened and the people quieted down when the fresh air rushed in. We got out as soon as we could. Too glad to get out, even tho' it was raining hard. Lucy, Mary, Mr Lovegrove and myself managed to keep together with some difficulties.

THE PLAN TO raise funds to build a special hospital for women was one to which Lady Loch readily lent her support, and the spectacular Chinese display, which everyone in Melbourne was talking about, helped to give extra publicity to the big fund raising bazaar which was to take place in the Exhibition Building a few days later.

Never had Melbourne people seen anything so spectacular as the Chinese procession that led up to the drama session in the evening. The next day's papers devoted long columns to it, but this more concise description appeared in the *Australasian Sketcher*:

 It occurred to the promoters of the bazaar that the Chinese had given famous entertainments on the gold-fields, which city people had never seen. The Chinese readily agreed to make a display of the dresses, emblems, and appointments of the combined resources of Sandhurst and Beechworth, and Mr. Kong Meng and Mr. Ah Mouy were so good as to guarantee the payment of all the expenses of bringing the accessories to Melbourne and the incidental outlay, so that the whole of the proceeds of the fête might be given to the hospital. The procession was made up of kings, soldiers, officers, guides, boys and girls, standard bearers, together with temples, pagodas, Sedan chairs, emblematic banners, and other articles of spectacular value. It was a motley throng. Nearly 1000 Chinese were arrayed in the most fantastic garb that even an Eastern costumier can design. There were mandarins, sleek and comfortable-looking, in flowing robes of bright blue satin, and warriors in gaiters and blouses, bearing

A DUEL TO THE DEATH

The Chinese Pageant at the Exhibition Buildings.

ancient weapons; the guide Heweii Hwai, arrayed in bright yellow, with his back covered with darts like the quills of a porcupine. But the dresses—curious, rich and varied as they were, everyone displaying as many colours as the rainbow—were only one of the sights of the procession. The varieties of head-gear constituted another, ranging as they did from hats similar to card baskets to others resembling nothing so much as conservatories in miniature. There were, besides, flags and banners of most curious device; faces disguised in paint; musical instruments, gongs and drums, carried in frameworks, borne by numerous men, and occupied by the chief players in the centre, while the instruments were beaten vigorously at every step of the march.

This march was a spectacle which appealed to everyone, young and old alike, but the dramatic production at night some people found terrifying. 'Quivis' of the *Argus* reported:

Shortly after eight, the performance for which I had been waiting, commenced, and it was different from anything of the kind I have ever seen or imagined.

Though I listened and looked patiently for over two hours, I do not feel competent to say whether there was a plot or not, but my private opinion is that every player came and went, and spoke and fought and sang and danced as he liked.

THE GRAND BAZAAR, which took place a few days later, was also a great success, though the Exhibition Building was not as crowded as it had been for the Chinese display. The receipts for these two functions amounted to over £7000, an immense sum in those days, and after meeting the overhead expenses, the sum of £6000 was handed to the treasurer of the Women's Hospital Building Fund, a result considered 'highly satisfactory'.

May 14th

Lady Stawell and the Miss Stawells left Government House.

May 15th

A children's party and cricket match. About thirty children to tea. Some left at 7 p.m. The boys had games and supper at 9.

May 16th

Lovely morning. Went to Christ Church, South Yarra. Mr Tucker's last Sunday.

May 17th

Went to see Mr Geary, who has sprained his foot badly—he says it is getting better. The ankle and heel are much discoloured. He will be disabled for some time I fear. We also went to see a nice old lady in the Domain, Mrs Comben. She met with a terrible accident, has been a cripple ever since. Supports herself by needlework.

May 18th

Mr Tucker left Melbourne by the P. & O. s.s. Carthage for the benefit of Mrs Tucker's health and their son, who has been very ill and needs change.

ADELAIDE

21 May–3 August 1886

THROUGHOUT THE AUTUMN of 1886, the Governor and his wife continued their busy round of official engagements, and the usual stream of visitors came and went, but for the Lochs themselves, the greatest pleasure of that season was to see their new residence at Macedon gradually taking shape.

The *Australasian Sketcher* gave a drawing of the house that was being built there, and provided its readers with some details of it.

 [Parliament had in its last session] voted ten thousand pounds for the purpose of providing His Excellency the Governor with a summer residence for his wife and family on the Southern slopes of Mt. Macedon. The building has been designed by the Public Works Office.

The present house will supply apartments for A.D.C.s, secretaries and servants. The new building will provide dining room, drawing room, and private room for the Governor, and a large entrance hall which will also be used as a sitting room; having doors opening on to a verandah one end, and on to the entrance vestibule at the other. There are school room, butler's pantry and serving room on the ground floor, and upstairs seven bedrooms, with the usual offices, bathroom etc.

The Governor's residence at Macedon, built in 1886. (National Library of Australia, Canberra)

The lower storey will be of brick and the upper floor of half-timber work. No plaster will be used, the whole of the interior will be lined with kauri pine. All interior woodwork is to be varnished and left in its natural colour. The style adopted for the house is largely favoured for country residences in England, and most suitable for the locality: Macedon is three thousand, two hundred and forty feet high.

May 21st

Sir Henry, Lady Loch and Master Douglas went to Macedon just for one night. The building is going on and is to be completed by September.

May 23rd

Sir Henry's birthday. Went to Christ Church for morning service and then the park to see Mrs Cotterell in the afternoon. She is not very well. Poor thing has a sore throat—looks pale and weak.

May 24th

Queen's Birthday. Lovely day. Sir Henry held a levee, which was well attended. Lady Loch, Mam'selle Heyman, the two young ladies, Master Douglas, Mrs Calla, Lucy, Mary and me watched the whole proceedings from the gallery at the end of the ballroom. We sat behind some tree ferns, were not seen by the visitors, who looked very brilliant in uniforms, and the judges in their wigs and gowns, the clergy from the colleges and schools in their many coloured stoles— made up a good picture. The band playing on the lawn and fine sunny morning made one wish more could witness the pretty sight. A review was held in the afternoon, to which Sir Henry, Lady Loch and all the family went. Sir Henry had a fall from his horse, who put his foot in a hole. Luckily Sir Henry got up and remounted at once, which was a great relief to the whole party. The saddle caught the shin and grazed it rather badly.

SIR HENRY's own birthday was followed the next day by the official Queen's Birthday. 'Probably in no part of the British dominions', declared the press, 'is the day observed with more heartiness than in the Australian Colonies. Lovely weather was enjoyed, the day being simply perfect for outdoor activities'. Emma, from her corner in the gallery, describes the scene in the ballroom, and the press gives us details of the afternoon's proceedings.

 After the levee at Government House the most important public incident of her Majesty's Birthday was the review held during the afternoon in Albert Park, before His Excellency the Governor, in his capacity of Commander-in-Chief . . .

🎔 The parade was very successful, no serious untoward incidents occurred and some features were introduced in the manoeuvres of a complex character, and not previously attempted . . . His Excellency arrived on the ground at three p.m., inspected the brigade drawn up on line in open order, and after the usual salutes from the batteries of field-artillery, and the feu de joie from the infantry, witnessed the march past from the saluting point. The concourse of spectators was very considerable, and the greatest order prevailed . . . An accident, happily of the most trifling character, but which might have been serious, befell Sir Henry yesterday just at the moment when he rode on the ground at Albert Park, where all the forces were drawn up in open order to receive him. His Excellency's charger, on ground which appeared to be perfectly level, dropped his foot suddenly into a hole, and fell, rolling over on his rider. Great consternation prevailed for a few moments, but matters soon set themselves right, and the Governor, unhurt, or, at any rate, not owning to any damage, remounted his horse, which had not been allowed to escape, rode on the parade ground, and 🎔 was received with the usual general salute.

May 26th

Birthday dinner for eighty. Reception after for 1000. Very successful. Party broke up soon after midnight.

🎔 An official dinner to celebrate Her Majesty's Birthday took place at Government House. The tables were exquisitely decorated with flowers which had been sent to Lady Loch from many conservatories in and around Melbourne. The Governor, in proposing the health of the Queen, which was the only one honoured, read the telegram he had received from the Queen in reply to the congratulatory message sent to Her Majesty on her birthday. At the conclusion of the dinner an At Home took place at which about a thousand guests were present, among whom was Lord Capel. The ballroom was

Sir Henry Loch, mounted on his charger. (National Library of Australia, Canberra)

admirably decorated with flowers, flags and foliage plants, and dancing was kept up till midnight. The company was a brilliant one and a very enjoyable evening was spent.

May 28th

Went to South Yarra to find Mrs Raynor, a sad case. Father, mother, son and daughter disabled thro' chronic rheumatic gout. The Benevolent Society are very good to them, but they seem glad of anything in the shape of food as they have no one to do anything except night and morning. Mrs Orr and maid arrived from Sydney in the s.s. Massilia. Mrs Orr, a cousin of Sir Henry's, is on her way to India to see her son.

May 30th

Very cold tho' fine. Went to Christ Church. Had to come out just before the others. My cough was troublesome. Walked home with Mr and Mrs Martin. Heard from Tom that Mrs Eliza Brown was no more.

May 31st

Lady Loch heard that Mr Geo. Liddell (her uncle) was dead. He has been ailing for some time and had reached four score years—poor old gentleman. I am very full of cold today. Voice almost gone.

June 1st

Mrs Orr left by steamer for India, and her maid, Mrs Fox. A dreadful wreck near Sydney on Sunday evening last. The Sycemoon [Ly-ee-Moon] from Melbourne. Eighty souls on board, only a few saved who happened to be on deck. The Sycemoon struck on the Green Cape and parted amidships. Not a woman or child saved, they were all below. Quite a sensation has been caused by this terrible calamity.

THIS WRECK, which occurred on a clear moonlight night, shocked all Australians, for she was one of the Australian Steam Navigation Company's best and fastest ships and so many people had used her to travel to and from Sydney and Melbourne. Disaster struck three hours after darkness fell; the captain had gone below for a nap, leaving the second officer in charge with instructions to call him when Green Cape light was sighted. This the officer did, but when the captain went on deck he found the vessel had drifted perilously close to the shore, and a few moments later she was dashed onto the rocks and broke in half. Over seventy people were drowned, but what shocked people most was that not a single woman or child survived, probably because they were down below. For the same reason, all the engineers and the firemen were trapped and drowned.

It was small comfort to the relatives of those who were lost to learn that the captain's certificate was cancelled and the mate's was suspended. But seldom has any disaster so touched the hearts of the people as this wreck, and relief funds for the survivors were opened in every city, large or small. Offers of help came from such diverse sources as the Albert Park Presbyterian Church, where 'a sermon will be delivered on the wreck of the "Ly-ee-Moon" and its lessons' (with a special collection), and the rather shocking 'Silk Stockings and Satin' company of Mr Frank Clark's, whose shows were billed as 'The Greatest and latest sensation in everything new and startling!' It offered a '"Grand Fashionable Matinee Benefit" with the proceeds all going for the Benefit of the Sufferers in the recent Ly-ee-Moon disaster'.

June 10th

A dreadful earthquake in New Zealand.

June 12th

A banquet for forty guests given by Sir Henry to Sir Wm. Stawell, who has just returned from a long visit for the benefit of his health.

SIR WILLIAM STAWELL was probably Sir Henry's oldest friend in Australia. He had met him first when he had come out as a young man to have a look round the colony, and when he returned in 1884 to fill the position of its Governor, he found it was Sir William who had been administering affairs here until he arrived.

He and Lady Stawell had stayed at Government House for a few days before they had sailed for Europe earlier in the year. They made the voyage as a rest cure for Sir William, and he had returned feeling quite restored to health. Unfortunately his second voyage in search of health, made in 1889, was not so successful, for he became ill and died at Naples.

June 13th

Did not attend service. My cough still troublesome. Had a turn in the garden with Benson, who was delighted.

June 14th

Went to Little Davies Street to see Mrs Raynor, who is so dreadfully afflicted with the rheumatism. We took some nice little delicacies from Lady Loch.

June 15th

My 51st birthday. Had some very good presents and kind messages from Mrs Calla, Mary, Lucy, Lady Loch, Sir Henry, the young Ladies and Master Douglas. My room looks so smart. Went to Fitzroy after dinner with Mr Hawkins to see Mr Green's Hall of Ferns, and afterwards to St Patrick's Cathedral to see where Archbishop Gooch [Goold] was buried as we were too late for the funeral. The church is unfinished. It will be very large when finished.

ARCHBISHOP GOOLD, who had come to Australia as a young missionary in 1838 had been consecrated as Melbourne's first Roman

St Patrick's Cathedral, Melbourne.

Catholic bishop when the See was created forty years later. He had filled this position with dignity, and was later to become the city's first Roman Catholic archbishop. He was keenly interested in education, and also in the colony's politics and, unlike the Anglican bishops, was prepared to take an active part in local political questions. But today he is best remembered for his plans for the great cathedral which he commissioned the architect Wardell to design. Although it was still unfinished at the time of his death, it was here that his impressive funeral was held.

June 17th

Miss Harbord and Captain came to stay for two nights on their way to England. Miss Herne has got a needle in her foot and walks so lame, poor girl.

June 18th

Dinner for forty-eight to Mr Murray Smith, Agent-General for the Colonies.

THIS WAS ONE of the many functions held in honour of the Agent-General, who, from his imposing office, had done so much to encourage the commercial development of the colonies and to assist them in their trading ventures. The press at this time contained many tributes to his ability, and one of the functions in his honour was a large complimentary dinner whose list of sponsors reads like a *Who's Who* of Melbourne.

June 19th

Captain and Miss Harbord left by French steamer Sydney. *Miss Herne left about 11 a.m. with the luggage. She is a bad sailor and dreads the voyage home.*

June 22nd

Went to see Mr Wise, who has been laid up, also poor Mrs Comben.

June 26th

Walked to Little Davies Street with Lady Loch to see poor Mrs Raynor, who is suffering, and her children, a girl and boy, with chronic rheumatism. The daughter is in the Home for Incurables. The son works when he is fit, and the husband. Yet both are afflicted with the same thing thro' living in a damp house.

EMMA WAS obviously a person of warm sympathies, and after being in Australia for only a few weeks was already visiting the sick and the blind, usually taking little gifts with her. How did she find these less fortunate people so quickly, for most newcomers exclaimed over the universal prosperity of the colony, and were surprised at the absence of beggars? A visiting MD, Dr Ashburton Thompson, wrote a long letter to the press saying that as he walked around he was 'struck by the appearance of active prosperity, and the absence of signs of poverty', and added 'I am among people who are active and intelligent'.

Emma frequently attended the services at Christ Church, South Yarra, and the church may have had a list of the sick 'for whom one's prayers are requested', or of lonely and housebound people who would like to be visited. Possibly the Miss Cross, who came to see Emma because they had a mutual friend in England, had told her about some of her neighbours who were struggling in the face of great difficulties. So Emma's list of disadvantaged persons increased, and she may have spoken of some of these sad cases as she attended to her mistress's wants, for now we find that she is carrying with her little gifts 'from Lady Loch'.

For the first few months after her arrival in the colony, Lady Loch's time, of course, was much occupied with her official duties, not to mention the needs of her own children, but as life settled into a routine, both the Governor and his wife began to take an active interest in Victoria's young people, especially the ones who were facing difficulties. Sir Henry had presided at concerts by members of the YMCA, and by the boys of the Try-Excelsior Classes, whose concert aimed to raise funds for the Gordon Institute, 'a club for the guidance and amusement of poor and neglected children', inspired by the work for boys done by General Gordon. Lady Loch, too, was interested in schools and had recently visited Coburg's Jika Jika Reformatory for girls, 'where she examined the school room, dormitory, lavatory, laundry, etc. very carefully and expressed herself much pleased with the clean appearance of the place'. She was accompanied on this tour, we read, by the Matron and Ladies' Committee, but it is not mentioned whether she saw the girls.

And now, with Emma, she had actually been inside one of those tiny terrace houses that lined the smaller streets and had seen just what the living conditions were like for Melbourne's less privileged inhabitants.

June 29th

Went to see poor Mrs Cotterell. She has had more trouble. Her husband's mother came from Gipps Land on a visit, had only been two or three days with them when illness came on, and after being unconscious for three days she died. The second daughter, Lucy, has been ill thro' a burn. The system all out of order. Harry is no better, so the poor woman has had her hands full.

July 1st

Lady Loch's reception [for visitors from] 'Fisk University'. The Jubilee Singers were here and sang some of their beautiful songs. 'I am Rolling thro' this unfriendly World' and 'Home Sweet Home' made one feel choky. Their voices are so sweet and sounded so well in the ballroom. There was a large attendance of visitors.

THIS YEAR Lady Loch's winter At Home was even more widely attended than her previous one had been, and at this reception she made an innovation. Instead of having Herr Plock's orchestra to entertain the guests with soft music, she asked the Jubilee Singers to provide the programme. These singers were probably the first band of Negro songsters to come to Australia, where their recitals were described as 'unique and inimitable, consisting of slave songs and spirituals'. Special children's matinées were given, on Saturdays, when admission prices were as low as one shilling, and Melbourne people so took these singers to their hearts that the season was extended several times. Their final advertisement announced that 'The Fisk Jubilee Singers will continue their series of concerts at the Town Hall for four nights longer, an entirely new programme is being given at each performance'.

The day of an At Home was always a very busy one for everyone at Government House, but the day that followed this one was to be even busier for Sir Henry and his ADC, for they had to be up at dawn to board a special train to Pyramid Hill where the Governor was to turn the first sod of a big irrigation scheme, a ceremony followed, of course, by a banquet, and they were not expected to reach Melbourne again until midnight.

July 6th

English mail. My poor Lucy heard her mother was dead. She had been ailing sometime with spasms and dropsy. Death took place on the 12th of May. We are truly sorry for poor Lucy. 'Tis sad to be so far away when those we love are snatched away. Lucy is bearing her sorrow in a true Christianlike spirit.

July 7th

Went to see Dr Turner about my hearing. He syringed the right ear and the hearing is better, tho' not quite right, so I am to go again on the 11th, when he again syringed and cleaned the passage wonderfully. I am hopeful all will soon be right, tho' he says I must go again.

IT SEEMS obvious from Emma's diary that her hearing was deteriorating. Her spelling of proper names had always been somewhat strange, but had become even more so this year, making it very difficult to identify some of the people or places that she mentions.

July 9th

A lovely day. Walked to Mrs Raynor's at South Yarra, then to Mrs Cotterell's, and on our way back called on Mrs Sidman for a cup of tea.

July 10th

Miss Cross came to tell us about her cousin's wedding at St Stephen's, Richmond.

July 11th

Miss Skene popped in for a chat. She is doing nothing just now.

July 15th

Mr and Mrs Geary came to see us, stayed to supper and we had a pleasant evening.

July 17th

A glorious, spring-like day. Went out for a turn in the grounds with Benson. Lucy went to church alone. I am still afraid of cold.

July 21st

Left Melbourne at 8.55 by special train for Adelaide. A lovely day. We had something to eat at Ararat, not at all good. Again at Horsham. Reached Dimboola about 5.30 and stopped at Bordertown for the night. Mr Millar and Mr Ladler, the Contractors, allowed Sir Henry and Lady Loch to occupy their six-roomed cottage for the night—all so clean and comfortable. Mrs Powell, the housekeeper, was so kind to us, and gave up her room to Lucy and me. We did not get much sleep: the roosters wake so early.

July 22nd

Up at 5.30, and left by special train for _____. All very tired. Country for 90 miles very flat and sandy, not a tree to be seen. 'Tis called the desert and Sir Wm. Robinson's State carriage was in readiness at

____ with a capital luncheon, which we all did good justice to. And then dozed till we reached Adelaide at 6 p.m. The soldiers turned out, and their band. Sir Wm. Robinson's ADC, several gentlemen, received Sir Henry at the station, and gave them a right hearty welcome. A dinner party at Government House. Had to unpack at once. Lady Loch attended a concert after dinner, and nearly fell asleep with fatigue.

WHEN THE LOCHS and their children travelled to Adelaide, one of the railway sections, the line to connect Horsham to Bordertown, on the South Australian border, was still under construction, and the directors of the firm that was building this line, Millar Brothers, very courteously vacated their house at Dimboola, and placed the house, and the housekeeper, at the Governor's disposal.

They were able to spend a comfortable night there, and although Emma found the roosters annoying, these birds probably disturbed the travellers much less than the crowds of men who thronged the hotels each night to spend their navvies' wages would have done. And the travellers were able to doze in their train next day as they sped across South Australia's drought stricken plains, which was fortunate, for a busy programme awaited them from the moment they stepped on to Adelaide's platform at sundown.

The *Adelaide Advertiser* informed its readers that the travellers had a pleasant journey, and that:

 On arrival the Vice-Regal party were met by the Premier and Treasurer, who cordially welcomed them. The police formed a line from the platform to the terrace where the Permanent Forces were drawn up as a guard of honour. A detachment of mounted police kept the roadway clear, and a troop of cavalry formed an escort. As His Excellency and Lady Loch entered the Governor's carriage the Military Band played 'Song of Australia' and the Permanent Forces presented arms. His Excellency drove off amidst the cheers of the large number of

Adelaide. Supreme Court (top), Botanical Gardens, and Museum and Art Gallery (bottom).

spectators who had assembled. In the evening Governor Robinson and his guests attended the Philharmonic Society's concert in the Town Hall.

In her diary Emma does not comment on Adelaide's Government House, possibly because she had so often, in the past, accompanied Lady Loch on her visits to the great houses of England that she took large rooms and lofty ceilings as a matter of course. But for most visitors to this exceedingly graceful house, their first glimpse of it was a memorable one. It was the work of two architects. The first drew up plans in the early days for a Georgian style residence to be built of wood, and these drawings were later amalgamated with the more elaborate plans of a later architect for a more imposing brick house. So well did the two plans blend that the general effect was of a spacious and dignified whole, free from the picturesque adornments that became so popular in the later part of the century.

Government House Adelaide July 23rd

Rather a dull day. Lucy and me went to the post office in the morning and through the principal streets. All is terribly dull and depressed. Good shops, but no customers. There has been a long drought, which has almost ruined many of the squatters. Then numbers of best families all in England for the Colonial Exhibition.

WHILE THE two lady's maids explored the main streets of Adelaide the next day, the Lochs carried out a full round of engagements, during which the citizens had a further opportunity of seeing the beautiful Lady Loch of whom they had heard so much.

 The Victorian vice-regal party now the guests of his Excellency the Governor, commenced doing the "lions" of the city on Friday. During the morning Sir Henry and Lady Loch, with Sir Wm. Robinson, visited the Botanic Gardens and were shown the principal objects of interest there. Her lady-ship was greatly pleased with the beauties of the floral king-dom which met the party at every turn. In the afternoon a reception was held at Government House . . . The oppor-tunity to those anxious to pay their respects to his Excellency and Lady Loch was largely availed of. The reception took place at Government House between the hours of 3.30 and 5 p.m., and during that time several hundreds of visitors attended. The weather was rather threatening, but despite this drawback the costumes of many of the ladies were striking and elegant . . . In the evening their Excellencies and Lady Loch and suites, attended the bachelors' ball in the North Adelaide Institute. The spacious hall was tastefully decorated, and a large party assembled. Dancing was kept up till a late hour.

July 24th

Went out in the morning with Lucy and young ladies to see the Arcade. Met Mrs and Miss Harper from Macedon. A dinner party for twenty-six and a concert after. Miss Markwell, Lucy, Master Douglas and I went up in the balcony to listen. Had to go in on all fours not to be seen. Sir Henry soon spied us out.

SATURDAY was to be even more strenuous for the visitors, their programme including among other events, two concerts! The first a matinée; and the second an evening recital at Government House, which tempted the maids and Master Douglas to crawl onto the balcony.

Sunday July 25th

Lovely morning. Lucy, Miss Markwell and I went to St Peter's Cathedral. Nice service. Rained hard all the afternoon, so all were compelled to remain indoors.

St Peter's Cathedral, Adelaide.

July 26th

Another wet day. Went out at 11.30 with Master Douglas to post some papers and get a little fresh air. Lady Loch and Sir Henry dined at the Chief Justice's—North Adelaide.

WHEN THE LOCHS had visited Sydney in a time of drought, they had brought the long-awaited winter rains with them, and in Adelaide they seem to have wrought a similar miracle. Monday was still wet, but the visitors carried out their full programme.

 Sir Henry and Lady Loch, with their two daughters, accompanied by his Honor the Chief Justice (the chancellor), paid a visit to the University on Monday. The visitors, under the guidance of the chancellor, were shown over the building, and took great interest in certain experiments in acoustics and in electricity, which were shown by Professor Bragg. Professor

Rennie received the vice-regal visitors in the chemical laboratory, and explained certain processes for extracting sarsaparilla and for analysing water, on which he was engaged at the time. Whilst passing the students' room the visitors were suddenly greeted by three ringing cheers from the undergraduates present—a reception as gratifying as it was unexpected. Sir Henry Loch gracefully acknowledged the compliment, and the chancellor presented Mr. Cecil Mead (the senior under-graduate present) to his Excellency. After a short visit to the library the party, having stayed for upwards of an hour in the University, left for the Art Gallery. Sir Henry was subsequently shown over the Public Library and Museum, and in the afternoon he inspected the Government Offices and the Post and Telegraph Offices. In the evening His Excellency dined with the Chief Justice at North Adelaide.

July 27th

Fine but cloudy. Lucy and I went off to find Mrs Holloway's friend at the Maid and Magpie, but failed to find her. Lucy and Miss Markwell went to Glenelg—returned about 6, and at 7.40 the young ladies and Miss Markwell went to the theatre to see The Mikado. *The young ladies just did enjoy themselves.*

July 28th

Lucy, Miss Markwell and me started off shopping in the afternoon. Lucy's friend, Miss Storm, came from Glenelg. A concert held at Government House for 250 guests. Nice music. We went up in the gallery to listen, but found the gas rather trying. The guests had all cleared off by 12 p.m.

ANOTHER FULL DAY for the Lochs, ending with yet another concert in the evening. A choral society that was based at Government House most surely have been unique!

On Wednesday his Excellency the Governor of Victoria . . . paid a visit to the Industrial School for the Blind . . . and was shown over the whole of the building, inspecting the various processes of brush and mat making carried on by those deprived of sight.

July 29th

Dear Miss Evelyn's birthday. A glorious day. We started at 11 a.m. for Marble Hill. Sir Wm. and Lady Loch in first phaeton, Sir Henry Loch, Master Douglas and the Secretary in another carriage, the young ladies, Lucy and me in a nice open buggy. Such a splendid drive of 13 miles. Good road all the way. The country looks beautifully green. Almond trees in full blossom in abundance. The roadside for some miles like a flower garden with red and white heath, native lilac, yellow gorse. The weeping willows must be beautiful in the spring. We reached Marble Hill about 1 p.m. We helped to put the luncheon on the table, then went for a stroll. Had our luncheon with Mr and Mrs Pound. Went all over the house, up the tower and round the garden to gather flowers for the table. Another start at 3.15. On our way home a man drove his cart against one wheel and broke the spring. We stopped at the blacksmith and had it repaired. Reached Government House Adelaide at 5 p.m. Dinner party for twenty-four and music after.

THE EXPEDITION to Marble Hill, the Governor's summer residence, had been postponed because of the rain, but Thursday was clear and sunny, a perfect day for a drive to the hills, past some of Adelaide's famous almond groves.

July 30th

Heavy, depressing morning. Began raining about 10.30. At 12 we started for the Houses of Parliament, Miss Markwell, Lucy, me and Mr Lovegrove. Found Mr Hines was out, so went on to the Picture Gallery. It is only a small collection. Some very good pictures (tho' I am no judge). Had a peep at the library and museum. As it was still raining we went back to Government House. It cleared up and we three started off to the Zoological Gardens. A small, but fair, collection of animals. Some lovely birds. After looking at all the reptiles and monkeys we walked home thro' the Botanical Gardens. The shady walks must look lovely in the summer. The Golden Wattle is in full bloom, and makes one long to pluck some. The Fern and Palm Houses are beautiful. We reached Government House about 5.30, very tired. I felt used up and, after dressing Lady Loch, Miss M____, Mr Crisford and me went to see the Micado [The Mikado]. *Sir Wm. Robinson lent us his box. I was unfortunately forced to come away before the piece was finished, felt so ill.*

On Friday morning his Excellency the Governor of Victoria inspected both branches of the police force at the barracks, North-terrace. Sir Henry was accompanied by the Chief Secretary (Hon. D. Murray), Captain Traill (Private Secretary), and Mr. Douglas Loch. Commissioner Peterswald commanded the forces, Inspector Hunt was in charge of the mounted police, and Inspector Sullivan had command of the foot. The men paraded in excellent order, and they presented the spectacle of a fine body of well-drilled and disciplined men. The mounted troopers were put through the ordinary formations and then the sword exercise, in both of which they acquitted themselves with credit. The foot-police after having been exercised in the usual movements, cleverly ran through the bayonet drill, showing both smartness and correctness. The Police Band was in attendance and performed a number of selections in good style. Just before the close of the parade rain commenced to fall, which, as his Excellency did not wish the men to get wet through, slightly curtailed the proceedings. Before leaving his Excellency complimented the band on their efficiency and the forces on the high standard of excellence they had attained. In the afternoon Sir Henry and Lady Loch were entertained at Torrens Park by Mr. R. Barr and Mrs. Smith . . . In the evening their Excellencies and Lady Loch witnessed the performance of "Our Boys" at the Academy of Music, by an amateur dramatic company, in aid of the Adelaide Hunt Club.

WHILE THE LOCHS had another round of engagements, ending up with the concert in aid of the Hunt Club, the staff had a leisurely day, going sightseeing between showers. Emma, despite being very tired, enjoyed Adelaide's Botanical Gardens which had been laid in a series of formal gardens by Dr Schomburgh.

And in the evening there was the excitement of watching *The Mikado*, the production which had kept Melbourne laughing for weeks. The antics of Mr Vernon who took the part of Ko Ko had filled the Theatre Royal night after night, but the maids would have considered the Theatre Royal prices beyond their pockets. And now they were to see it from the Governor's private box! Something to write home about indeed.

July 31st

Not very bright, but fine. Had to keep quiet all day. Lucy went to Glenelg at 2 p.m. After she came home she took my temperature, found it was nearly 102. Lady Loch sent for a doctor, who came at once and prescribed for me. He seemed to think it was the digestive organs. Had a restless night, tho' much better this morning, I am thankful to say.

WHILE EMMA was laid low with a temperature, the Lochs carried out another round of engagements, Lucy presumably taking Emma's place in dressing Lady Loch in the various elaborate costumes that these functions called for.

Sir Henry began the day with an inspection of the forts Glanville and Largs, and of the gunboat *Protector*, which gave a demonstration of its fire power, hurried on to the Mayor's Parlour in Port Adelaide for loyal toasts, and again had to hurry away for a complimentary banquet tendered to their Excellencies in the Town Hall, which seems to have been a very happy occasion.

Government House, Adelaide.

The banquet given by the Ministry in honour of Sir Henry Brougham Loch was a timely and pleasant compliment to a man of more than ordinary mark. Apart from his official position as Governor of Victoria, the visit of a gentleman of such distinction and ability would claim special recognition. Sir Henry Loch had earned laurels in the service of his country long before the Colonial Office placed him at the head of the Victorian Government. The heroic part he played in the Chinese war touches the sympathies of all true Englishmen, and gives him the right to the esteem of everyone who can appreciate courageous devotion to duty in the face of extraordinary difficulties and hardships. Sir Henry is a popular Governor in his own Colony, and well he deserves to be. As the representative of a sister State, with which South Australia has always maintained friendly relations, he received the welcome due to his rank and station, but the man himself evoked manifestations of goodwill and friendly feeling which could not but prove gratifying to him. It is not in after-dinner speeches that men such as Sir Henry Loch are seen at their best. He is a man of action rather than words, but still at

Saturday's banquet our distinguished visitor spoke remarkably well.

August 1st

Dr Thomas came at 10 and said I might get up, which was a great relief as I like to do my own packing. Felt rather shaky all day, but got thro' many letters and packed and rested by turns. A supper for eighteen, music after.

August 2nd

Left Government House at 7.45 and started at 8 prompt. A guard of honour was drawn up for Sir Henry. Many gentlemen were waiting to wish Sir Henry and Lady Loch a safe and pleasant journey. Mr and Mrs Harper; Mr Labertouch, Secretary for Railway in Victoria; Mr, Mrs and Miss Lavine; travelled in the special. At most of the stations people assembled to have a look and cheer. We had a splendid luncheon in the dining saloon as we travelled; provided by the Government and prepared by Mr Hines, Caterer, Adelaide. We had turkey, salad, jellies, champagne, coffee, everything that the heart could wish for. Arrived at the Dimboola Cottage about 4.30. Mrs Powell gave us some excellent tea and we started for Horsham. Here Sir Henry, Lady Loch and family put up for the night. A nice clean hotel. We all slept like tops.
    Christina's Wedding Day.

August 3rd

Got up at 7 and, after a nice cup of tea, dressed Lady Loch and packed up. We left Horsham at 9.30. Sir Henry was treated most loyally. A guard of honour, brass band and a crowd of people who shouted lustily as the train moved off. At Stawell there was quite a demonstration. Children drawn up in line, and some hundreds of people waving flags, etc. The station was very well decorated with flowers and wattle. The ladies of Stawell presented Lady Loch with a most flattering address: the Mayor also read an address of welcome, the children sang the National Anthem, and tho' the rain pelted down, they braved the elements and shouted till their little throats must have been sore. One of the gentlemen brought us some champagne to the carriage, which we enjoyed. We reached Melbourne at 6.28, and the Big House about 7, thankful to be home safe and sound once more, and to find the mail had arrived and a nice lot of letters to be read.

The Last Pages

13 August–24 October 1886

ALTHOUGH THE GOVERNOR and his family returned from Adelaide to find Melbourne still wet and cold, and some of their staff still in bed with sore throats, the few days of Adelaide's clear sunshine and the beauty of its almond blossom had given them the feeling that spring would soon be here.

August 13th

Lady Loch and Sir Henry went to Macedon for the night. Lucy and myself went to Melbourne soon after dinner, in the carriage with the young ladies. We did some shopping, then went on by omnibus to Northcote to find Mr Edwards (Mary's brother). Failed to find him. It seems he has moved and we know not where.

August 14th

Mary not well. A sore throat. Dr Turner hopes with care she will soon be all right.

August 15th

Showery. Lucy went to church alone. I did not feel very well. Only had a little walk in the grounds.

Shoppers in Collins Street, Melbourne.

August 16th

A cold, showery day. Miss Edith christened a boat at Footscray, named the Lady Loch. *Unfortunately, the* Lady Loch *would only move a few feet instead of gliding into the water like a swan. After waiting nearly two hours in the wet and cold to see if she would move, the company went to their banquet and gave up trying to induce the obstinate vessel to move until tomorrow, when fresh efforts will be made to launch her. Mr Bigsby arrived. Mary still in bed. Very poorly, her throat very painful.*

THE LOCHS' two little girls had grown rapidly since they came to Australia, and when Miss Edith, who was now eleven, had been asked to perform a very important ceremony, we can imagine the excitement. Of course the girls had been used to watching official functions of all kinds, and during their parents' recent visit to Adelaide had even accompanied them on occasions such as their inspection of the University. And now Miss Edith had been invited to christen, and to launch, the largest ship ever built in Australia.

This ship, for which permission had been sought, and granted, to name it the *Lady Loch*, had been built for the Government at a shipyard in Footscray. Elaborate arrangements had been made for the visit to commence at half past three in the afternoon so that when the ship glided down the slipway into Saltwater Creek, she would get the advantage of the full tide in the stream. The viceregal party and the two hundred distinguished citizens who had been invited, were asked to assemble at the Customs Wharf at two o'clock, when they would be taken down to Footscray in two large launches.

The day was cold and grey, with a strong southerly wind and frequent showers of icy rain and, as the *Age* reporter observed, 'Disasters never come singly'. The rain came down in torrents as the launches negotiated that unlovely stretch of the river and they soon found the waterway blocked by a disabled steamer that had run aground. But they eventually reached the shipyard where:

 A spacious tent was close at hand for the reception of the Vice-regal and Ministerial party, the Harbor Trust and their friends, the municipal authorities, prominent citizens and other invited guests. The inhabitants of the district mustered in their thousands on the opposite shore.

These onlookers on the opposite bank were waiting patiently in the rain to see the fine ship entering the water. The work of knocking away the shoring began at the time arranged for the ceremony and the bottle of champagne hung at the bows, ready for Miss Edith to break it as she christened the vessel. But it soon became apparent that there was a serious hitch in the proceedings—the boat failed to move! After an hour's shouting and struggling, during which the visitors became bemused, an announcement was made. As nightfall was approaching, and the tide was running out, it would be impossible to launch the vessel till the following day. So Miss Edith named the *Lady Loch* amidst loud cheers, and the company, having seen that:

> ... the position was hopeless, with true British pluck adjourned to the luncheon long deferred, in the marquee. Fully two hundred guests sat down, and this portion of the programme of the day's proceedings was at any rate most successfully carried out, the creature comforts provided being on a scale commensurate with the occasion.

Sir Henry, in replying to the loyal toast, made a witty speech which soon had all the company laughing. He referred to all the feminine qualities that the ship possessed, and said that 'true to the traditions of her sex, she had obstinately refused to glide out at the word of command and display herself to the public gaze at a moment which she considered inauspicious'. He was sure that when the sun was shining and conditions were favourable, she would be more amenable to the wishes of her admirers.

August 17th

Dr Turner thinks Mary is a little better today, tho' she looks white and weak.

August 20th

Mrs Ryan from Macedon arrived.

MRS RYAN was one of the Lochs' neighbours when they were at Macedon. It was she who had hurried down to Government Cottage to calm fears about the bushfires during their first summer in Australia, and to assure Lady Loch that the cottage was not in danger despite the fearsome flames on the surrounding slopes. The Ryans had a large house set in acres of beautiful garden, and their staff were always included in the expeditions that Sir Henry arranged for his helpers during their time at Macedon.

August 21st

Dinner party for eighteen. Mary all right. Able to work today.

August 22nd

Went to see poor Mrs Raynor, who is very unwell, not able to raise herself in bed. Dinner for sixteen. Master Douglas not well, sore throat again.

August 23rd

Beautiful day. Went to see Mrs Hawkbridge and poor old Mrs Comben for a few minutes this morning. Heard Lord Castlerosse was engaged to be married to Miss Baring.

August 27th

Parliamentary Dinner. Sixty members dined. Lady Loch held an evening party after for 1200 guests. Almost like a ball. I was almost knocked up. We had not finished at the buffet till after 1 a.m. It was kept up with great spirit and all seemed much pleased.

Horsham.

August 29th

Lovely morning. Went to Christ Church. The Miss Herberts came to tea.

September 3rd

Second Parliamentary Dinner and evening party for 1200. Very hard day for us all. Went off well. Dancing kept up with great enthusiasm till the National Anthem was played.

September 5th

Went to Christ Church in the morning.

September 8th

Started at 8.50 for Horsham. Rather a cold journey. Rained the greater part of the journey. Arrived at 5 p.m. Crowd of people at the station. We, Mr Lovegrove and I, went in a cab to the Royal Hotel. Flags and arches in all directions. A regular crowd at the hotel to *receive the Governor and Lady Loch, who arrived half an hour before time. All had a good meal and slept like tops.*

September 9th

Up early. Sir Henry and Lady Loch went off to see the hospital after breakfast. Returned at midday, had luncheon and went off in a carriage and four to see the Agricultural Show. I sat out and worked on the balcony. It was warm and sunny. About 5 all returned, and the rain fell in torrents directly they had reached the hotel. A banquet was given at the hall for 100 guests in honour of the Governor's visit. All went off well.

THE LOCHS had spent a comfortable night at one of Horsham's hotels on their way home from Adelaide, and when they were leaving the next morning, hundreds of people had rallied round, despite the early hour, to cheer them on their way. Now the Governor had returned for the Agricultural Show, and the *Age* correspondent reported that when he and his party arrived, just before five o'clock, they had received a hearty welcome, the town being gay with flags and with a magnificent triumphal arch erected in the main street. Horsham was a busy little town in the centre of the Wimmera district, much of which had recently been thrown open to selectors, and although the town itself only had two thousand residents, the surrounding district was developing rapidly. Although the viceregal party had travelled through heavy rain to reach Horsham, the reporter was able to record that:

The second day of the Horsham show passed off very successfully. The weather was beautifully fine, the attendance exceeded 3000, and there would have been 5000 but for the bad state of the roads caused by the recent rains. The Governor and Lady Loch, Mr. Dow, the Minister for Lands, and Mr. George Young, M.L.A, were amongst the visitors. The Australian Natives presented an address to the Governor. The vice-regal party visited the hospital and the gas-works. The principal attraction of the show was the trial of hunters.

September 10th

Left Horsham at 9.30 a.m. for Ballarat by special [train]. Reached Ballarat at 2.30 and drove to Bishopscourt, close to the Lake Wendouree. A nice comfortable place. The Bishop and Mrs Thornton very kind. Dinner party and large meeting in Ballarat about the new cathedral they want to commence. All the party attended. Sir Henry addressed the meeting, also the Bishop. A goodly sum was subscribed on the spot.

FROM HORSHAM a special train carried Sir Henry and his suite across to Ballarat. When Bishop Thornton had stayed at Government House some months before, Sir Henry had been so impressed by his vision of building a great cathedral in Ballarat that he had promised to go across and preside at a public meeting to launch a cathedral building fund.

Detailed preparations had been made for this visit with its important meeting, and one supporter had actually obtained a Manx flag to fly at his hotel so that the Governor would feel that he was among old friends! All the people who had been unable to catch a glimpse of the Governor on his earlier visit, because of the appalling weather conditions that had prevailed, were determined to see him this time—and of course the church people hoped that the crowds who were anxious to see the Governor would come to hear his speech at the evening's Public Meeting in the Academy of Music.

On this occasion Sir Henry had perfect weather for his visit, and the *Star* reported that:

His Excellency was met at the station by Bishop Thornton, the Hon. Colonel Smith and Mr. J. Russell (mayor of the Town of Ballarat), M's.L.A., Mr. Thompson (mayor of the City) attired in his robes and decorations of office, as well as by a number of church dignitaries and other prominent citizens. A guard of honor, composed of members of the 3rd Battalion Victoria Militia, was drawn up on the station under Captain Laidlaw, and as the vice-regal party stepped on to the platform the Militia band played the national anthem. By the courtesy of Bishop Moore, that prelate's fine carriage was placed at the disposal of his Excellency, who, with Lady Loch, was driven first to Christ Church and subsequently through the gardens to Bishops-court, where the party were last night the guests of Bishop and Mrs. Thornton.

In the evening Professor Kelly gave a magnificent display of fireworks from the new Post Office tower in honor of the vice-regal visit. By preconcerted signal the display started when the party came into Sturt-street, and was kept up until they entered the Academy of Music. The red lights were particularly brilliant, and the shells and rockets were also excellent. A fine fall of golden rain, representing the Falls of Niagara, was also an effective display, as was the representation of the Lal Lal Falls, a fine effect being produced by steel filings. The bombardment of Alexandria was likewise a brilliant spectacle. The crown at the Unicorn hotel was alight, as were several other illuminations in the city. During the day bunting was flying from all the public and many of the private buildings, the Manx flag being displayed at one of the hotels.

After this spectacular display, people crowded into the hall, and we read:

The Academy was well filled, upwards of 1500 persons being present. As his Excellency the Governor entered the building, the Militia Band struck up "God save the Queen", the audience rising to their feet, and remaining standing until the conclusion of the anthem. As Sir Henry Loch appeared on the platform he was greeted with prolonged applause, which he suitably acknowledged.

His Excellency, who was received with cheering, expressed his pleasure at being present to aid the object of the meeting. Those who professed to believe should show their belief was more than surface deep; they should contribute toward the propagation of Christian doctrines. He referred to all denominations, and thought they should assist each other in erecting suitable buildings for worship. It was the object of all to provide beautiful edifices in which to worship. A more opportune time for urging could not be chosen than when the accommodation in churches was insufficient. Public sentiment demanded that the public buildings should be fine, and they saw banks vieing with each other in the matter of architecture. Were they to be backward in such a matter? By spreading the contributions over five years, the Bishop provided for contributions from the poorest. But something more was wanted—sympathy; in fact, this was the principal thing, and without it success could not be achieved.

Sir Henry did his part to ensure the success of the appeal by promising a donation of £125, and Sir George Verdon, one of his Macedon neighbours, followed with one of £25.

Unfortunately the Lochs' proverbial good luck seemed to have deserted them this year. The ship that Miss Edith was to have launched refused to enter the water, and the cathedral that Sir Henry hoped to see dominating Ballarat failed to appear on the skyline. True, the crypt and chapter house, whose foundations he saw laid the following year, still stand, a handsome bluestone structure, but it has been sold by the church authorities and a sign informs the public that it is now 'The Hot Gossip Night Club'.

September 11th

Left Ballarat at 10.30 for Melbourne. Lovely day. Reached Government House soon after 2 p.m. Found the mail had just arrived by s.s. Ganges.

EMMA OBVIOUSLY enjoyed the peace and quiet of Bishopscourt, in its lovely setting by the lake. Perhaps it reminded her of the calm of a Cathedral Close in England. The large rambling house, which had been offered to the church at a very moderate price, when Bishop Thornton had first arrived and was desperate to find somewhere to live, was in a beautiful position among the trees, and was approached by a long avenue of elms. Sadly, the house has now been demolished and its garden subdivided—the original grounds contain three residential streets, St Aidan's Drive, Lindisfarne Crescent and The Boulevard.

September 12th

Lovely summers day. Went to Christ Church and in the afternoon to see Mrs Cotterell. All the children at home and well, tho' baby looks delicate.

September 17th

Left Government House at 3.30 and Flinders Street Station at 4. The Saloon carriage was so heated from the sun I felt parboiled and so glad when Master Douglas said we were close to Parwan, the station we got out at for Greystones. Mr Molesworth Greene was at the station with an open buggy and Lady Loch sat on the box seat with Mr Greene. Sir Henry, Master Douglas, Mr Fort and myself behind. A beautiful drive across country for 7 miles at the rate of 12 miles an hour. Was most enjoyable. The air seemed so cool after Melbourne. We reached Greystones about 6.30. Such a nice home, and so beautifully furnished. Had a refreshing cup of tea, then unpacked. Dressed Lady Loch for 7.30 dinner and read till supper time. I felt so tired and worn out—got off early to bed and slept well.

THE VISIT TO Greystones, near Bacchus Marsh, was another restful break in Emma's constant round of packing and unpacking, pressing and mending, and she seems to have been more impressed by the house and its treasures that she had been by any of the other big homesteads she had seen. Greystones, which still stands today, had formed part of the huge Glenmore station of the pioneering era. When the station was sold, the Greenes had bought the lightly timbered plains beside the river, and the Greystones homestead stood on the bank, with extensive views of

Station Peak, Corio Bay, the Dandenong and Plenty Ranges, round to Mount Macedon. A contemporary account of the homestead describes it as being:

> ... in the rural Gothic style of architecture, and was commenced in 1875. It is built mainly of bluestone, with facings of Darley sandstone. There are little corners and nooks about the grounds, met with at turns in the winding paths and on the terraces, that would make admirable little "bits" for a sketch-book, especially in colour, and the old grey house itself, with its creeper-o'ergrown verandah, is always a feature in the landscape. Inside, Greystones is roomy and comfortable, and furnished as it is with all that is pleasant to the eye, may in these days be taken as a typical Victorian country home.

September 18th

Another lovely day. The garden looks so pretty and the beautiful scarlet passion flowers all twining round the verandah. The blue sarsparilla in another corner. Another lovely shrub with immense bunches of pink blooms all round my window makes me think again and again how lovely the flowers and shrubs are in this highly favoured country. I went for a little turn in the morning. Found the sun too hot for walking. Sat under a tree for a while and read.

Sunday September 19th

Another real summers day. Lady Loch, Sir Henry, Mr and Mrs Molesworth Greene, the Misses Greene and Colonel, went to church. Miss Berry showed me thro' the house. There is much to see. So many pretty things collected together from many parts of the world. We then went to see the tennis court and garden. Came back about 1 p.m. After a rest and dinner, started again to the kitchen garden and on to the hill where we get a splendid view of Geelong, and a fine sea view. After tea, packed up.

Monday September 20th

Up at 6. Left Greystones at 8.30. All very kind. The quiet rest is very good for one. Reached Melbourne at 11, where the dust and heat are almost suffocating. I wish they would water the roads. The dust is enough to blind one.

September 22nd

Mr and Mrs Edward Trotter arrived from New Zealand about 8.30 a.m. At 12 noon Lady Loch, Mr and Mrs Trotter, Miss Edith and Miss Evelyn started for Mt Macedon. Sir Henry and Master Douglas went by afternoon train.

September 23rd

Lucy and me went off soon after breakfast to see poor Mrs Raynor. She was glad to see us. We have not been for some weeks. I am afraid their son is not likely ever to be able to get his own living .

September 24th

Went to see poor old Mrs Comben in Domain Road about more needlework. She has much to do still for different ladies who are very good to her. Sir Henry returned from Macedon for a dinner.

September 25th

Lady Loch, Mr and Mrs Trotter and the young ladies returned from Macedon. In the afternoon Archdeacon Julius, Mrs Julius, their son from the college, nurse and baby arrived. Dinner party for twenty in the evening.

THE LOCHS returned from their few days at Macedon in time to greet Archdeacon Julius and his wife who had arrived from Ballarat to spend a few days as the guests of the Governor. Julius had been one of the principal speakers at the meeting to launch the cathedral appeal, and had made a great impression on the Lochs, as his preaching too, was to make on Emma. As well as their baby and the nurse, the couple had with them their son George, who was a boarder at Melbourne Grammar. Both father and son were destined to make their mark, Churchill, the father, as Lord Bishop of Christchurch in New Zealand, and George becoming an eminent scientist who was knighted for his research and his many inventions. One of these, invented before World War I, is now used by countless millions in every country under the sun, the Totalisator.

September 26th

Beautiful morning. Mrs Trotter's maid (Miss Gibbs), Lucy and me went to Christ Church. Archdeacon Julius preached a most excellent sermon. Quite a treat for us all.

September 27th

Got a letter from Latham, Georgey Kayes, announcing the sudden death of Mrs Edwards from heart disease.

September 29th

Archdeacon Julius left for Ballarat.

September 30th

Mr and Mrs Molesworth Greene arrived on a visit. Mrs Trotter has kept to her room all the week. Very warm day.

October 1st

Sir Henry laid the Memorial Stone of the Houses of Parliament at Melbourne. The day was gloomy, heavy showers fell, and some thunder, tho' not heavy, was heard at intervals.

Houses of Parliament, Melbourne. The elaborate dome was never built.

VICTORIA's Parliament House had been built in several stages, and although it had been used by the Legislature for some years, it was felt that the completion of the final stages should be marked by a ceremony. So Sir Henry was asked to lay a memorial stone in the front of the imposing structure and the event was reported in great detail in the papers.

 The laying of the ceremonial stone of Parliament House was celebrated yesterday with a more than ordinary amount of Oéclat. The weather was not all that could be desired on so important an occasion, and at one time it was believed that the event would be an exceedingly tame affair; but the rain ceased most opportunely about noon, with the result that the ceremony was witnessed by an enormous concourse of people. A more truly representative gathering could not be conceived, and a large number of the most prominent citizens took part in the demonstration. The attendance of ladies was very large, and the platforms erected for their accommodation were fully occupied. There was a good military display as well, the mounted rifles escorting his Excellency and suite from Government House to Spring-street, where he was received by a guard of honor composed of a detachment of the Victorian artillery, two companies of militia and the Naval Brigade.

Sir Henry carefully tapped the stone into place with the trowel which had been presented to him. This trowel was of gold with a handle of blackwood, 'on the blade of which was engraved a suitable description and a pictorial representation of the completed Houses of parliament, the whole being a very pretty piece of workmanship'.

Under the stone was placed a sealed bottle containing newspapers of the day and other items, and the ceremony being concluded. the company adjourned for the banquet, which was one of the largest ever to take place in the history of the colony.

The banquet was held in the Exhibition-building. When the guests began to arrive, the doors were not open, and about 500 persons had assembled before admission was obtained. The result was that some uncomfortable crowding took place; and after undergoing this the guests had the gratification of receiving a lecture from the ticket-collector, who bluntly informed them that their conduct was disgraceful. This was the only unpleasant incident in the day's proceedings. The tables had been laid in the western transept. There was a cross-table along the northern side, and 34 other tables, affording in all accommodation for 1,588 persons. The building presented a brilliant appearance. Distributed on the tables were 288 pots of flowers, and 112 bouquets of flowers. These were provided by the caterer (Mr. H. Skinner), but the general decorations were carried out by Mr. H. Morgan. The gallery fronts and the pillars were draped with curtains. Between each of the pillars were banners, emblems, and trophies of flags. The walls and the ceiling were similarly treated, and on the platform were a number of tree ferns and pot plants. The effect was excellent,

Melbourne Exhibition Buildings.

and when the guests were seated the scene was a remarkable one. The caterer states that this was the largest banquet which has ever been laid in the colony. There were over 1,500 ladies and gentlemen present. There were 180 waiters in attendance, and altogether 222 persons employed in the building. The platform was occupied by a powerful band, under the baton of Mr. Julius Siede.

It is strange that after being laid with so much pomp and ceremony, this stone was so soon forgotten; and even its position was unknown to later generations. However, as the centenary of the occasion came round, the old records were scanned, and the stone's position was finally confirmed. It is at the base of one of the huge sandstone columns at the front of Parliament House.

October 4th

Mrs Julius, nurse and baby left Government House for Ballarat. Mr and Mrs Molesworth Greene left for Bacchus Marsh.

October 6th

Sir Henry, Lady Loch and Mr Fort went to Bacchus Marsh for the Agricultural Show at Bacchus Marsh.

THIS SHOW gave the Lochs an opportunity to see the Molesworth Greenes again, and they spent a restful night at Greystones before driving across for the Show next day. Bacchus Marsh people were excited at the thought that they would soon be connected to Melbourne by train, for the rails had been laid as far as Parwan, and only had three more miles to go, to reach Bacchus Marsh itself. The *Age* reporter informed its readers that:

The second annual show held under the auspices of the Bacchus Marsh Agricultural and Pastoral Society took place in the yards, near the town yesterday. The weather was not altogether favourable for an outdoor gathering, as a rather high, cold wind prevailed, and one or two heavy showers of rain descended during the day. Still, the attendance was fair, though it is certain that the visitors from the well settled surrounding locality would have been more numerous had the weather been more inviting. The number of Melbourne visitors was greater than was the case last year, and it is probable that at future shows the metropolitan contingent will be still larger, as the railway will soon be opened to Bacchus Marsh, making that picturesquely situated township within very easy journey of Melbourne . . .

His Excellency the Governor, accompanied by Lady Loch, arrived on the grounds soon after noon, having driven over from Greystones, the residence of Mr. Molesworth Greene, whose guests they had been since the preceding day. On their arrival in the showyard, Sir Henry and Lady Loch were presented with addresses of welcome from the Bacchus Marsh shire, of which Mr. Molesworth Greene is president, and from the Agricultural Society. After inspecting the exhibits, his Excellency and Lady Loch were present at the show luncheon, where the president of the society, Mr. T. Cain, presided.

October 7th

Returned from Bacchus Marsh. Reached Government House at 7.30.

October 10th

Went to Christ Church for morning service. Mr Hancock gave us a capital sermon.

October 12th

Mr and Mrs Trotter went to Bacchus Marsh. Returned on the 15th.

October 16th

All up at 5.30. Sir Henry and Lady Loch went by early train to Macedon to settle about painting, papering etc. Returned at 4.30.

THE NEW Government Cottage at Macedon was by now almost completed, and the Lochs were enjoying choosing the colours for the interior walls. They had decided that as far as it was possible they would leave all the woodwork unpainted, revealing the natural colours and the interesting grain of the native woods. When Victoria's Parliament House was completed, much of the furniture for it was constructed of blackwood, and the universal admiration of these furnishings had brought blackwood, and other native woods, very much into fashion.

October 17th

Caulfield races. Sir Henry, Lady Loch, Master Douglas, Miss Stawell, Capt. Traill, Mr Fort, Mr Sturgess, went at 12 p.m. Fine but rather cold and blowing hard. Children's tea party and sixteen to dinner. Rather a full day.

October 18th

Wet and cold. Lucy went to church. Miss Gibbs walked with me round the grounds.

October 19th

The Bishop of Adelaide arrived and his Chaplain.

THIS WAS Bishop Kennion whom Sir Henry had met when he visited Adelaide, and they had soon found that they had many interests in common. The Bishop was a Northcountryman, but already had links with South Australia before he came to Adelaide, for his wife was a younger sister of Sir James Ferguson, the colony's Governor in the late 1860s and 1870s. Kennion was a man of great energy, who not only built over fifty new churches in his diocese, but succeeded in attracting clergymen to fill their pulpits. He also worked for the young people in Adelaide, founding Kennion Hall as a home for boys, and taking a particular interest in the city's newsboys.

October 20th

Mr Baring and servant came about 11.30.

October 22nd

Mr Baring left by steamer Carthage *for Columbo. The Bishop of Ballarat and Mrs Thornton came.*

October 23rd

Sir Henry and Lady Loch rose early and started for Macedon by special train at 9 a.m. Mr and Mrs Trotter and Miss Gibbs left at 3.30 p.m. for Queenscliff. The Bishop of Adelaide and Mrs Kennion left for Sydney—also the Bishop of Ballarat and Mrs Thornton. Empty house for a day or two.

October 24th

Wet, showery day. Not a good prospect for Hospital Sunday. A good congregation at South Yarra. Canon Vance preached well for the sick and needy. Miss Shirley came in the afternoon. Lucy and Mary attended the Flower Service at Christ Church. A great number of people in the Gardens, and band playing, tho' the rain is falling pretty frequently. I fear there will not be much gathered in for the hospitals today.

HOSPITAL SUNDAY was one of the events that obviously had a great appeal for Emma, and in fact many people looked forward to it from year to year as an occasion when they heard beautiful music and saw armfuls of exquisite flowers brought along for people in hospital, and when they could open their hearts, and their purses, to help the sick.

A glance down the 'Church Services' column of any Melbourne paper showed what musical treats were in store: one church promised Haydn 'Imperial Mass' with full orchestra, another Beethoven's 'Mass in C' with full orchestra and a charity sermon. In the Town Hall there were to be two services at the request of the mayor, with the controversial Dr Charles Strong as preacher, and in many suburban churches the collection plates were to be taken round by the mayor and councillors in their official robes. There were outdoor events too, a 'Grand Open Air Service' in the Botanical Gardens Reserve, and recitals by such diverse bands as the Albert Park Fife and Drum Band, the Melbourne Temperance Military Band and the Windsor Fire Brigade Band.

Emma records in her diary that on the day when all these open air concerts were to take place, rain was falling 'pretty frequently', and Monday's papers confirm this. The *Age* states that:

Saturday and Sunday were the days set apart for the fourteenth time for the annual collection throughout the city and suburbs in aid of metropolitan charities. Melbourne has never been behindhand in works of charity, and the steady advance of this fund, year by year, is a substantial monument of the rightly-directed liberality of the community. Never since the initiation of the movement has there been a year which has shown a falling off. On the contrary, with each recurring annual period there has always been a large increase . . .

The weather on Saturday and Sunday was not of a character to attract people either to the public places set apart for the making of collections or to the churches. Instead of the bright sun of last year there were bleak winds and cold showers, which disposed people to remain at home rather than to brave the elements. The arrangements for the collection were made with the customary completeness but it is greatly to be feared that the fund has suffered by the inclemency of the season.

FINAL YEARS

WITH HER DESCRIPTION of Melbourne's Hospital Sunday 1886, Emma came to the last line of the last page of her note book. What a pity that no one presented her with a second black note book, where she could have continued the story of her time in Marvellous Melbourne. But despite being ended somewhat abruptly, her diary has left us with two very clear pictures—a portrait of the perfect lady's maid and of the perfect mistress.

I wonder if any reader of Emma's diary noticed in its pages the gradual development of a romance? In the early pages of the diary there are constant references to Mr Hawkins, the butler—the pleasure of pacing round the *Coptic*'s deck on Mr Hawkins' arm, his cheerfulness in all circumstances, the bravery with which he bore the burns on his face after the disastrous dinner party, and how much the rest of the staff missed him while he was recovering from this accident. There are accounts of Emma going to church with him, and of a sunny afternoon spent on the beach with him. But in the later parts of the diary there is not a mention of Mr Hawkins: was this because he had ceased to be merely 'Mr Hawkins' to Emma, and had suddenly become her, 'dearest Robert', a term of affection too precious to be mentioned even in the hidden pages of the diary?

Lord Loch told me, however, that in the end Emma and Mr Hawkins were married and 'lived happily ever after'—well, not quite for ever, of course, but Emma certainly lived on until the 1920s, still visited in her retirement flat by the Loch family, who always spoke of her as their 'dear Titty'.

And what of Lady Loch and Sir Henry? With each year they spent in Melbourne their popularity had grown, and when, at the end of Sir Henry's term as Governor of Victoria, in 1889, they sailed for Cape Town, where he was to become Governor of the Cape Colony, they were farewelled at a series of elaborate parties. They were showered with gifts as tokens of appreciation of the friendships they had made, and of the many good causes they had espoused during their years in Victoria. Lady Loch was presented with a diamond tiara, a replica of the one that graced—but did not save—Marie Antoinette's head, and the 'young ladies' were each asked to accept a diamond pendant.

When they reached South Africa after a pleasant voyage on the *Damascus*, the Lochs, who had been amazed by the enormous crowds that welcomed them in Melbourne, were met with an even larger reception in Cape Town. Their five years in Cape Town were very successful, and their popularity was unprecedented. In a Christmas number of the South African weekly paper, there were no less than six large photographs of the Governor and his household.

On completion of his term in the Cape Colony in 1895, Sir Henry returned to Britain and was granted a baronetcy, taking the title Lord Loch of Drylaw, the Scottish electorate that his father had represented for so long. Lord Loch lived only until 1900, but Lady Loch, having celebrated her ninetieth birthday with her twin sister at a great party in London, lived on until she was ninety-six, surviving her twin by one year.

Master Douglas grew up to be a Captain of the Kings Body Guard in the Yeomen of the Guard, and had a distinguished career in World War I, despite being severely wounded. He married a daughter of the Marquis of Northampton. He was, of course, the second Lord Loch, and was succeeded by his elder son, George Henry. When this son died, leaving only a baby daughter, the title passed to Master Douglas's younger son, Spencer Loch.

He was a Major in the Grenadier Guards in World War II, but as both his sons died before their father, his death notice in *The Times* contained the sad words—'the fourth, and last, Lord Loch'. Lady Loch and his daughter still take an interest in all that goes on, and Lady Loch has been most generous in donating family papers to State Archives in various parts of the world where the family had lived, and I personally have to thank Lady Loch for some of the illustrations in this book.

And what of the two 'young ladies'? Miss Edith married her first cousin, a son of Lady Loch's elder sister, Teresa Earle. Teresa may perhaps have looked with envy at her twin sisters' brilliant marriages and interesting lives, but I doubt it, for her pleasure lay in the simpler things of life. She and her husband lived comparatively quietly, dividing their time between a town house and an old country house in Surrey, but her husband then inherited a large fortune, and Teresa made a fortune. She was sixty when she wrote her first book, *Pot Pourri from a Surrey Garden*, and it brought her instant fame, running into countless editions, and was followed by five sequels. It is sad to relate that her husband was killed in a road accident the very day that her first book was published, but she, like her twin sisters, lived to enjoy a happy old age.

It was Teresa's grandson (Edith's son), Lieutenant Colonel Charles Earle, who cherished Emma's note book and who so kindly gave me permission to copy it and to publish it. On his death in recent years, the black note book was inherited by his son Richard Earle, who also inherited his great grandmother's love of gardening, and lives now in a house called Jessamine Cottage, in Somerset. He too, has helped me generously with details for this book.

Little Miss Evelyn's life was not such a happy one as her sister's. She married Lord Charles Gordon-Lennox, but after a few short blissful years he was killed in action on 10 November 1918, the last day before the Armistice. She lived on alone until 1944, when she was killed, again by enemy action, during an air raid on London.

So the final curtain went down on the family we came to know so well from the pages of Emma Southgate's diary.